The Analyst in the Inner City

Relational Perspectives Book Series
Volume 3

Relational Perspectives Book Series

Stephen A. Mitchell & Lewis Aron
Series Editors

Volume 1

Rita Wiley McCleary
Conversing with Uncertainty:
Practicing Psychotherapy in a Hospital Setting

Volume 2

Charles Spezzano
Affect in Psychoanalysis:
A Clinical Synthesis

Volume 3

Neil Altman
The Analyst in the Inner City:
Race, Class, and Culture Through a Psychoanalytic Lens

In Preparation

Lewis Aron
Interpretation and Subjectivity

Emmanuel Ghent
Process and Paradox

Donnel Stern
Unformulated Experience

Peter Shabad
The Echo of Inner Truth:
A Psychoanalytic-Existential Synthesis

The Analyst in the Inner City

Race, Class, and Culture Through a Psychoanalyic Lens

Neil Altman

THE ANALYTIC PRESS

1995   Hillsdale, NJ   London

Published by
The Analytic Press, Inc.
Editorial Offices: 101 West Street
            Hillsdale, NJ 07642

Typeset by Innovative Systems, Long Branch, NJ

Library of Congress Cataloging-in-Publication Data

Altman, Neil, 1946-
   The analyst in the inner city : race, class, and culture through a
psychoanalytic lens / Neil Altman
      p.   cm.
   Includes bibliographical references and index.
   ISBN 0-88163-173-6
   1. Psychoanalysis–Social aspects. 2. Urban poor–Mental health
services–United States. 3. Psychiatric clinics–Sociological aspects. 4.
Psychodynamic psychotherapy–Social aspects. 5. Managed mental health
care–United States. I. Title.
[DNLM: 1. Psychoanalysis. 2. Urban Health–United States. 3.
Community Mental Health Services–United States. 4. Psychology,
Social–United States. WM 460 A4693p 1995]
RC506.A48   1995
616.89'17–dc20
DNLM/DLC
for Library of Congress   95-23629
                                                                    CIP

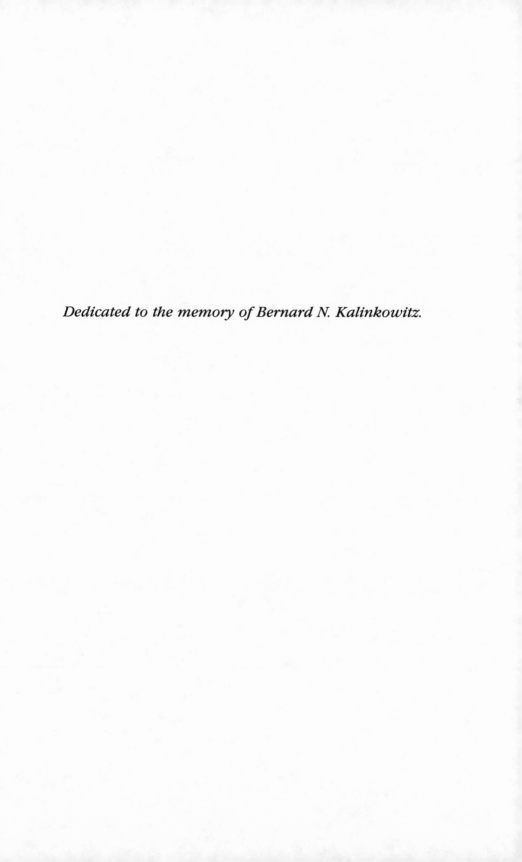

Dedicated to the memory of Bernard N. Kalinkowitz.

CONTENTS

ACKNOWLEDGMENTS

For much of the time that I worked in inner-city public clinics, I was in psychoanalytic training at the New York University Postdoctoral Program. In order to attend my classes, I would often leave work in the middle of the day, get on the subway in a poor section of the Bronx, and emerge 20 minutes later in an affluent section of Manhattan. After sitting for two hours in the instructor's well-appointed office, I would get back in the subway and return to the Bronx. It felt like culture shock to go so quickly from one world to another. Likewise, I felt I had a split professional life: on one side, psychoanalysis and my private practice, and, on the other, the Bronx and my work there. I always suspected that my participation in each world informed my work in the other, that my psychoanalytic training deeply influenced my work in the Bronx and that my experiences in the Bronx and the commitments that led me to work there influenced the kind of psychoanalyst I was. Only after I decided to leave the Bronx, in 1990, did I begin to articulate the links between my psychoanalytic work and my work in the Bronx. This linkage took the form of a paper I wrote called "Psychoanalysis and the Urban Poor," which appeared in *Psychoanalytic Dialogues* in 1993. Writing this paper was a form of integration of my experiences in the inner city, as I did the psychic work of preparing to leave behind that phase of my professional life. Since leaving the Bronx, I have been writing virtually nonstop on topics stimulated by my experiences there. This book is the product of that writing and constitutes an extended period of processing of those experiences.

I wish to acknowledge the contributions of those who have supported and encouraged me on the long path that led to the writing of this book. I feel extremely fortunate to have had more than one mentor in my life, people who believed in me and encouraged me to develop and pursue my own vision of a meaningful professional and personal life. In my graduate and postdoctoral education, Bernard N. Kalinkowitz, to whose memory this book is dedicated, was extremely supportive of my efforts to find ways to use my training in underserved settings. My decision to take a placement in a single-room-occupancy hotel during my first year in graduate school seemed to please and worry Bernie. He was concerned that

I was a young, naive student from the Middle West who would have a rude awakening upon encountering the reality of New York City; nonetheless, Bernie clearly loved the choice I made, and I felt that it reflected some of his own deeply held values. During some of the more lonely and beleaguered times I spent in the Bronx, a phone call to Bernie unfailingly restored my spirits.

Stephen Mitchell has been my editor, and so much more. In his capacity as editor, Steve has had a gift for offering a challenging critique of my work in the context of appreciation and faith in me as a writer. Since I showed him my first tentative efforts at psychoanalytic writing, his belief that I could write has been an important factor in my ability and willingness to believe in myself. Steve's passion and love for ideas and for the process of thinking and writing has inspired me. When we have disagreed, there is enjoyment in the exchange, a sense that I have his support whether I see things his way or not. I cannot imagine an editor who would more effectively have promoted my development as a writer. Steve has also been most encouraging of my interest in psychoanalytic writing that has social relevance.

I spent over 15 years doing clinical and supervisory work, as well as teaching, in the Bronx. Many people supported me, taught me, and stimulated me in my work there. Eli Leiter was my "boss"; he was always available for intellectual stimulation, laughter, complaints, and the ventilation of feelings that is vital in the preservation of sanity under difficult conditions. Luz Towns-Miranda was a friend who, along with José Sanchez, helped me navigate treacherous administrative waters so as to accomplish what I wanted to do. I also want to acknowledge the following people with whom I worked and who contributed to this book through helping engender a creative and productive atmosphere in the clinics where we worked: Naomi Adler, Richard Briggs, Bette Clark, Lisa Director, Carol Eagle, Barbara Gochberg, Samuelle Klein-Von Reiche, Laura Neiman, Cecile Ortiz-Rodriguez, and Carol Wachs.

I appreciate greatly the help of the following people, who took the time to read all or part of the manuscript and to offer thoughtful, critical, and helpful suggestions: Margaret Black, Muriel Dimen, Richard Fulmer, Adrienne Harris, Anita Herron, Steven Lubin, Wendy Lubin, Cecile Ortiz-Rodriguez, and Kirkland Vaughns. Lennard Davis offered valuable help in finding a title that captured the complexity of my project in an evocative way.

My wife, Roberta, has shared my social concerns for 26 years, since our time together in the Peace Corps in India. I read almost everything in this book to her as soon as I wrote it, in states ranging from doubt and insecurity, to pride and excitement. She was patient enough to put up with my doubts, despair, and excitement at all hours, late at night and early in the morning. She made many crucial suggestions for improvements. I am lucky to have had her intelligence and wide experience in the public sector available to me "on site" as I wrote and revised the book.

Finally, I want to thank my daughters, Lisa and Amanda, for their patience with my states of preoccupation and their interest in what I was doing. Each, in her own way, has been part of the strength and inspiration on which I have drawn in order to do this work.

PREFACE

For psychoanalytically oriented clinicians working in the public sector, these are times of crisis and opportunity. Historically, psychoanalysis has largely eschewed concern with inner-city public clinic work. On one hand, with their requirements for a particular educational background and a Calvinist tolerance of frustration, classical and ego psychological versions of psychoanalysis largely excluded people of lower socioeconomic status and nonmainstream ethnicity. On the other hand, the classical ideal of analytic anonymity could not be approximated in a public clinic, where therapists had to perform multiple functions for their patients, including bureaucratic and advocacy functions. Public clinic administrations, trying to serve large numbers of people, often did not look kindly on intensive treatment. Public clinics, especially in the inner city, have thus not seemed hospitable to psychoanalytic work. Psychoanalysts concentrated on private practice, where conditions more nearly fitted the classical ideal and where, not incidentally, there was more money to be made. The exceptions to this pattern were analysts who stayed in the public sector in order to train interns and residents. Their focus on those few inner-city patients who were bright, educated, or middle-class only reinforced psychoanalysis's reputation for elitism.

In recent years, developments have been even more discouraging for people who hope to bring a psychoanalytic approach to the inner city. Funding agencies have increasingly emphasized cost-effectiveness in mental health treatment. When efficiency in symptom relief is the criterion for effective treatment, psychoanalytic treatment easily appears to be at a disadvantage compared with psychopharmacology and behavioral techniques (I argue later that this is so only if one adopts concrete and short-sighted standards of cost-effectiveness). Most recently, the emphasis in public mental health has been on intensive case management, in which case managers follow chronically mentally ill, or otherwise at-risk, patients in their communities to advocate for their needs and to encourage treatment compliance. The goal is to avoid hospitalization, far and away the most expensive treatment modality. When the locus of mental health work thus moves out of the office, it becomes difficult to see the relevance of psychoanalysis per se as a treatment. (I argue later that, nonetheless, the psychoanalytic perspective is invaluable in such work.)

There are, at the same time, encouraging developments: recent revisions of psychoanalytic theory and technique make public clinic work much more compatible with a psychoanalytic approach. Relational and interpersonal psychoanalytic criteria for analyzability emphasize how the patient can use the analytic relationship, rather than particular forms of verbal intelligence and the capacity to tolerate frustration per se. The analyst's stance is not calculated to produce frustration in the patient, as is the case with classical technique, nor is there necessarily an attempt to minimize behavioral interaction. The multiple roles that therapists must fill in relation to public clinic patients pose less of a problem when psychoanalysis does not require anonymity and abstention from action in relation to the patient.

Contemporary psychoanalytic theory and practice thus potentially bring public clinic therapy into the psychoanalytic domain; however, just at the moment when psychoanalysts have become better prepared to do therapy in the inner city, psychotherapy has become deemphasized in favor of seemingly more cost-effective modalities. What role might there be for psychoanalysis in a world of biological psychiatry, behavioral psychology, and intensive case management? Have psychoanalysts become dinosaurs, fighting a losing battle against extinction as their ecological niche disappears?

I think not, but the survival of psychoanalysis depends on analysts' believing in what they have to offer in this brave new world and acting resourcefully to expand the niches in which they make their contribution. For example, an understanding of transference and countertransference is clearly absolutely indispensable to an intensive case manager. Intensive case managers make home visits, take a great deal of responsibility for their patients, and get involved in many areas of their lives. The setup, to an analytically trained eye, clearly pulls for reenactments of parent–child interactions. Powerful emotional reactions on the part of patients and case managers are inevitable. Case managers may appear to their patients as omnipotent rescuers, controlling and punitive intruders, potential lovers, rapists, friends, and on and on. Case managers, who are often on call 24 hours per day, may experience their patients as overwhelmingly demanding, intrusive, frustrating, abusive, seductive, and so on. Case managers, at least as much as office based therapists, need analytic understanding of their interactions with patients if they are to manage them appropriately. There is a role, then, an *indispensable* role, for analysts in the training, supervision, and support of case managers. Assuming this role depends on analysts' expanding their sense of what they have to offer beyond the traditional private-practice, office-based role. Analysts need to be able to apply their understanding of transference and countertransference and the ways in which these phenomena can be worked with therapeutically to the complex, goal-driven, community-based interactions that case managers have with their clients. To a traditional psychoanalytic sensibility, the active, directive stance of the case manager and the in-home site of the interaction make the case manager's work an implausible object of psychoanalytic consideration. It takes a more contemporary, relational sensibility, accustomed to more flexibility with respect to the kinds of interactions that fit within a psychoanalytic frame, to see the potential for enriched understanding generated by bringing a psychoanalytic eye and ear to this community work.

My project in this book is part of a larger contemporary project of integrating the social with the psychological within psychoanalytic theory and practice. Sullivan and his followers in the American interpersonal tradition took the lead in the middle part of this century with their reformulation of Freud's theory in social terms. Relational theory has taken the project a step further by integrating British object relations theory, with its focus on the ways in which interpersonal experience becomes internalized. We have moved from an "asocial" view of the psychoanalytic interaction (Hoffman, 1983) to one that takes account of both the analyst's actions and his subjectivity (Hoffman, 1983; Aron, 1991, 1992). In France, Lacan (1977), took another path toward the integration of the social and the psychological by conceiving of the mind—the unconscious, as he put it—as constituted and structured by language (Dimen, personal communication, 1994).[1] The "postmodern impulse" (Barratt, 1993) in psychoanalysis leads one to see the mind in the context of socially shared discursive practices, that is, the ways of thinking available at

---

[1] I am indebted to Muriel Dimen for pointing out that Lacan regarded the social domain, as represented by language, to be invariant. In this sense, his conception of the social is fundamentally different from my own, according to which the structure of the social domain is specific to a time and place. As pointed out by Dimen (personal communication), however, Lacan's postulation of a universal and patriarchal symbolic domain offers one way to introduce the category of the social into psychoanalytic thought. By arguing that the unconscious is structured like a language, Lacan unintentionally gave us a handle to think that differently structured languages might make for differently structured minds.

a given time and place and the social power arrangements reflected therein (Foucault, 1980). Along these lines, feminist psychoanalysts have pointed out how patriarchal society structures the ways we have available for conceiving of gender. Gender as it is constructed on the social level constitutes gender as a psychological phenomenon from this point of view.

In a variety of ways, then, psychoanalysts have been struggling to "see the social and the psychological at the same time" (Harris, personal communication, 1994; see also Cushman, 1994, and Samuels, 1993, for similar efforts). In considering the role of psychoanalysis in the inner-city public clinic, I am taking on another aspect of this project. I am attempting to take account, psychoanalytically, of the social context of therapeutic work in the inner city in a way that will be of relevance to clinical practitioners. This effort entails taking account, *psychoanalytically*, of class, culture, and race and the dynamics of a public clinic and of a larger community. In this effort, I seek ways to conceive of these factors within a psychoanalytic perspective and to find the ways in which they operate in the clinical situation.

Recent decades have seen a heightened interest in, and awareness of, the ways in which foundational values and assumptions permeate theory and practice across disciplines. Traditional concepts and technical practices in psychoanalysis have come to be viewed as saturated with the mores specific to a time and place. Viewing matters in this way opens up opportunities for taking a critical attitude toward the status quo in psychoanalysis and in society. The consequence of failing to place psychoanalysis in historical context has been the enshrining of a set of concepts and practices. Conservative currents in psychoanalysis have come to predominate, while psychoanalysis has become a conservative force in society. Freud could postulate an equation of femininity with passivity, masculinity with activity; feminist writing shows us here the reflection of the preconceptions of a particular historical period that are contingent and thus open to critique.[2] Similarly, traditional analytic developmental theory has built a pejorative attitude toward homosexuality into psychoanalytic theory (Mitchell, 1981; Lewes, 1988; Blechner, 1993; Lesser, 1993; Schwartz, 1993; Frommer, 1994). Part of what analysts thought was subsumed in their "neutral" analytic stance is now

---

[2]Freud himself was too complex-minded to accept his own equation (see footnotes in Freud, 1905, p. 143; 1930, pp. 105–106) although he did not think about gender stereotypes as being culturally specific.

thought of as an often highly prejudicial set of assumptions about people—analyst and patient. Once we begin to view our categories and practices as contingent, that is, constructed within a particular cultural context, we can turn a critical eye onto the forces and factors leading us to construct gender and sexual orientation, for example, in a particular way within society at large, as well as within the analytic situation.

We have ignored class, culture, and race as powerful elements in the psychoanalytic field only by being unreflectively embedded in our society's arrangements with regard to these categories. Postmodern theorists tend to focus on those who are marginalized as a way of heightening awareness of taken-for-granted aspects of mainstream culture. It is harder to take heterosexuality for granted if one is homosexual or spends time thinking about homosexuality. Marginalizing homosexuals serves to reinforce our sense of heterosexuality as "natural," God-given. Similarly, culture, class, and race can be quite invisible if one lives in many parts of America. We can fail to reflect on the ways in which these categories are constructed and the social and psychic consequences and purposes served thereby. In limiting itself to affluent private practice, psychoanalysis traditionally has created an environment for itself that is the functional equivalent of a homogeneous American suburban environment with respect to culture, class, and race. Psychoanalysis has its own value-laden and culturally embedded framework, which can remain invisible so long as people whose frameworks are different are excluded. Once we include African-Americans, Latinos, the lower social classes, and the culturally nonmainstream, differences are highlighted. If we neither exclude nor marginalize these "others," we are faced with the challenge of reflecting on the processes by which difference and hierarchy are constructed. To focus on psychoanalysis in the inner city, then, is to move to the margins of what has been traditionally encompassed by psychoanalysis. My project is, thus, to contribute to bringing social class, culture, and race into the psychoanalytic domain. I want to stimulate psychoanalytic thinking about the construction of these factors on social and personal levels, especially in the clinical psychoanalytic situation. If, as I suggest, defensive psychic functions are served by constructing these categories as we do, to think psychoanalytically about how we use social class, culture, and race, is to expand the range of our consciousness.

I suggest, then, that psychoanalysis has developed as an exclusionary discourse. Classism, racism, and ethnocentrism embedded in our theory are manifest, at the level of practice, by the exclusion of nonmainstream members of our society as "nonanalyzable." The excluded "other" also represents the psychically disowned. We have thus built psychic defense, projection, and introjection into every psychoanalytic interaction via the implicit acceptance of ground rules (e.g., "talk, don't act") that arise within an exclusionary discourse. In this sense, classism, racism, and ethnocentrism structure every psychoanalytic interaction, just as they must structure every interaction in an exclusionary society. Simply to speak of psychoanalysis in the inner-city highlights, or renders conscious, the implicit biases of our theory and practice, just as to speak of "heterosexuality as compromise formation" (Chodorow, 1992) highlights the heterosexist biases in our discourse. I do not set out here to transcend bias in psychoanalytic theory; I believe bias of one sort or another is inevitable, just as psychic defense is inevitable. Rather, the psychoanalytic project in this respect is to commit ourselves to an endless process of seeking to highlight and reflect upon the implicit assumptions that structure our work.

I further address the social context of psychoanalytic work by focusing on the public clinic, its dynamics and interdisciplinary relationships, as a part of the psychoanalytic field. With a systemic perspective, I highlight how the dynamics of society with respect to race, culture, and class, the dynamics of an inner-city public clinic, and the dynamics of a therapeutic dyad within such a clinic reflect one another. In this way, I bring together, within an overarching perspective, the social and the psychological, the individual and society, bureaucracy and the clinical interaction.

This book, then, has two centers of gravity. I want this book to be of practical significance to the clinician working in the inner city. At the same time, I am concerned with what we can learn about psychoanalysis and its theory by taking analytic work into the inner city. I intertwine the practical with the theoretical in a way that highlights the inseparability of the two. By linking these two projects in one book, I offer my own source of inspiration, my own way of finding meaning in this stressful and often frustrating work at the margins of our society, our theory, and our practice.

I begin with a series of vignettes intended to set the stage for the discussions in later chapters. My intention is to give the reader a "feel" for the inner-city public clinic, in the context of the community, the intrastaff relationships within the clinic, and the clinical work that takes place. These clinical vignettes also serve as illustrative material for the discussions in later chapters.

In Chapter 2, I present multifaceted background material necessary for the reader to be oriented to later discussions. This chapter begins with a history of psychoanalysis in the public sector, along with factors that have led analysts to avoid the public sector in general. Next, I present a theoretical frame of reference that draws heavily on contemporary relational and neo-Kleinian perspectives and that is well suited for the work of integrating social and psychological factors in inner-city therapy. I argue that a two-person, a social-psychoanalytic, perspective is necessary to accommodate such intrinsically social factors as race and social class within a psychoanalytic frame of reference. Further, a projective-introjective framework provides a model for conceptualizing the psychic functions served by categorizations based on race, culture, and social class. Finally, I give an introduction to postmodern currents in psychoanalysis that inform the perspective I have taken in this book. Postmodern concerns with the instability of identity and with the construction of social categories are quite compatible with my theoretical perspective and heavily influence my approach to social class, culture, and race.

In Chapter 3, I look at race, culture, and social class in detail. My concern in this chapter is both theoretical and clinical. Theoretically, my goal is to place these social phenomena within a psychoanalytic framework. I show how the social system and the individual psyche reflect each other. This project entails a consideration both of the ways in which social class, race, and culture imprint themselves on the individual psyche and of the ways in which psychic operations are reflected in how society is structured. I demonstrate how these social phenomena make their appearance in the clinical interaction, with examples of implications for practice. I use a three-person psychoanalytic model, in which the third term refers to the social context in which the analytic work takes place. With this third term, one is able to take account of such factors as the social system that structures both psyches in the analytic situation and that is necessary to be able to understand fully such phenomena as racial prejudice.

In Chapter 4, I apply my projective-introjective, three-person psychoanalytic model to a social issue at the core of my concerns in this book: the private-public split in capitalist society, as reflected in the bifurcation of public from private practice in psychoanalysis. "Public" and "private" come to have psychic significance; for example, in the United States, the public sector comes to represent what is devalued: poverty, difference, strangeness, and so on. Here, as elsewhere in this book, I use psychoanalytic understanding to put a social phenomenon into a fresh perspective, to show how the social is inherent in the psychological and how the psychological is inherent in the social.

In Chapter 5, I turn the lens of this perspective onto the public clinic. Here I seek to integrate the social with the psychological by considering the dynamics of a public clinic, with its interdisciplinary relationships, for example, from a psychoanalytic perspective. Further, I consider how these dynamics are reflected in therapeutic relationships taking place within public clinics.

Finally, in Chapter 6, I offer some thoughts on the future of psychoanalysis. Psychoanalysis offers a humane and complex-minded response to human suffering at a time in history that is marked by increasing degrees of dehumanization and a search for painless, "quick-fix" solutions to problems. The age of "managed care" threatens the survival of psychoanalysis but also makes its survival essential as a counterforce, an alternative vision of psychological treatment. The viability of psychoanalysis will be best served by maximizing the extent to which humanistic values inform our theory and practice and by expanding the domain in which psychoanalysts make their contribution. Both these goals are served by exposing, grappling with, and countering the elitism of psychoanalysis wherever it appears. Psychoanalysis, as labor-intensive as it is, can never be undertaken with large numbers of people. This fact does not make psychoanalytic elitism inevitable. The elitism that does exist is addressable by bringing racial, cultural, and class differences within the psychoanalytic domain and by being active in the public sector, as therapists and consultants, so as to bring the psychoanalytic vision to bear on work with people from a wider variety of cultural and socioeconomic backgrounds. In the theoretical sphere, analysts can be aware of the ways in which the definition of the required frame for psychoanalytic work and certain criteria of analyzability introduce superfluous exclusivity. Analysts can also be aware of how they, in an elitist effort at differentiating psychoanalysis from psychotherapy, have at times portrayed their work as being concerned solely with understanding as opposed to change. All these factors make psychoanalysis vulnerable to being set up as the villain in the managed care narrative that pits guardians of cost-efficiency against wasteful, self-indulgent therapists. Such a development does not further the psychoanalytic critique of the idea that complex human problems can be solved simply and expeditiously, without unpredictable consequences and complications.

1 / CLINICAL EXPERIENCES FROM A PUBLIC CLINIC

Life in the Inner City

Life in the inner city entails a greater burden of stress, loss, and trauma than life in working-class-and-up communities. These conditions predispose to psychopathology (Brown and Harris, 1978) and complications in parenting young children (Halpern, 1993) and form part of what is enacted and experienced in the transference and countertransference when one works psychoanalytically with inner-city patients. The upper-middle-class therapist who goes to work in an inner-city public clinic frequently enters, psychologically, a realm of trauma and loss that she may have been able to avoid, to some degree, in her own life. The countertransference, to the extent that one is open to the experience, brings to the therapist more than the usual doses of anger, fear, and despair.

Poverty places stress on people in many ways, for example, inadequate housing with little or no heat in winter or protection from rats and other vermin; relatively greater exposure to crime of all kinds, especially violent crime; poor educational and employment opportunities; inadequate income for the essentials of life, not to speak of entertainment or distraction; racism; the exposure of one's children to the temptations of drugs and crime. Impoverished people have more children, on average, than middle-class people and are more likely to raise them without support of a coparent. Fathers, with the deck stacked against their ability to take on a traditional provider role, often come and go, creating experiences of loss and abandonment for mothers and children. The primary caretaker of children is more likely to be very young in the inner city. Trauma, of both the cumulative, chronic type and the acute type (being the victim of, or exposed to, violence and physical or sexual abuse), is relatively common. The sequelae of trauma (van der Kolk, 1987), posttraumatic stress disorders and dissociative disorders are also widespread and transmitted from generation to generation, as is child maltreatment (Lyons-Ruth and Zeanah, 1993). When these people—

1

adults, parents, children—enter our offices, they enter with the full range of transference expectations born of trauma. The analyst must expect, in the transference, to take on the role of rescuer, victim, abuser, and neglectful parent, in the ways Davies and Frawley (1992) and Gabbard (1992) have shown to occur in the analysis of adult survivors of childhood sexual abuse.

Adversity can also breed uncommon strength, as documented in the studies of "resilient" children (Anthony and Cohler, 1987; Neiman, 1987). Inner-city people may also be buffered from the effects of stress in certain ways unavailable to other people. For example, residents of inner cities sometimes retain the extended family or community support network of their native country. It is not uncommon in the community where I worked, for example, for an entire block or a building to have families from a village in Puerto Rico or the Dominican Republic. Members of families often share parenting responsibilities. Support from church or mosque and its fellow members and clergy is commonly available and utilized. There are also traditional healing methods (e.g., the religiously based systems known as *espiritismo* and *santeria*) widely available in the inner city. Inner-city people may bring to the therapy situation great resources, as well as expectations of a healing relationship that may be unfamiliar to the middle-class North American mental health professional.

Inner-city life typically entails complications in the development of ethnic identity, a crucial aspect of personal identity formation. Immigrant people are involved in a complicated process of assimilation into American life while preserving ties to the cultures of the native land. Splits within families often occur when adolescent children assimilate in a way that disturbs parents who are more rooted in the "old country." Adolescent assimilation may reflect a wish to differentiate from parents that itself is culturally specific to the United States and that may be interpreted by parents only as unwarranted defiance. (See the case of Rosa for a description of how the prospect of assimilation and differentiation led to internal conflict for an adolescent.) The form of American culture into which inner-city adolescents may wish to assimilate is "street culture," which is especially disturbing to parents worried about drugs and crime.

The stabilization of ethnic identity is especially difficult for members of discriminated-against groups (Herron, 1994). As children become aware of their group's and family's relatively powerless position within society at large, it may be complicated to sustain the sense of pride in one's family and group that reinforces a strong sense of identity. On the other hand, as awareness of societal discrimination has grown in the last three decades, there have been increasing efforts at reinforcement of awareness of the strengths of nonmainstream cultures in our cities. There is also richness available to immigrant groups and to the culture as a whole from the cross-fertilization among the peoples who are creating the current American mosaic.

Personal Background

My experience doing therapeutic work in the public clinic was conditioned, inevitably, by who I was and what I brought with me to my work there. The personal information I provide in this section helps set the stage for the clinical material to follow.

Since beginning my graduate training, I had always worked in the public sector. I was raised upper-middle-class, white, privileged. What drew me to work with culturally, ethnically, socioeconomically different people, the poor? On a broadly cultural level, one might say that I had a traditionally Jewish social consciousness. I was also a member of the 1960s generation that had lived amid the civil rights movement, the women's movement, the anti-Vietnam War movement. I had been a Peace Corps volunteer in India, where I became fascinated with culture as a phenomenon and with the capacity for cross-cultural relatedness that I discovered in myself. Living in India reinforced an impatience, which I had felt as an adolescent, with the limited horizons of the homogeneous American suburban community in which I grew up. I had been acutely aware, at least since college, of social inequities and uncomfortable doing nothing to address them.

On a more personal level, the meaning to me of work in a poor community was conditioned by events before I was born. My mother grew up in a poor neighborhood. Her father was a cigar maker. After he died, my grandmother made her living from a grocery store in front of their apartment, which was in a racially mixed community. My father, on the other hand, came from an affluent family across town. His father, legend has it, had big cars even in the middle of the Great Depression. My father swept my mother up in one of those cars and took her away from her modest circumstances into the lap of luxury.

My experience working in poor communities was, in significant ways, shaped by connections with both of my parents. On one hand,

I have a sense of having connected with my mother through having worked in an environment that I identified with her.

On the other hand, I had an identification with my father as a "white knight" who would ride into the ghetto with his big car and rescue the inhabitants. Work in the ghetto allowed me to feel special and admirable. This feeling helped compensate for whatever feelings of insecurity I had as a therapist and made it seem more desirable to avoid competition for jobs in more affluent neighborhoods, jobs that were more sought after by many of my peers.

In short, working in poor communities had resonances with various aspects of my background and associated fantasies about myself and other people. These personal considerations, along with my social commitments, made my public clinic work a complex, multifaceted experience.

Snapshots of Work in the Public Clinic

A Tipsy Telephone Call

In the child psychiatry clinic where I worked, the staff took it for granted that men, whether fathers or surrogates, would not participate in therapy. For example, when the initial call came to the clinic from a parent or another referring person, the staff member who took the call routinely said that the *mother* should bring the child to the first appointment. I protested from time to time that the father or stepfather should be invited to the first session, but my suggestion never caught on, and I never followed up as persistently as I might have. It was also very common to discover, in the course of doing an intake, that the father has abandoned the mother and child or children, was abusive, abused drugs and alcohol, or any of these. As part of the overall treatment plan for the family, I would make some attempt to engage this man. Often, he would respond positively to the invitation to meet me but later would not be consistently involved in the therapy. In extreme cases, I would end up working with mothers around crises in which they were being physically abused by their husbands or boyfriends. After one such crisis, I continued treating a woman individually. She once brought her cousin to see me, who also had a troubled son and an abusive husband.

One day I got a call from these two women from a pay phone on the street. They were, I thought, tipsy. As one of them began to talk to me, they both began giggling uncontrollably. Some readers may have already made connections with my personal history; as I began treating these patients, however, I was only dimly aware of any connections. But when I got this flirtatious call from my two patients, it was as if the veil were drawn away. I could not avoid seeing my role here as the male knight in shining armor who had come to rescue these two damsels in distress from their evil male villains. I had to acknowledge the ways in which I may have been acting in a seductive manner and the ways in which I had portrayed myself as the "good" man, counterposed to the "bad" men with whom they had relationships.

At the time this incident took place, many years ago, I did not have the conceptual tools I have now to understand the dynamics of the situation. In hindsight, it seems to me that the phone call was a somewhat dissociated (taking place as it did in an altered state of consciousness) commentary on the transference-countertransference situation in which my patient and I colluded to let her husband be the "bad" man, with me as the "good" one. The phone call did several things: it exposed this splitting operation, while simultaneously revealing my own not-so-good aspect, that is, my competitiveness with their husbands. By undermining my sense of being the virtuous "white knight," the phone call was a potential corrective to the defensive splitting operation in which we were engaged through heightening my awareness of how I was positioning myself in relation to these women and their husbands and by providing an opportunity for inquiry into my impact on these patients.

Food in the Public Clinic

It should not be surprising that food and eating are issues in therapy that takes place between a relatively affluent therapist and poor patients in a public clinic. In the clinic where I worked, food easily became a focus because the clinic kept food on hand for the children to have as snacks and because the clinic threw holiday parties for the patients at which food was present in abundance.

Certain children, especially severely deprived children who had experienced multiple losses in their lives, became preoccupied with food. In a typical scenario they would request more of this and more of that. At a certain point, the therapist, who might initially have been comfortable with the idea of a snack, would start to become uncomfortable. The child seemed to be inordinately greedy or seemed ready to take so much of the food that there would be little left for others. The therapist might say, "Why don't you start with two packs of cookies, and we can get more later if you're still hungry?" At this point, the child might say: "How about three? And an apple or two? I need juice too. I'm very thirsty and hungry. I didn't eat the school lunch today." If the therapist turned away for a second, he or she might become aware that the child had stuffed his pockets with food and drink. If the therapist tried to push the point that enough was enough or said something like, "We're not going to have much time left for our session if you keep eating or taking more food," a power struggle would ensue. The therapist ultimately had the resources to prevail in such a power struggle, but it would feel as if an activity that initially had seemed to be an act of generosity had been transformed into a hostile and depriving act.

What is going on in such situations? While I am sure that some of the children were genuinely hungry, most certainly were not *that* hungry. The children's behavior could be seen as reflecting an institutional transference configuration. That is, the clinic was often seen as part of the social service network, which includes welfare, Medicaid, and Social Security. These agencies, which control much of the income of impoverished people, fit the mold of what Fairbairn (1952) called "exciting" and "rejecting" internalized object relationships. That is, these agencies are seen as having enormous resources that they can make available to poor people but that they often withhold. As part of this social service network, the assistance of the mental health clinic and its staff is often enlisted by patients in their efforts to obtain one sort of benefit or another. An upper-middle-class therapist working in the public system is, in this transference configuration, easily perceived as the guardian of social service resources.

From this point of view, the children in the snack room might be seen as playing out this institutional transference. The child and therapist find themselves inadvertently orchestrating an enactment of the exciting and rejecting object transference. One might say that there was no need for the therapist to pull the child away from the food so the session could start. The therapeutic interaction was going on, in a very powerful way, around the food itself.

Why did the clinic have food on hand for the children? Of course, one might say that there is a need to offer snacks to families who otherwise might not be able to afford them, however, it was a rare family in which the children were not usually loaded with snacks, no matter how economically besieged their families. We had more self-interested motives for having that food available. For example, one therapist once said to me that giving food to her patients made her feel that at least she was able to do one clearly helpful thing for them. They had so many intractable problems, she said, that she often felt useless. The food, for a brief moment, counteracted that feeling. The clinic administration believed that having food in the clinic would bring in more patients and increase our billable visits. This aspect of the situation became particularly apparent at Christmastime, when the clinic put out a spread for the patients that would have rivalled a corporate Christmas party. Why?

The Christmas party idea always came up in the context of a discussion about how to keep up our billable visits during the Christmas vacation. How does one get families to come to the clinic during vacations? The plan: feed them. Sure enough, patients came to see their therapists on the day of the party by the hundreds. I was sometimes serving food and I would notice something I found strange: many of the patients did not want to eat. They looked embarrassed. Some, to be sure, ate quite comfortably, and others, usually children, were quite unrestrained as they loaded their plates. How are we to understand the reluctance of some of the patients to eat? Was this a reaction formation against greed? Perhaps. But, in addition, some people may have been wondering, Why is a mental health clinic feeding us? One answer would have to be: Because we get reimbursed for seeing you at a rate much higher than the cost of feeding you. Or, Because it counteracts our feeling of helplessness as we confront the problems you face. With the situation thus laid out baldly, it seems no longer a mystery that many of us, patients and staff, felt awkward.

We were meeting our own needs, then, in feeding our patients. By implying that we were looking out only for the welfare of our patients, we were perpetuating a myth, similar to one cited by Racker (1968), that the therapist is high-minded, healthy, altruistic, and giving, while the patient is sick, needy, and dependent. Searles (1979a) notes how therapists may need their patients to be sick so they can feel healthy. Providing food to our patients may have helped us feel resourceful and healthy, at the cost of perpetuating our patients' feelings of being sick, poor, helpless, and needy. Thus, the patients may have felt condescended to, one down, in relation to us. Stereotypes based on social class and race may have been covertly maintained in the relationship between the clinic and its patients. If we had been able to facilitate our patients' exploration of our motives in providing food to them, perhaps in exploring their embarrassment at holiday parties, we might have discovered a mutuality to our relationships that would have counteracted such stereotypes.

A Numbers Game in the Public Clinic

A patient in a public clinic began her session by saying: "You're lucky I came today." The therapist was struck dumb. She *had* been feeling lucky the patient came that day. Why? The therapist worked in a clinic in which staff were expected to see 35 patients per week. If they failed to do so, their performance was judged negatively. The week had been going poorly for the therapist—it was Wednesday and she had seen only 10 patients. The therapist had been conscious of feeling relieved that the patient showed up, increasing her chances of looking good to her superiors or at least avoiding trouble.

What did the patient know about this aspect of their interaction? It is not likely that the patient knew the specifics of the therapist's situation, but it *is* likely that the patient would be at least dimly aware that the therapist's needs, as well as the patient's, are served by the patient's participation in the treatment.[1] Her comment was a potential opening to an exploration of her fantasies and perceptions about the ways in which she was meeting, or not meeting, the therapist's needs and how she felt about that situation.

Missed Appointments

Linda was referred to a public mental health clinic because she had been feeling nervous. She was brought into a hospital emergency room the previous night by her sister after losing her temper and throwing dishes at her boyfriend. She was angry because she suspected that he had another woman. Linda's sister, on her behalf, said that she needed pills for her nerves. Linda had several times in the past received prescriptions for "nerve medicine." She tended to take them irregularly, regardless of how they were prescribed. The emergency room resident, having seen Linda before and knowing that she tended not to follow up on treatment, decided not to give her a prescription that night and to send her to the outpatient clinic the next morning. She was seen there by a psychology intern who talked with her for a long time. The intern heard a story of parental

---

[1]Friedman (1988) provides a discussion of the various needs of the therapist that are typically met in the therapeutic situation. Searles (1979a) discusses how patients try to "cure" their analysts, that is, meet the analyst's needs so that the analyst can better meet their needs. Ferenczi's (1932) thoughts along these lines led to his experiments with mutual analysis. Hoffman (1983) and Aron (1991, 1992) emphasize the potential awareness patients have of the subjectivity of the analyst and the vicissitudes of patient responses to this awareness.

abandonment as a child, of numerous betrayals by parents and boyfriends. The patient expressed a great deal of anger at many people in her life. The intern pointed out that the latest betrayal, by her boyfriend the previous night, was only the latest in a long series of previous events and so struck a very raw nerve. The patient acknowledged the intern's comment and promised to return the next week to talk with her again, without asking for medication. She said that talking to the intern had made her feel much better.

The next week, Linda did not show up, much to the disappointment of the intern, who felt she had established a strong and meaningful connection with her in their first meeting. Since Linda had no phone, the intern wrote her a letter. There was no response for two weeks from Linda. In the third week, however, the intern was called by the receptionist to say that Linda was in the waiting room to see her. She knew that she had no appointment but would like to see her for just a minute. The intern felt confused, irritated, worried. When Linda came into her office, she apologized for not returning to the clinic and explained that she had been getting the runaround from welfare and that she had decided to apply for SSI (Supplemental Security Income; a Social Security program to provide money to people who cannot work because of a physical or mental disability) on the basis of her mental condition. Would the intern please send her medical records to the Social Security Administration on her behalf?

The intern felt quite disoriented. Linda's actions seemed to be an indirect, yet powerful, communication of hostility and despair, provoking similar feelings in the intern. She had thought that this woman could benefit from psychotherapy. Linda seemed to be settling for crumbs from life. Why accept the status of a mentally disabled person so easily? Was she trying to exploit the system? Perhaps, in her world, there were no options. You either find a secure source of income from the "system," or you do not eat. What should a would-be psychotherapist say to Linda? The intern felt caught between rejecting her, on one hand, and colluding with her exploitativeness, hostility, and despair, on the other. Should she go along with her request as a temporary expedient to establish a relationship with her? Would a rejection undermine any chance that Linda would come back? Would acceding to Linda's request be a collusion with Linda's devaluation of herself and her exploitation of the system? Which course of action would less seriously undermine a therapeutic relationship? Besides, Linda did not really seem to want psychotherapy. Should the intern urge it on her? Linda did not come from a background where people go for therapy when they are in trouble. Perhaps the intern needed to start with her where she was and work toward being a therapist. But along the way, how does one avoid foreclosing one's ability to take a therapeutic stance in the future? The intern, trying to deal with all these thoughts, not to mention her feelings and her anxiety, asked Linda about the experiences that led up to her decision to apply for SSI and whether she saw herself as being able to work. The intern inquired about how Linda would feel if she got SSI and also conveyed her opinion that the patient could benefit from psychotherapy and that perhaps psychotherapy would lead Linda to see other options in her life. Linda agreed to give it a try and left with another appointment.

The issues raised by work with a patient such as Linda can be approached from a relational perspective by asking: Who am I in this patient's object world? That is, the therapist assumes that the transference involves his being seen by the patient through the template of the patient's internalized object relations. For Fairbairn (1952), for example, the transference involves the patient's seeing the analyst as an exciting object (i.e., tempting, promising), as a rejecting object, or both. Such transference configurations are pulled for in very powerful fashion by the situation in public clinics.

When a patient of lower socioeconomic status, such as Linda, walks into a public clinic, from her point of view she enters another of the institutions that control crucial aspects of her life. A frame is already established for the therapy that is about to occur. A hospital or a hospital clinic is part of the network of institutions and bureaucracies that include public assistance, Medicaid, and Social Security. These institutions both provide and frustrate. At least, they are the potential source of provision. In fact, a person dealing with one of these systems is likely to encounter an overworked, harassed clerk whose mandate is not to provide benefits to anyone who cannot demonstrate impeccable qualifications of need. Could there be an external situation better calculated to evoke an inner world peopled by exciting and rejecting objects? In Fairbairn's picture of the inner world, the self is seen as split into two: a needy, desirous self (which he calls the libidinal ego) attached to the exciting object and a need-rejecting self (which he calls the antilibidinal ego) attached to the rejecting object. Thus is depicted the combination of desperate need and hatred of both self and other that is felt by many poor patients as they apply for, or are asked to come for recertification of their need for, public assistance.

As Linda requested help from the intern with SSI, the intern found herself identified, despite their conversation about her life, with the entire tantalizing social welfare system. In principle, is this situation different from any other transferential situation? Perhaps there are echoes here of what one would presume was Linda's experience with a parent. As one considers the therapeutic possibilities in this situation, Linda herself becomes an exciting and rejecting object. A would-be therapist would like to engage her in an examination of these issues, but she is so elusive. Countertransference is induced, which, as Bollas (1987) points out, can be the analyst's entrée into the patient's inner world.

Let us examine one likely transference-countertransference configuration that can be created by a patient such as Linda when she misses appointments. Particularly when there has been a session that stimulates hope for productive work together, such a patient can leave the therapist feeling rejected, abandoned, and angry. The therapist may, after many such experiences, bypass such feelings and say to herself, in effect, Good; now I have time to relax or catch up on my reading. She may hesitate to call the patient, if it seems too much like pursuing her. On the other hand, she may feel that she is abandoning the patient, perhaps in a retaliatory way, if she does not pursue her.

From an object relations perspective, what we are dealing with here can be seen as the patient's way of processing her own experience of unreliability on the part of important people in her life. As the therapist feels rejected, abandoned, or angry in relation to the patient, the therapist is sampling the patient's own experience. The situation provides the opportunity to feel one's way into the patient's object world, into her experience. This is a process described by Bollas (1987) as follows: "The patient not only talks to the analyst about the self; he also puts the analyst through intense experience, effectively inviting the analyst to know his self and his objects" (p. 250).

Sometimes there is an added twist to this scenario. After missing several weeks, perhaps after the case is closed in the clinic, the patient may show up without an appointment, as Linda did. The patient may, in addition, be in crisis. With some patients, this pattern can become the modus operandi in the clinic. In extreme cases, patients may come *only* in crisis, without appointments, and rarely, if ever, keep the appointments that are offered to them. From an object relations perspective, one can find in such a situation the patient's attempt to maintain contact, a connection, with people who are experienced as basically rejecting, unreliable, and ungiving. That is, a crisis coerces a response. A crisis dramatizes the need of the patient to such an extent that a caretaking response is virtually guaranteed. Ogden (1986) makes a similar point in stating that self-other boundaries are blurred in a crisis. For Ogden, crises are a way of reestablishing the "unmediated sensory closeness" characteristic of Melanie Klein's paranoid-schizoid position. In the later depressive position, whole object relatedness is associated with a sense of isolation, which can be reversed when a crisis brings people together. Ogden writes: "Crises are not events which take place between separate people. They are events in which patient and therapist are 'in it together'" (p. 213). In responding to crises, the therapist experiences the patient's way of maintaining, or attempting to maintain, object ties in a depriving environment.

The therapist is in a very uncomfortable position as she begins to empathize with, and sample, the patient's experience of abandonment and despair. The "burnout" with which therapists in public clinics struggle is akin to a generalized "burnout" that can be observed in poor patients. In other words, one is tempted to withdraw, to give up, in the face of the anxiety, sense of futility, and despair that are engendered both by the patient's psychological situation and by the overwhelming social problems that impact on him or her. One way of coping with these feelings is to question the suitability of psychoanalytic therapy for inner-city patients. One may thereby justify not engaging the pain of these patients' lives, while taking the focus off one's own sense of helplessness and futility.

From an object relations perspective, missed appointments, crises, and so on are the ways in which the therapist becomes what Greenberg (1986) calls an "old object," a modern representative of an internalized object. The therapeutic issue is whether the therapist can also be enough of a "new object" for the patient to allow for change to occur in the patient's inner world as a consequence of the analytic work. In Fairbairn's (1958) terms, can the analyst avoid being "press-ganged" into the patient's internal object world, like everyone else in the patient's life?

This is a knotty problem with any patient. It is not easy to find the proper balance between being an "old" and a "new" object in the patient's world. In the case of a patient from the lower socioeconomic classes, an additional complication is that deprivation is an ongoing and real factor in the patient's life. The therapist's position as a modern version of the internalized exciting and rejecting object is reinforced by the socioeconomic differential between patient and therapist, by the therapist's position as part of the social service network, and by the real power he or she potentially has as an advocate.

CASE DISCUSSIONS

Rosa

Rosa was a high school senior who came to the clinic with panic attacks and severe, intermittent depression, triggered by a recent breakup with a boyfriend. She was a bright young woman who went to an elite high school out of her neighborhood. Her mother and father were first-generation immigrants from the Dominican Republic who had lived here for about 20 years. Rosa's mother was a bright woman, but moody and sometimes quite depressed, who had never learned English. She stayed home raising her five children, of whom Rosa was the oldest. The father, an intelligent and energetic man, had worked his way up from being a stock clerk in a store, to the store manager. Rosa began therapy talking mostly about her anger that her ex-boyfriend had left her for another young woman they both knew. Rosa was enraged, depressed, with suicidal thoughts. I began seeing her twice a week.

After the first few sessions, Rosa began missing appointments. A pattern developed between us: Rosa would come to one or two sessions and then miss one. At first she would call to cancel. Something had come up at school, or she needed to be at home to help her mother. After some time, she began missing sessions without calling. I felt disappointed, sometimes angry, when she would cancel. She was an articulate and upwardly mobile person, someone with potential that I thought I could help nurture. I felt much more hope about our work than I felt with many of my other patients in the clinic, who often seemed to me more mired in despair, unable to escape intractable life situations. When she began missing sessions, I felt as if she were betraying what I thought was our joint project.

After the pattern of keeping and missing appointments had established itself, I developed a characteristic conflict about how to follow up on the missed appointments. I felt caught between intruding by pursuing her and abandoning her by seeming to ignore her absence. I also felt caught between revealing to her, by an overly eager phone call, how much I wanted her to show up and revealing to her, by withholding contact, how angry I was. My compromise solution was to wait a day or two to see if she would call; if she did not, I would write her a letter noting that she had missed an appointment and saying that unless I heard otherwise, I would expect to see her at our next appointment. Rosa would show up at the next appointment with some concrete reason she had been unable to come to the appointment and apologize for having forgotten to call me.

After a couple of months, Rosa did not respond to one of my letters, so I wrote again asking her to contact me about her plans for our next appointment. After a week's delay, Rosa called, saying she had not gotten my first letter and asking for a new appointment.

When we met, I asked Rosa what she had been thinking about our work while we had not met. She said she had been feeling better and thought perhaps she did not need to come so regularly. I asked her if she had considered contacting me to tell me so. She said that she felt uncomfortable about it: she anticipated I would think that she needed to continue her sessions, and that since I was the doctor, it was not her place to disagree. I asked her how she thought I had experienced her absence, and she said that she had actually thought about me at one point and wondered how I would fill the time when she did not show up. When I pressed her to speculate about my state of mind, she said she thought I was probably angry to be "stood up." I said perhaps this was not unlike what she had felt, although more intensely, when her boyfriend had "stood her up," and she agreed.

In the next session, Rosa expressed anger at her mother for insisting that she be home at midnight the previous weekend when she had gone to a party. She felt that her mother could not accept that she was pretty much grown up. What if she wanted to go away to college the next year? Would her mother even let her go? Rosa felt that her mother had no life of her own, that she would go into a depression if Rosa did not stay home with her. I suggested that Rosa might feel similarly about me, that she had to hide her thought that she was feeling better and might not need me anymore. Rosa agreed and said that she had also been feeling angry at me for pursuing her when she thought she was making it clear by her absence that she did not want to come to her sessions, at least on a regular basis. Her mother and I were both standing in the way of her developing autonomy. Over the next few sessions, none of which were missed, we had the opportunity to explore her guilt about wanting to be more independent. She felt that she was leaving behind her mother, as well as her childhood friends, in going "downtown" to school.

In subsequent sessions, we also talked about how Rosa saw me as potentially facilitating her growth away from her mother, because I was White, a professional, and a man and because we were trying to remove obstacles to her independent development. Thus, her work with me was threatening whether she saw me as representing her mother or as an alternative to her mother, like her upwardly mobile father. Here there was another problem. Rosa suspected that her father had a covert sexual interest in her. She felt that her father felt more of a kinship with Rosa than with his wife. For example, the two of them would speak English together, excluding the mother. Anxiety about her father's sexual feelings toward her, as well as oedipal guilt, was thus activated in relation to me as father-transference object. Rosa denied anxiety about sexual feelings between us, but I suspected that this issue was too threatening to take up at that time.

Rosa continued her treatment, on and off, until she graduated from high school. She went to college away from home, dropped out, reenrolled near home, and called me from time to time in distress about ways in which she felt she was sabotaging her success. I have not seen her for two years at this writing.

This case example illustrates many aspects of clinical work in impoverished neighborhoods. Issues of socioeconomic status, ethnicity, culture, and gender also significantly contributed to the transference-countertransference matrix in which we worked. Missed appointments and my response to them had a crucial catalyzing function in developing a shared understanding of this matrix. I return to many of these issues in subsequent chapters.

José

José was a 16-year-old high school junior when I began to see him. A year earlier he had been removed from his mother's home and placed in a group home by the City Department of Child Welfare. José, his mother, and his brother had been found living in a park. The mother had been having a psychotic episode. José had been referred for therapy because of severe compulsive rituals and obsessive thoughts. These resolved quickly upon entering therapy, although he remained prone to seemingly unprovoked feelings of impending doom.

As I got to know José, I learned that his mother had had several other psychotic episodes through the years and that he had taken on major responsibility for raising his younger brother. José would not go to school unless he was sure that things were under control at home. José never knew his father.

Upon entering the group home, José was placed in an alternative school, where he could get individualized instruction and attention to his emotional needs. He was very bright. Despite having missed so much school over the years, he excelled. He had a gentle, unassuming manner that endeared him to his teachers. They spent a lot of one-on-one time with him and gave him special help and attention. José eventually graduated as valedictorian of his class, and received a scholarship to go to college.

I saw José once a week for a year until he graduated. He spoke softly and undemonstratively, yawning a lot. I, too, found it hard to keep my eyelids from drooping when I was with him. As the year went on, José began having intrusive thoughts about hurting his mother. He was horrified. I tried to encourage him to tolerate these thoughts and to differentiate them from actions. One day, however, José came in and told me that he had thrown a rock through the window of his mother's new apartment. Now I was horrified, too, and I began to feel that I had been too quick to assume thoughts and actions *could* be differentiated for José. I also developed a new appreciation for his rage and how the somnolent atmosphere in the sessions may have been a cover for these feelings. I now had to find a way to approach José's angry feelings without complacently assuming that verbalization would ensure control or that we could handle what would emerge if we opened this Pandora's box. I found myself respecting, even welcoming, José's defenses in a way that sometimes seemed antianalytic or an acting out of my own anxiety about the level of his rage. This issue never felt fully resolved between us; as we continued our work, rage receded as an issue as José's life became quite stable and satisfying; it seemed he had created a new family for himself with his group home counselors, his high school teachers, and me.

When he graduated from high school, however, José began dismantling his support network. He decided to move out of the group home, although he would have been allowed to stay as long as he was in college. He moved in with one of his high school teachers who (quite inappropriately, I thought) offered José a room in his house. He decided to drop out of therapy, although I felt uneasy about his leaving therapy at a major transition point in his life. I thought that José was managing abandonment feelings connected with high school graduation and the end of his time at the group home by retaining the connection to his teacher and leaving the group home before it could ask him to leave. I also thought José might be preempting an anticipated abandonment by me. My comments to this effect were quickly dismissed by José. I began to feel that he was disengaging from me, perhaps in a manner reminiscent of how it felt to him when his mother would disengage from him.

I next heard from José about six months later. He had not entered college and planned to work for a year and save some money. He had started work as a stock boy in a store and had so impressed his superiors that he was promoted several times. He had also started to drink heavily. He called me after he missed work one day without calling in, the day after receiving a major promotion. In addition, he had begun stealing liquor from the former teacher from whom he was renting his room. He thought he was probably about to be caught and thrown out. He saw that he was sabotaging his success and thought it was time to come back to therapy.

I had an administrative, as well as a clinical, problem at this point. Since José had terminated his treatment, he needed to be reregistered as a patient. Being 18 years old, however, he was no longer entitled to be a patient in the Child Psychiatry clinic. I was able to obtain an exception for José, however, and he was registered as a patient so that I could see him. My next problem was that he would have to receive a psychiatric evaluation as part of the intake process for all new and returning patients. My team psychiatrist, however, refused to see him. He said that he no longer should be seen in the child clinic, that he was an adult and should be seen in the adult clinic. I was enraged. At the same time, I was wary of creating or reinforcing an alienating polarization between the psychiatrist and me. On a political level, I had to recognize that the psychiatrist was above me in the clinic hierarchy. In a showdown between us, he would prevail. My rage was thus fed by a sense of helplessness. I also believed that the psychiatrist resented what he perceived as the arrogance of psychologists who considered themselves to be the better clinicians. There was truth to that perception. I felt the psychiatrist was using his institutional power in an ongoing struggle between the professions. If I were to have any control over this situation, I would have to find some way to ally with the psychiatrist.

Thus, I acknowledged the validity of some of the psychiatrist's concerns. There were too many patients for the clinic to handle, so it did make sense, in this way, to deny admittance to those who were adults, and José had given up his place in my caseload when he interrupted his treatment. Clinical and administrative considerations often pulled one in opposite directions. Such conflicts formed the basis of alienation between clinical and administrative staff. In this case, however, the psychiatrist was a clinician, not an administrator, so I could only conclude that he did not want the responsibility or the work I was asking him to assume. If he had asked me to do likewise, for example, if he had asked me to see an adult medication patient in therapy or to test that patient, I would have said no as well. Thus, I established some sense of alliance with the psychiatrist within myself. Acknowledging the psychiatrist's point of view, I nonetheless made a case for continuity of treatment by calling his attention to the dynamics between José and me and how he would have transformed me into an abandoning object if we were to send him away. The psychiatrist acknowledged that this was an unfortu-nate outcome but said there was no reason José could not work this problem out with another therapist. He flatly refused to see José. I appealed to his supervisor, the chief psychiatrist, who had supported me in the past when I had conflict with other psychiatrists. (This was certainly part of the resentment my psychiatrist felt toward me.) In this case, the supervisor upheld the psychiatrist's decision. (This was part of an ongoing realignment of the balance of power in the clinic, that is, a consolidation of psychiatric control, which I discuss in detail in a later chapter.) I had to refer José to the adult clinic.

At the adult clinic, I inquired as to whether I could see José there. The administrator was sympathetic but could not guarantee me an office for an hour a week. I would have to come in early and see if anyone was out sick. There were residents and interns who also had no regular office who would be competing with me for office space. In the end, José was not registered in the adult clinic either when it was discovered that he lived outside the catchment area of the hospital. He was referred to another hospital, where, José informed me, there was a waiting list several months long. I next heard from José about a year later after he had been arrested for assaulting a woman with whom he was living. I tried to help him find a clinic where he could be seen. After this contact, I never heard from him again. In this case a confluence of factors, ranging from José's internal object world, to administrative problems, to the interprofessional dynamics in this clinic, combined to reinforce a reenactment of José's experience of parental abandonment. I return to some of these issues when I discuss interstaff relationships in public clinics.

Nancy

Nancy had first come to our clinic after giving birth to a baby at the age of 14. The obstetrics department social worker thought she was depressed and considered her at risk for neglecting her child. The baby's father, a drug abuser, was not taking responsibility. Nancy lived with her mother, who received public assistance, one older and two younger brothers, and one younger sister. One brother was in prison for selling drugs. Another brother was reported by Nancy to be a regular user of heroin and crack cocaine. He rarely went to school. The sister was doing well in school. Nancy's father was in prison in Jamaica for murder.

Nancy presented as quite depressed on her first visit to the clinic with her baby. Her mother accompanied her and was sullen, seemingly angry at Nancy. She and Nancy argued over who was in charge of the baby. Nancy's mother did not come for any of the follow-up appointments. Nancy came twice and then missed two appointments without calling.

This was the sort of situation in which I often made home visits. I felt some uneasiness about making home visits, not only because I had been schooled in the ways of analytic reserve. I had concerns about the potential seductiveness of making a home visit, in terms of appearing to promise more than I could deliver as a clinician, that is, of implicitly promising to become like a member of the family. On the other hand, I felt that this was a difficult-to-involve patient and family and that a home visit often created a bond that made it more likely that people would come to the clinic.[2] I also found that it deepened my experience of public clinic work to visit people's homes in this community. I often found myself recoiling from imagining what it was like actually to live in this community. It was easy to avoid thinking about these matters after working in this community for some time; I would drive in, sit in a comfortable clinic office all day, and go home to my doorman luxury building, which was five miles, but light years, away. Walking into the vestibule of a building in this inner-city neighborhood, going through the front door, which was always unlocked, walking nervously past people who were "hanging out" on the sidewalk or in the lobby of the building, using a decrepit elevator—all these experiences gave me a powerful, if limited, sense of this community from the inside in counterpoint to the usual "ivory tower" experience.

In this case I decided to make a home visit. My anxiety was somewhat mitigated at first by finding that Nancy lived on the ground floor (I would not have to brave the elevator) and by seeing her smiling face greeting me out the window as I approached her

---

[2] Fraiberg (1987) has written about mother–infant work done exclusively via home visits.

building. Outside her door was the shadow of a *mezuzah* (discolored
paint where the traditional doorpost marker of a Jewish household
had hung, probably decades earlier). I entered the apartment and was
immediately struck by the emptiness of the space. It was a large
apartment, with a large living room, into which I was shown. The
living room had one chair and no other furniture. Nancy brought
another chair in for her to sit on, offered me some coffee, then
disappeared into the kitchen. Shortly afterward, Nancy's mother
appeared carrying the baby. At some point I got a glimpse into the
kitchen and saw what looked like a brand new washing machine and
dryer. At that time in my life, I did not have such appliances in my
apartment. How does a family that lives from welfare check to
welfare check afford a washing machine and dryer? I thought that
perhaps this was part of the spoils of the boys' drug dealing and
perhaps a source of the mother's collusion in the continuation of this
side business. I had wondered why the mother could not stop her
sons from getting into such trouble and why she was not more
aggressively seeking help for her family. Perhaps she had mixed
feelings about the whole thing: on one hand, wanting her sons to
make it in the workaday world of schools and jobs, not wanting them
to be antisocial, not wanting them to end up in jail like their father.
On the other hand, how does one live on what welfare provides?
How does one resist the little luxuries that are available when a child
or two get involved with drug distribution or selling? How feasible
did it seem that her children could make a decent living from a job?
Perhaps the mother was a pragmatic or cynical woman who knew
how things worked in the real world in which she lived. Had there
never been furniture in this apartment? I had been in many other
apartments of welfare recipients in which there was furniture. Was
the furniture sold to support someone's drug addiction? Had a
decision been made to buy a washing machine and dryer and forgo
other furniture? How would I find out the answers to these questions? Was I being suspicious and unsympathetic to these people? If
I were more sympathetic, impressed by their poverty and deprivation, would I be overlooking their sociopathy or perhaps their
competence in "making it" in the ways that were open to them? How
could I get to know Nancy and her life situation unless these
questions were answered?

In any case, my first home visit to Nancy and her family did seem
to create a bond between us: Nancy came to the clinic more
regularly, and I saw her mother from time to time. Over the months,
their attendance would become irregular from time to time, and then

I would make another home visit. Sometimes I imagined that a pattern had developed in which Nancy would induce me to make a home visit by missing appointments, so I would thereby demonstrate my caring and concern. I also wondered whether we were colluding to deny the limits of my involvement with Nancy and her family by re-creating the illusion that I was a member of the family through these home visits.

My ability to make such home visits ended abruptly when the state Medicaid office decided not to reimburse clinics for visits that took place off-site. We could no longer make home visits or school visits to observe children in the classroom and talk with their teachers. Nancy stopped coming to the clinic after she was raped in another part of town. I saw her on an emergency basis the day after the rape. She had been seen at the hospital and referred to a rape crisis team there. Nancy was in a traumatized and disorganized state. It was not clear what had happened to her. Nancy did not show up for subsequent appointments. I could not call her, since the apartment had no phone. I wrote to her and received a response from her mother that Nancy was too frightened to go out. A few weeks later, I heard from her mother that Nancy had disappeared with a boyfriend and left the baby with her. That was the last contact I had with this family.

Nancy's inconsistent attendance at the clinic reflected an internal object world characterized by devaluing and traumatically abandoning relationships. Upon entering this world, I was faced with my own feelings of being abandoned by Nancy and her family, as well as the prospect of being insufficiently available to them myself. In choosing to make home visits, I was trying to be a "new" and "good" object. I tend to be wary of such efforts and believe that "old" and "bad" object relationships must also be engaged for deep analytic work to be accomplished. In this case, however, as in so many others that present in inner-city public clinics, to fail to reach out often means never to engage the patient or family at all. Old object relations tend to establish themselves despite, often through, one's efforts to be "new" and "good." In this case I became an old object not only because of the limits on my availability inherent in my role as a clinician but also because of the limits on my availability imposed by public-sector bureaucratic regulations. I ended up, perhaps, promising to be available in ways I could not sustain, as I had feared. Part of the problem here is that clinical considerations such as I had in mind were not factors for those who administer the Medicaid program. I return in later chapters to these administrative issues, as well as transference-countertransference issues that arise around home visits.

In the course of my therapeutic work with Nancy, in the second year of once-a-week treatment, she reported a dream in which she surreptitiously put her hand in my pocket and found a $100 bill. This session was the first in which I had asked Nancy for dreams. Her explicit associations to the dream had to do with thinking that perhaps she was about to come into some money, but she had no idea how I might be involved. She went on to talk about feeling resentful that the father of her year-old baby was failing to provide financial support as promised. She said that she hoped to locate her father, who had been released from prison, she thought, and might be somewhere now in the community. He had always been support-ive when she was a little girl, she said with tears in her eyes, but every man in her life who was ever supportive let her down sooner or later.

At the end of this session, I wrote out a slip for Nancy that allowed her to receive bus fare from the clinic receptionist. Patients such as Nancy who are on Medicaid are entitled to reimbursement for their travel expenses to medical appointments. On this occasion, Nancy took the slip and then asked me if I would write out slips for two of her younger brothers, who had accompanied her to the clinic and were sitting in the waiting room. I hesitated. I was in the habit of writing a slip for one of her brothers who accompanied her, because Nancy said she never ventured out alone in the neighbor-hood where she lived. I felt some justification, but I also felt uneasy about giving bus fare at all. One of Nancy's brothers, who lived at home, was a daily drug user, despite having no visible source of income. The two other brothers probably used drugs as well, at least occasionally. Was it right to give money for bus fare to her brother when I knew that he was probably spending considerable sums on drugs? With these thoughts in mind, I said I could give a slip for bus fare only to Nancy and one brother. Only after Nancy left did I note the parallel between the dream and the request for extra bus fare at the end of the session.

How are we to understand this dream, along with the ensuing events in the session? On one hand, they suggest that the patient saw me quite literally as a source of money to be exploited. From the perspective of Fairbairn's theory, as mentioned before, our attention is called to the way in which the therapist in the dream is portrayed as an exciting object. The exciting quality can be linked to the therapist as the bearer of money, as a sexually exciting object, or both. The dream, in fact, seems to imply an identification of sexuality and money, or nurturance, more broadly. The therapist as rejecting object also seems inherent in the dream. Why else would Nancy need to take the money from me surreptitiously? The way in which the session ended, in fact, seemed to leave me in the role of depriving object. From this perspective, then, the bus fare issue has provided a focus for the manifestation of the patient's internal object world in the therapeutic setting. The therapist has become an "old object." The therapeutic problem is how to shift one's position away from enacting the internal drama with the patient, to examining with the patient the nature of the dream and the ways in which the script is written.

I would like to call attention to the way in which the administrative structure of this clinic plays a role in this vignette. The fact that the therapist fills out the bus fare slip means that he is put in the role of deciding who gets reimbursement and who does not. From a classical point of view, the therapist's neutrality and anonymity are compromised when he is in the role of dispensing or withholding money. The transference becomes uninterpretable because the therapist has taken action in reality. From this perspective, the bus fare decisions should be made by clerical or administrative staff to preserve the therapist's neutral position, so that the patient's transference fantasies can be properly analyzed.

From a relational perspective, the administrative issue brings us back to the question of how the therapist can strike the proper balance between being an old object and being a new object for the patient. As with Nancy, when the therapist manages the dispensing or withholding of money, the stage is set for the patient to see the therapist as an exciting and rejecting object. A focus is provided. Is this a desirable development from the point of view of the treatment? In some cases, it may be so. The bus fare issue may provide a focus for the analysis of these transference issues when the patient sees the therapist primarily as a new object. In other cases, the therapist may already be seen, in an excessively concrete way, as an exciting and rejecting object. The socioeconomic differential between patient and therapist makes it quite likely that many patients see the therapist in this way. In these instances, the therapist's involvement with bus fare may "heat up" the transference feelings further and work against the development of a view of the therapist as a new object. It may become difficult to find any sort of detached perspective from which to view, with the patient, the transferential perceptions that have developed.

Child Abuse

Josephine was referred to our clinic by a child abuse prevention program. She had hit her child on at least one occasion, leaving a bruise that had been noted by her son's school. The school made a report to the local child welfare agency, which referred her to a child abuse prevention program, the mission of which was to keep families together, to prevent placement of the children. The bureaucratic goal here, I believe, was to save money on foster care and other forms of residential placement. In order to accomplish this goal, child abuse prevention workers were to be available 24 hours a day to intervene in whatever way necessary to prevent further child abuse.

Josephine had been raised by her mother as an only child. She did not know her father. Her mother had many boyfriends, with whom she was preoccupied, so that Josephine felt quite neglected. At age 14, Josephine became pregnant with her son. She and her mother got into severe conflict over her decision to have this baby, and Josephine ended up leaving home and going to live with the father of the baby. He became physically abusive to Josephine, and she left him at age 16, getting her own apartment with her son while being supported by an older man with whom she had entered a relationship.

Josephine missed several appointments when she first began treatment with me. As was required by the clinic's agreement with the child abuse prevention project, I informed the worker, who began accompanying Josephine to her appointments with me. After several such accompanied visits, Josephine began coming to appointments on her own. She came, at first, with her son. She used the time, however, almost exclusively to talk about her own life, about how she had no support from her mother, and about difficulties she was having with her boyfriend, the older man, who seemed to have quite a bit of money. She talked of feeling enraged with her son when he demanded attention at times when she felt unsupported by her mother and boyfriend. She had abused her son on an occasion when her boyfriend had not called her for a few days. Josephine missed about half of our sessions but always responded to a phone call. I felt no need to involve the child abuse prevention worker again. After a while, she stopped bringing her son. She was able to discipline him without physical means, and she seemed to be moving forward in her life. She had gotten a job and felt quite proud of herself.

After seeing Josephine for about a year, having decided to leave the clinic and go into full-time private practice, I was in the anguishing position of having to tell her, along with my other patients, that I would be leaving her and our work. I told Josephine about my departure in a session two months before I left. She said she understood; she thought that I was moving ahead in my life as she was in hers. Josephine, however, did not show up for her next several sessions, and she did not respond to my phone calls. Eventually, it seemed that I would not even have the opportunity to say good-bye to her. At this point, I decided to inform the child abuse prevention worker that I was leaving and that Josephine had missed our last few appointments. I asked the worker to encourage Josephine to come to the clinic to say good-bye and so I could inform her of arrangements to be transferred to another therapist.

On my last day seeing patients in the clinic, Josephine arrived, accompanied by the child abuse prevention worker and her son. Her son had a large bruise on the side of his face. Before seeing Josephine, I asked the worker if she had reported this new incident of abuse. She said no, that she saw no need to report it, since Josephine had generally been doing so well. I felt very uneasy, however, since I was required by law to report the incident if it had not already been reported. The child abuse prevention worker refused to report it, and so in my last session with Josephine I had to tell her that I was going to report the bruise on her son's face. She was furious with me and said that she had just gotten her life together and that this incident would set her back. She would have home visits again, people looking over her shoulder, and, perhaps she would even lose her son. I tried to talk about the recurrence of her abusive behavior toward her son in terms of the impact on her of my abandoning her by leaving the clinic. Josephine sat sullen, not speaking. In this way, we said good-bye.

In retrospect, I believe that Josephine saw the child abuse prevention worker and me as a team, as an attentive, caring mother, preoccupied with, and protective of, her. Her son represented both his father, who had abused Josephine, and her own needy self, in relation to which she took a violently repressive attitude. In relation to her son, she enacted her identification with her own abusers. At first, Josephine thrived with the attention we paid her. When I told her I would be terminating the treatment, she reacted at first by mobilizing an independent, self-reliant, nonneedy side of herself. Staying away from me for weeks thereafter both expressed and defended against the arousal of rage against me as an abandoning object. In this context, when I pressed Josephine to come for a final session and called in the child abuse prevention worker, I became a persecutory object. The alternative, which seemed even less desirable to me, was to leave without processing the termination with Josephine at all. Despite my knowledge that I would be perceived as intrusive and persecutory, I was stunned to see the bruise on her son's face—a concrete sign of her rage at me and her own deprived, abandoned self. I felt the pain, in some ways, more acutely than I would have if my own face had been punched. It was as if Josephine were showing me what she felt I was doing to her in leaving her. The child abuse prevention worker, knowing she had been drawn into the force field between Josephine and me refused to be drawn in further by calling the child welfare authorities. She may have had other reasons for not wanting to call: further child abuse in one of her families might have seemed like evidence of a failure on her part to her superiors. A final consideration is that by hitting her son, Josephine may have been unconsciously mobilizing further care from the child abuse prevention worker, who had largely withdrawn from the case.

Thomas

Thomas was 6 years old when he was first referred to our clinic by the agency through which he had been placed in foster care. Thomas's mother, Ms. B, 22 years old, had suffered several psychotic episodes requiring hospitalization and outpatient follow-up. She had left her two children, Thomas and a 3-year-old sister, home alone for two or three days immediately prior to her latest hospitalization. As a result, the child welfare administration was called, and Thomas and his sister were placed in separate foster homes. I began seeing Thomas after his first set of foster parents returned him to the foster care agency after he had been with them for three weeks. They said Thomas had been quiet and well behaved for the first week but that he had started stealing things, usually small change, from the foster parents' bedroom. He also was reported to "steal" food from the family's refrigerator and hoard it in various places in his room. They were not willing to tolerate this behavior and told Thomas they would send him back if he did not stop. The next day, they caught him in their room picking through some of their things and sent him to the foster care agency as they had promised.

When I began seeing him, Thomas was temporarily in a group home while the agency sought out new foster parents. After the first session or two, in which he was reserved and wary, Thomas relaxed and became very active and involved with the toys in my office. He seemed to attach to me very strongly, a bit too strongly and too quickly, it seemed to me. He ran into my office when I came to get him from the waiting room. Sometimes I found him waiting outside my door when I went out to get him, so eager that he could not wait. He resisted leaving as sessions ended and found one thing or another he still had to do. Thomas claimed to be starving as we began sessions; we always spent several minutes in the snack room negotiating over how much food he would be allowed to have. (See section on food earlier in this chapter.) At the very beginning of sessions, I felt Thomas was very glad to see me and I to see him. Within minutes, however, there was a feeling of conflict and exasperation over food. Once we got back to my office, Thomas was so active and distractible that it was fatiguing to try to keep up with him. The sense of conflict and exasperation returned as I tried to end the session. I often thought that Thomas had created a situation in which I felt like rejecting him and his demands. I found myself almost pushing him out of my office at the end of sessions when I had another patient. In my more reflective moments, I would think that we had re-created some of the feeling of being rejected and abandoned by his mother. I would occasionally try to comment to Thomas on his feeling that he never got enough from me or that he must have felt pushed away at times with his mother as he did with me as our sessions ended. I was never sure I was not talking to the wind, a whirlwind, in his case. It was a constant struggle to use my experience with Thomas to understand him, rather than simply to reenact his traumatic past, and to try to find a way to let him know that I was doing so.

Over a period of three years, Thomas went through two more foster homes. He made a good adjustment in one home after a period of testing and provocation. This family wanted to adopt a child, however; Thomas was not available for adoption because his mother's parental rights had not been terminated. When another child became available for adoption to this family, Thomas was sent back to the agency again. In the next family, Thomas was expelled within a month after he cut the cord on the family's television set. As the search began for a fourth foster home, I emphasized to the foster care worker how important it was to give prospective parents a realistic sense of what Thomas was like, how he tended to be provocative at first and how later he was very lovable but also active and demanding. Parents needed to know what they were committing themselves to before they took Thomas; otherwise, there was the prospect of an indefinitely long series of attachments followed by loss. After several months in a group home, during which I could see Thomas only intermittently, a family was found that seemed realistic about him, yet willing to take him on. I began seeing Thomas again regularly.

Thomas's mother had been fighting in court during all this time to get him back. Although she had little money, a prominent attorney had taken an interest in her case. Despite her willingness to go to court, Thomas's mother almost never showed up for scheduled visits with him. She also failed to show up for appointments with me that I scheduled with her. As a result, her motions to have Thomas returned to her were always denied. Nonetheless, she refused to give up her parental rights so that Thomas could be adopted. After scheduled visits with his mother at which she would not appear, Thomas would be especially provocative with me and with his foster family. Our sessions over time became more and more characterized by conflict, anger, a sense that I was depriving him.

In the fourth year, the foster care agency, with my encouragement, decided to move in court to get Thomas's mother's parental rights terminated. The foster family, meanwhile, proved to be as patient with Thomas as they had promised. They were fundamentalist Christians, and their lives were centered on the church. Thomas resisted going to church and acted up when he was there, but nothing seemed to disturb the stolid commitment of this family. I met regularly with the foster mother, who came dutifully to the sessions and reported on some of Thomas's activities but did not seem very attuned to his feelings. Her husband came for the first session to meet me. He said little and never came again. I would call him from time to time to get his observations of Thomas.

One day, unexpectedly, the judge removed Ms. B's attorney from the case for reasons that were never clear to me. Soon thereafter, he terminated Ms. B's parental rights. Thomas's foster family immediately applied to adopt him. There was a dramatic change in Thomas when the adoption became final: he became much calmer, less provocative, more thoughtful and reflective, better related with me in sessions. There was little frenetic activity, no more desperation about getting more food, a willingness to leave at the end of sessions with a sense that there would be another session soon. Thomas also suddenly became an enthusiastic member of his family's church. A few months later, Thomas, the foster family, and I agreed that it made sense for us to terminate the treatment. At our last session, Thomas invited me to come to Sunday services at his church. I was moved by his invitation and happy to accept. A few weeks later, I found myself sitting in the pews of a fundamentalist Christian church in the Bronx, listening to the preacher, and contemplating what life would be like if one felt that one could be transformed through faith at any moment. Being in this church exposed me to a sense of purpose and inspiration that I had not often encountered sitting in a clinic in the South Bronx. Especially, I was impressed by the men. I had seen many women of strength and determination who brought their children to the clinic. Men were too often conspicuous by their absence. In the church I saw men on the pulpit and in the congregation who could give a boy something promising to look forward to in growing up to be a man. I was grateful to Thomas for inviting me to see what kind of life he had entered.

In this case, therapeutic work with Thomas had to be coupled with case management work with the foster care agency and the foster parents. Thomas's problems were internalized, in the sense that he tended to reproduce an internal world of abandoning objects by provoking rejection by caretakers. As an analyst has to "work through in the countertransference" (Pick, 1988) to avoid unreflectively playing the part assigned to him by the patient, so the foster parents needed to be able to take perspective on Thomas's provocative behavior so as to manage it without rejection. As Thomas's analyst, my job was to see my impatience, exasperation, even rage at Thomas in the light of the internal situation he was enacting with me. It seemed essential to help the people in his support network to do the same thing. Ultimately, Thomas seemed exceptionally responsive to the commitment and stability provided by his adoptive family. Religion seemed to offer a structure that assisted this family in containing the feelings that Thomas tended to induce in them, so that they could steadfastly maintain their commitment to him in the face of all manner of provocation. Once Thomas felt secure with them, he adopted the church as his own containing structure. His parting gift to me was to invite me into this new world of his where we both felt he could stay at least long enough to grow up. After years of trying to engage Thomas and the people in his environment in my world of psychoanalytic therapy, it felt good to be on their turf and to try to make sense, in my own terms, of some of what I found there.

2 / THEORETICAL, HISTORICAL, AND SOCIOLOGICAL BACKGROUND

Psychoanalysis and Social Issues

As early as 1919, Freud acknowledged that psychoanalysis had become a treatment for the well-to-do. He attributed this fact to "the necessities of our own existence" (p. 166). He had a vision, however, of a day when

> the conscience of the community will awake and remind it that the poor man should have just as much right to assistance for his mind as he now has to the life-saving help offered by surgery; and that the neuroses threaten public health no less than tuberculosis and can be left as little as the latter to the impotent care of individual members of the community [p. 167].

Freud looked forward to the day when clinics would be built, to which "analytically trained physicians" would be appointed. He envisioned that the treatment would be free. Freud also thought that analytic treatment would have to be adapted to these new conditions. He thought psychotherapy might have to be combined with some

> material support. . . . the large-scale application of our therapy will compel us to alloy the pure gold of analysis freely with the copper of direct suggestion. . . . whatever form this psychotherapy for the people may take, whatever the elements out of which it is compounded, its most effective and most important ingredients will assuredly remain those borrowed from strict and untendentious psychoanalysis [pp. 167–168].

Freud evidently was not daunted by the prospect of working with people who were different socioeconomically or culturally, for he wrote in the same paper, "I have been able to help people with whom I had nothing in common, neither race, education, social position, nor outlook upon life in general" (p. 165).

Freud reveals here a democratic sensibility, a discomfort with a restriction of psychoanalytic treatment to those well-to-do patients who satisfy the analyst's material needs. In contemplating psychoanalytic treatment of the poor, Freud assumes, with some implicit defensiveness, that material help and direct suggestive techniques will be necessary. He does not elaborate on these assumptions, but it seems that Freud thought that material needs had to be met before psychological issues could be addressed, that material deprivation would make it more difficult or impossible for poor patients to tolerate analytic abstinence, or both. This latter consideration may also account for his assumption that suggestive techniques, insofar as they gratify the patient's dependent wishes, may be required with poor patients. Freud may also have felt that poor people were less capable of independent functioning. He compares the analyst working with the poor to Emperor Joseph (Freud, 1913), who, as Dimen (1994) points out, lived among the poor in order better to understand their needs. Dimen writes: "It would not, of course, have occurred to either the emperor or the physician what we take for granted today, that poor people might actually have been able to articulate at least some of their own needs" (p. 80).

Freud's vision of a more democratic psychoanalytic treatment was put into practice, on a small scale, at the Berlin Psychoanalytic Society. Members of this society offered one free treatment of a patient. Training cases for candidates were also drawn from this clinic.

The Frankfurt School

Beginning in the 1920s, a group of intellectuals, philosophers, for the most part, came together to form the Institute for Social Research in Frankfurt. (See Jay, 1973, for a comprehensive discussion of the Frankfurt school.) Their project was critical social theory from a Hegelian, that is, dialectical, and Marxist perspective. A psychoanalytic point of view was added by Erich Fromm, who joined the philosophers Max Horkheimer, Theodor Adorno, and Herbert Marcuse. Marcuse and Norman O. Brown developed their own integration of Freudian thought in some of their work. "Critical social theory" seeks to transcend uncritical embeddedness in current socioeconomic structures and arrangements. Following Hegel, the

Frankfurt social theorists posited a gap between appearance and essence, so that whatever is "given" exists in dialectical relation with its opposite at another level of analysis. Philosophical positivism and idealism, seeming opposites, both, by contrast, split appearance from essence and privileged one over the other. Positivism regards appearance, that is, the observable, as ultimate reality, whereas idealism so regards essence, the world of the abstract. The Frankfurt school theorists strove for a middle ground in which the gap between appearance and essence would provide a space within which one could examine the given of the social world from an outside perspective. Therein lies the potential for a "critical" social theory. The Frankfurt school theorists regarded both positivist and idealist philosophical stances as leading to social quietism, to uncritical acceptance of the status quo, the given.

In providing a standpoint from which to engage in critique, dialectical thinking further provided a standpoint from which to engage in resistance to the established social order. Marxism, with its revolutionary bent, was consistent with the commitment of these philosophers to praxis, that is, action in the world conceived of as inseparable from critique. Thus, philosophical idealism was rejected as unengaged with the world of appearance in which praxis can take place. Their Marxist perspective led the Frankfurt school theorists to focus on capitalism as the socially given, with critique drawing on the socialist alternative.

Psychoanalysis was integrated by Brown (1959) and Marcuse (1964), building on the work of Wilhelm Reich (1945). Reich had attempted to join psychoanalysis with leftist social theory. Building on Freud's (1930) depiction of conflict between id impulses and society, internalized as the superego, he developed a picture of the individual in conflict with an oppressive social and economic system. Reich thought that the repression of sexuality was responsible not only for individual neurosis but also for massive compliance with repressive and exploitative capitalistic social and economic forces. The liberation of libido would result in individual freedom to resist these forces. Reich, thus, established the id as the locus of an oppositional point of view toward the socially given. Repression of libido was identical with the process by which people were inducted into a damaging social order. Reich's emphasis became pragmatic and therapeutic as he turned his attention to ways in which to liberate libido, in terms of orgastic energy (the orgone box).

Brown's (1959) and Marcuse's (1966) concerns remained theoretical. They posited a primal unity in which the life force, eros

(Marcuse's preferred term) or libido, suffused the entire body. For historical reasons, this primal unity was broken. That is, in order to accommodate the demands of social living, libido had to succumb to repression and sublimation. In this process, libido was removed from its connection with the body and was spiritualized, in a way that diminished its life-giving power. Further, the patriarchal family structure demanded that libido submit to genital primacy and robbed the nongenital parts of the body of their connection with the life force. Such a deadening of most of the body paved the way for the devitalized or alienated work required in a capitalist society according to a Marxist point of view. Marcuse (1966) believed that some degree of repression of eros was necessary for any sort of civilized living but that the perpetuation of particular oppressive social orders entailed extra, or "surplus," repression (p. 35). Marcuse envisioned the lifting of surplus repression so as to release pregenital sexuality, a liberation of the polymorphously perverse. He felt the time was ripe, at this point in history, for such developments because of the very success of the technical rationality that requires the repression of infantile sexuality. That is, in the state of abundance that modern civilization has produced, there is less need to organize people's psyches in the service of the domination of nature. For Brown and especially Marcuse, a return to pregenital sexuality, to what Freud called polymorphous perversity, promised to restore the primal unity of the body with the life force. In the process, the alienating, oppressive impact of society would be overcome. The tendency of the repressed to return, as demonstrated by Freud, meant that the pressure of pregenital impulses in the unconscious was a constant, socially subversive force. In the depths of his mind, the individual is opposed to society, as Freud had believed. Brown and Marcuse did not share Freud's tragic vision in this respect; they believed that the liberation of the repressed impulses would lead to a beneficial transformation of society and the individuals in it.

For Freud there was an inherent opposition between unconscious sexual impulses and social order in general. For the Frankfurt school theorists, on the other hand, these impulses are subversive only with respect to oppressive societies organized around domination, capitalist society in particular. In their ideal socialist society, there would be no necessary opposition between sexual impulses and the social order. Freud's formulation has the virtue of simplicity: libido is immediately pleasure-seeking and, as such, is indifferent, if not hostile, to the requirements of any social order. No social order could ever be derived from unmodified libido, as conceived by Freud. This socially oppositional quality made libido a revolutionary force for the Frankfurt school. For this reason, Marcuse and others opposed the neo-Freudian revisionists who were positing a more socially oriented core to the individual. For Marcuse, object relations psychology was inherently adaptationalist. Yet, Marcuse conceives of the socialist order as derivable from unsublimated eros. He thus requires a conception of eros as inherently socially structured. Here I believe that Marcuse's thought is fundamentally at odds with Freudian drive theory but that Marcuse sidesteps these contradictions by using Freud's concept of eros. Freud defined eros in a way that made it seem potentially object seeking; libido, however, derived from eros, is pictured as striving solely for pleasure. Ultimately, I believe, Marcuse's reading of Freud as a revolutionary thinker (using Freud's concept of libido as recalcitrant to social influence) is incompatible with his reading of Freud in which eros is posited as the potential force behind the building of a socialist society.

Consider the various ways in which Freud conceived of the instinctual core of the individual. The structural concept of the id, on one hand, is associated with a seething cauldron of formless energy, pressing only for gratification. Eros, the life force, on the other hand, is conceptualized as striving for unification. As a force toward structure-building and organization, eros would seem to be conceivable as the force underlying object-relating. Eros is certainly not associated with the chaos and disorganization one might associate with the Freudian id. The latter qualities are rather associated with the death instinct, the source of the id's aggressive energy. Libido, or sexual energy, can be seen as object-seeking or pleasure-seeking, as striving for unification or chaos, depending on its conceptual context. As id impulse, it is pleasure-seeking; as derivative of eros, it seeks unification and thus object relatedness.

Returning to the concept of the id, it is not obvious how its liberation would lead to the egalitarian, socialist vision of society that appealed to these theorists. It is difficult to see how the liberation of a seething cauldron of formless energy could produce a society that would be anything but anarchic. Partly for this reason, Freud posited a necessary antagonism between the individual and society. This formlessness also promised liberation from oppressive social structures for the Frankfurt school; the problem remains, however, of bridging the gap between the liberation of this energy and the emergence of a society structured along particular lines. One must assume that they thought either that id energy *is* inherently organized along the lines intrinsic to a socialist society or that another sort of socializing process would be brought to bear on the liberated id energy. In the prior case, the id is not truly formless, nor is it a truly personal core, untouched by social influence. In the latter case, the Frankfurt school theorists would be proposing a better form of socialization, from their point of view. This alternative, however, would undermine their advocacy of liberation from sublimation and a return to the body or to polymorphous perversity. Such liberation would merely be a prelude to a new socialization along socialist lines. One would then have to argue that socialist socialization is better than capitalist socialization and, further, that the antagonism between the individual and society would no longer occur in socialist society; such an argument can be made, however, without advocating liberation of the id. The arguments of Brown and Marcuse are most powerful if one identifies the socialization process itself with induction into a repressive social order; one then needs to assume, however, that a return to the body, or to eros, would inherently and inevitably lead to an egalitarian, socialist society in order to avoid proposing simply a new form of socialization. In this case, however, we are back to the id as inherently structured and social; that is, we would no longer be working with the Freudian id as formless energy. It was important to Brown and Marcuse to retain Freud's presocial core of the individual (see Marcuse's [1966] postscript to *Eros and Civilization*, in which he criticizes neo-Freudian revisionism as leading to an adaptationalist psychoanalysis), but it seems that their own social vision requires a socially oriented core.

Marcuse dealt with this problem by using Freud's (1920) later conception of eros, rather than the structural notion of the id. As a force aiming toward combining "living substance into ever larger and more durable units" (Marcuse, 1966, p. 128), eros tends toward bringing things and people together. In this connection, Marcuse cites Freud's (1922) reference to a "social instinct." Marcuse now had a way of beginning to conceptualize how the liberation of the individual core would foster the building of social organizations. He proposes an inherent "libidinal morality" by citing Freudian notions of "instinctual barriers to absolute gratification" (Marcuse, 1966, p. 228) and the ways in which the superego, insofar as it allies with the id, is not "unambiguously the representative of the reality principle" (p. 229). Having posited an inherent libidinal morality, Marcuse then is able to foresee that in his ideal society there would be no socially imposed repression of the instincts necessary to maintain order; only the individual would impose order on his instincts. The death instinct would not interfere with Marcuse's ideal society because, as the conditions for instinctual gratification were improved, the death instinct's striving for quietude, or nirvana, would simultaneously be gratified.

Marcuse does not make a convincing case for the plausibility of his vision of the development of an ideal society, nor does he adequately deal with the complexities involved in integrating Freudian id psychology with the concept of eros and with his sociopolitical commitments. With respect to the plausibility of his vision, he does not adequately specify the nature of the "libidinal morality" that would preserve social order once eros was released. With respect to the issue of theoretical integration, he seems to require a concept of a relationally organized personal core to be consistent with his social vision; he finds such a core in eros, as a force striving for the unification of living substance; to the extent that libido operates under the influence of eros thus defined, it must be inherently "object-seeking" (Fairbairn, 1958) rather than pleasure-seeking. Such a conception of eros, however, seems inconsistent with his conception of a presocial individual core, oppositionally oriented to social oppression. Brown and Marcuse tried to sidestep problems inherent in integrating Freudian theory with Marxist social theory. Their inability to do so reflects problems in both Freudian theory (i.e., how to conceive of the individual as having a deeply personal core that is also relationally structured) and Marxist theory (i.e., how to conceive of a socialist order as uniquely suited to human nature and needs).

Erich Fromm (1941, 1947, 1955, 1970) dealt with some of these problems by dropping Freudian id psychology and substituting a variant of interpersonal psychoanalytic theory with a culturalist orientation. Like Brown and Marcuse, Fromm saw a tension between the individual and society. Fromm cast this tension in fundamentally different terms. For Fromm, it was not a question of deeply individual id impulses running up against societally derived repression; rather, Fromm's vision was of a society that failed to provide conditions under which the individual could actualize her potential for love and productive activity. For Fromm (1947), healthy living is defined by the development and actualization of these potentials, the achievement of what he called the "productive orientation." He viewed the thwarting influence of society in Marxist terms. That is, capitalist society creates a context in which people's characters are molded along lines required for the smooth operation of a market economy. These "social characters" represent, for Fromm, deformations in the sense that they interfere with the capacity to love and to engage in productive activity as he defines it. Nineteenth-century capitalism, which put a premium on saving and accumulating wealth and capital, produced the "exploitative character" and the "hoarding character."[1] Twentieth-century capitalism requires consumption and responsivity to advertising and an attitude toward one's work as a commodity to be bought and sold. This socioeconomic system, accordingly, has produced the "receptive" (consuming) character and the "marketing" character, within which one treats oneself as a commodity to be promoted and marketed. Following Marx, Fromm regarded these orientations to one's work and one's self as producing deformations of human nature; each entails the alienation of the person from his work and his self. Fromm followed Marx (1867) in conceiving of work as embodying the relationship between people and nature. That is, work is the process by which human beings transform nature, turn nature to their own purposes, while being transformed themselves by their interaction with the world. "The 'labour process' is thus the . . . essence of the human condition itself" (Kovel, 1988, p. 170). The meaningfulness of work, deriving from this personal interaction with nature, is lost in capitalist society; work becomes a commodity, something to be bought and sold. People work for money, rather than for the sake of some more direct transaction with nature. Their work becomes a part of someone else's (the capitalist's) project. The personalities molded to fit within such a system can reflect only the alienation built into that system.

Fromm (1955) believed that central elements in Freudian theory, such as Freud's conception of the drives and the Oedipus complex did not validly reflect human nature but were, rather, artifacts of capitalist society. Parent-child oedipal competition was reframed as a reflection of the competitive characteristics required in a market economy (pp. 74-75). Drive theory was seen as a reflection of the capitalist construction of the human being as "a system of desires and

---

[1]The hoarding character is analogous to Abraham's (1924) anal retentive character, based on the Freudian notion of the anal stage of libidinal development. In the Freudian schema, character had libidinal roots, so that a personality type reflected the nature of the libidinal stage active at the time of its evolution. For Fromm, on the other hand, character had its roots, in part, in the socialization process, under the influence of the socioeconomic system into which people had to be molded to fit. Thus, while the behaviors referred to by the "anal-retentive" character and the "hoarding orientation" may be similar or identical, the concepts are fundamentally different.

satisfactions" (p. 149).[2] Fromm believed that a failure to recognize the historically contingent nature of Freud's theory would lead to a universalization of capitalist values that would cut off the possibility of critique. In this way, for Fromm, Freud's influence was conservative and adaptationalist.

Fromm (1955) envisioned a "sane society" in which people would be free to have a "productive" character or orientation to life, in which people would be able to develop their capacities to love and to work in unalienated fashion. Fromm's sane society was organized into small work groups in which people would be able to work collaboratively, sharing control of their working conditions and the distribution of the fruits of their labor. Viewing exploitativeness and competitiveness as prototypical of a patriarchal system, Fromm turned to Bachofen's (1968) conception of matriarchal society as a model for his sane society. For Fromm, thus, there was no inherent conflict between the individual and society; such conflict was an artifact of a particular socioeconomic setup that stifled and distorted human development. In Fromm's ideal, socialist society, there would be conditions under which people could actualize their productive potential.

If Fromm saw human nature as essentially loving and productive, how did he account for the occurrence of destructive aggression? Fromm (1955) did not regard destructiveness as a primary force in human nature. Like contemporary self psychologists, he thought of nonproductive aggression, that is, aggression not in the service of the defense of oneself or one's growth, as secondary and derivative. That is, Fromm thought that violence and destructiveness were a by-product of the thwarting of human potential. In the sane society, there would be no cause for destructive aggression.

If human nature is essentially growth-oriented, how does Fromm account for the emergence of societies that thwart human potential in the first place? At this point, Fromm (1941) introduces an element in the human psyche that makes people liable to collude with, or

---

[2]This analysis has been extended by Cushman (1994), who argues that the "empty self" analogy of self psychology and of some of the British object relations theorists fits hand in glove with late capitalist ideology. That is, an empty self is seen as requiring a "commodity," be it selfobject experiences like mirroring in self psychology or objects to internalize in Kleinian theory. The analytic experience, in analogous fashion, is seen as providing the missing experience or function for the patient to internalize, that is, consume. More broadly, Cushman believes that psychoanalytic theory posits a self-contained individual, the concept of which he regards as specific to the modern West.

even opt for, social arrangements that inhibit their development. This element is existential anxiety, which arises when people are faced with their fundamental aloneness in the face of death and the uncertainties of existence. In order to avoid this anxiety, people are willing and eager to "escape from freedom," to cast their lots with authoritarian leaders who provide them with the illusion of being taken care of, the illusion of a "god" who can serve as buffer between individuals and the hazards of life, followed by their inevitable demise.

Fromm, then, sees human beings as essentially in conflict between an inherent tendency toward growth and existential anxiety. Once they have opted for the illusory protection of an authoritarian leader and an oppressive system, a vicious circle is established through the propagation of social characters which are adapted to the existing order. Much of Fromm's writing can be read as an effort to raise popular consciousness about our defensive retreat from freedom, in order to tip the balance toward productive growth and thus enhance the potential viability of a "sane society." It seems implicit in Fromm's work that, with the proper perspective, existential anxiety can be borne by human beings without resort to magical solutions.

Fromm provides a remarkably lucid and comprehensive account of the interaction between psyche and society; however, he draws an overly sharp distinction between the two. For example, consider the concept of the social character. This concept recognizes the influence of social factors on the psyche. In conceiving of this influence as a *deformation* of the psyche, however, Fromm draws a fairly sharp line between the psyche per se and the psyche as shaped by certain kinds of social influence. There is a similarity to the Winnicottian notions of true and false self here: like Winnicott, Fromm has a notion of the psyche in pristine form and the psyche as distorted by social influence.

The parallel with Winnicottian theory can be carried further: just as Winnicott believes that in the proper kind of analytic holding environment there *is* no social influence on the patient beyond facilitation of the maturational processes (Winnicott, 1958b), Fromm believes that in the right kind of society the psyche is not *influenced* by social forces; rather, society functions as a kind of facilitating environment for inherent psychic maturational potential. In this way, there is a limit to the interactionism in Fromm's view of the relationship between mind and society. Society contributes to the form of the psyche only when it deforms it. There is an analogy to the classical, as well as the Winnicottian, psychoanalytic position in which the analyst's participation is notable only when there is interference with the patient's process. There is also an absolutism in Fromm's position: a commitment to the validity of a particular kind of socioeconomic environment that is beyond questioning because it is presumed to fit with the requirements of human nature. Note that such a point of view depends on having an essentialist view of human nature, that is, that the essence of human nature remains constant, regardless of its particular manifestations in various contexts.

For Fromm, this stance is, of course, consistent with his socialist commitments. Does Fromm's socialism constitute a bias, in terms of his view of human nature and the relationship between psyche and society? Would there have been a way for Fromm to have developed a more fully interactive, less absolutist picture of the relationship between psyche and society without sacrificing his socialist values? I believe the answer is yes on both counts. With respect to bias, one must first recall that capitalistically inclined social theorists also believe that their theory fits with human nature, in this case, conceived of as essentially acquisitive, greedy, and individualistic. Capitalists would argue, as did Smith (1776), that capitalism is a system that harnesses human nature for the common good. How are we to choose between these two views of human nature with their divergent implications for social theory?

If one adopts a model of the mind as essentially interactive with its environment, it would follow that love and productivity in Fromm's sense, as well as individualism, acquisitiveness, and greed, are all part of a multifaceted human potential that manifests diversely within a field composed of self-in-interaction-with-environment. Fromm, as well as other Frankfurt school theorists, resisted such a fully interactive conception of the psyche-in-society because he feared that it would rob social theory of its revolutionary implications. That is, if psyche is inherently embedded in society, how is one to conceive of the individual's critiquing, or revolting against, the established order? Fromm and his colleagues were wary of adaptationalist psychologies. It thus became important for them to retain some conception of the self as untouched by society. For Marcuse and Brown, as we have seen, the concepts of the id, libido, and eros served this function. For Fromm, the essentially loving, productive self underneath, or apart from, the socially distorted self served the same function.

One can conceive of a socially embedded self that retains a critical perspective on its own embeddedness. With respect to the psychoanalytic dyad, contemporary theory tends to view patient and analyst as each partially embedded in the context created by the other and by the psychoanalytic situation itself. At the same time, each is viewed as at least potentially capable of reflecting on his interaction and on the way in which each participant takes shape in relationship with the other. The self-reflective capability of human beings makes it possible to be simultaneously engaged and embedded and also reflective and critical.

There is no reason that commitment to socialist values or to any other value system need be buttressed by essentialism about human nature. One need not claim that socialist society constitutes the human "ecological niche" in order to argue strongly for its desirability. Recognizing the human proclivity to be greedy, domineering, exploitative, and destructive, as well as loving and productive, in fact might set the stage for a more powerful argument in favor of a social system that would reflect and encourage the latter tendencies. Recognizing that socialist values constitute a bias, in the sense of a particular point of view about what people need, as opposed to an objective assessment of those needs, is not necessarily a problem. It becomes so in a positivist framework in which bias is conceived of as transcendable. Bias is a problem, of course, even in a nonpositivist framework, if it is held to dogmatically.

I have so far argued against Fromm's essentialist vision of human nature from a field-theoretical position in which it makes no sense to conceive of human nature as separable from its environment. I should add that other objections might spring from a Kleinian (as well as a late Freudian) position. From that point of view, destructiveness and hate are as intrinsic to human nature as love. From the Kleinian point of view in particular, a "sane society" could emerge only through the integration, not the denial, of hate and destructiveness. In the Kleinian schema, concern for other people arises, in the "depressive position" (Klein, 1975c), as a result of the child's dawning awareness that the parent he loves and the parent he hates are the same person. Winnicott (1958a) reformulated the position as involving the awareness that the nurturing mother whom the child desires to attack greedily is the same mother who takes care of the child. This awareness gives rise to guilt and a desire to make reparation for one's destructive urges. Fromm's productive orientation, from a Kleinian point of view, would rest on the reparative impulse; it would depend on the recognition and integration of what

Kleinians regard as inherent destructiveness. From a Kleinian point of view, Fromm's view of human beings as essentially benign forces him to locate destructive forces in the external world, that is, in capitalist society. A kind of splitting gets set up, which Kleinians would see as a defensive activity designed to protect the loving and the good from the hating and the destructive. Such splitting would, in fact, work *against* the kind of integration that can give rise to reparative activity. Looked at from a Kleinian or Winnicottian angle, socialism would grow out of concern about inherent greed, hate, and destructiveness, rather than providing a means for the eradication of these impulses. (Alford, 1989, provides an elaboration of this position.)

This Kleinian perspective remedies some problems in Fromm's theory. The idea that there is inherent destructiveness in man gives us a more direct account of how oppressive societies come to be than is possible given Fromm's view of man as essentially benign. A Kleinian perspective allows us to see the destructive aspect of activities that might seem, at first glance, constructive. Alford, for example, points out that, to the Kleinian mind, there is a destructive side even to "forcing" nature into our human categories. For the Kleinian, human activity inevitably requires us to wrestle with the dialectic of destruction and constructiveness. Ultimately, the Kleinian view of human beings paints a more complex-minded, multifaceted picture of the human psyche as inherently conflicted yet capable of integration, as destructive and ruthless yet capable of love and constructive activity. The Kleinian view seems consistent with a Frommian account of how certain historical conditions stimulate destructiveness but is inconsistent with his view that an alteration of social conditions could eliminate this destructiveness.

The Transplantation of Psychoanalysis to the United States

During the 1930s as the Nazis consolidated their power in Germany, most psychoanalysts moved to England and the United States. Once here, psychoanalysis took a turn away from political and social involvement. Some such involvement survived, at first largely through the efforts of Otto Fenichel (see Jacoby, 1983). Fenichel organized a group of leftist analysts and circulated a newsletter. In the McCarthy era, however, Fenichel, who was not a citizen, began to fear that he would be deported. He ceased his political activities.

The association of psychoanalysis with leftist politics, in general, did not survive the transplantation to the United States. Psychoanalysis, more and more, became a treatment reserved for the highest social classes (Hollingshead and Redlich, 1958). Poor people, working-class people, people seen in the public sector came to be viewed as unsuitable candidates for psychoanalysis, in contrast to Freud's views. What about the American scene led to this rigidification of attitude about the applicability of psychoanalytic therapy?

On a purely economic level, one can point to the prominence of the capitalistic, entrepreneurial spirit in American life. The business aspect of the private practice of psychoanalysis became increasingly important. Seeing well-to-do patients was an inherent part of having a successful practice. Having poor, low-fee patients is incomprehensible in this framework, unless one has no access to higher-fee patients. Psychoanalysis also came to be defined as a medical specialty, a subspecialty of psychiatry, a path to affluence for its practitioners, as are other medical subspecialties.

The ego psychological turn that psychoanalysis took in the United States had a complex impact on the scope of psychoanalytic treatment. Conceiving of psychosis as resulting from the withdrawal of libido from object attachments, Freud had thought relatively disturbed patients were not able to form a transference attachment and were thus not amenable to psychoanalytic treatment. A focus on the ego, rather than the id, thus opened up new ways to think about how to treat relatively disturbed patients psychoanalytically. In this sense, the scope of psychoanalytic treatment widened. On the other hand, to the extent that what resulted was conceived of as "ego-supportive," treatment of disturbed patients came to be thought of as psychotherapy instead of psychoanalysis. In a purist effort to define psychoanalysis in contrast to psychotherapy (including the plethora of competing nonanalytic psychotherapies that developed over time in the United States [Friedman, 1988]), criteria of analyzability for analysis proper may have correspondingly rigidified as the criteria for psychoanalytic therapy loosened.[3]

Ego-based criteria for analyzability tend to restrict the scope of psychoanalytic treatment in certain ways. Ego strength as a criterion of analyzability requires characteristics that are culture- and class-specific. For example, frustration tolerance is naturally defined as a

---

[3]Otto Kernberg (1975, 1992) is a prominent exception. Although his framework is ego psychological to a significant degree, he integrates Kleinian concepts related to splitting. His emphasis on splitting in borderline patients leads him to reject supportive treatments for disturbed patients as likely to reinforce splitting by presenting the analyst as "good." Kernberg thus favors psychoanalysis with limited use of parameters, rather than psychotherapy, for borderline patients.

strength in a context where the Calvinist, Protestant ethic predominates. People who are different in culture or class from the upper-middle-class, white analyst of European origin are more likely to be seen as nonanalyzable. Ego psychology, oriented to the dimension "strength–weakness," is prone to seeing "defect" or "deficit" rather than "difference."

Technical prescriptions tended to rigidify in the United States. Freud, to be sure, was inconsistent about technical flexibility. On one hand, he provided the metaphor of the analyst as surgeon or as blank screen, doing nothing but interpreting. On the other hand, there are the well-known examples of Freud's offering food to his patient the Wolf Man or doing analysis while climbing mountains with Ferenczi. Freud, in his effort to establish psychoanalysis as scientific by 19th-century standards, sought to eliminate the analyst's personal influence on the patient. He sought to establish that the therapeutic action of psychoanalysis rested on more than mere suggestibility. How is one to reconcile this position with his occasionally quite personally involved behavior with his patients? Lipton (1977) and Gill (1982) argue that his apparent contradiction is resolved by noting that Freud made a distinction between the technical aspect of the analytic relationship and nontechnical personal relationship. Anonymity and neutrality are technical principles that do not rule out nontechnical behavior, anymore than the surgeon's technical detachment rules out a sympathetic visit to the patient postoperatively.

Analysts in the United States in the 1940s and 1950s, according to Lipton, departed from Freud by applying technical principles to all analyst behavior and thus required a much more thoroughgoing detachment. Lipton, as well as Stone (1961), believed that the outcome was often interference with rapport between patient and analyst, without which analytic collaboration was impossible. One might attribute this development in American psychoanalysis to the need to establish the scientific respectability of psychoanalysis in an American medical context. Freud, on the other hand, despite his desire to attain medical respectability, could argue that a training in the humanities was the best preparation for psychoanalytic work (Freud, 1926). In the United States, lines were drawn more rigidly around pure psychoanalysis, in which the analyst ideally did nothing but interpret. If there was to be any suggestion or directive intervention of any kind or concrete help, the work was to be classified as psychotherapy. In psychoanalysis proper, such an intervention was regarded as a "parameter" (Eissler, 1958), at some point, requiring reduction through interpretation.

Thus, psychoanalytic treatment was divided into two tiers; on one level was pure psychoanalysis, and on the other level was the baser stuff of psychotherapy. A corresponding hierarchy was established with respect to patients. Patients with "strong" egos get psychoanalysis, while patients with "weak" egos get psychotherapy, or psychoanalysis with parameters. The patient with poor frustration tolerance, for example, who is prone to action rather than reflection, requires directive intervention to forestall acting out. The patient with limited verbal skills who tends not to talk about feelings needs direct help naming feelings (Pine, 1985). Since, as I have noted, the definition of ego strength occurs in a cultural context, the culturally or socioeconomically different patient, if accepted into analytic work at all, is not likely to get the elite version of the treatment. The elite status of psychoanalysis as a treatment modality is thus protected by reserving the "pure gold" for elite patients. The hierarchical class structure of society is thereby replicated in the analytic subculture.

Once technical prescriptions are seen as applying to all analyst behavior, analytic work in a public clinic context comes to seem a contradiction in terms. Insofar as the analyst necessarily performs multiple functions in relation to the patient (e.g., advocacy with social welfare agencies, approval of requests for transportation money) they are inevitable gratification of the patient and compromise of the analyst's neutrality. Clinic bureaucracies may impose conditions upon the treatment, for example, with respect to frequency, that are not compatible with technical prescriptions. In this regard, similar problems are not regarded as an insuperable barrier to analytic treatment when poor patients are not at issue. For example, training analyses at traditional institutes often include a high degree of compromise of the analyst's anonymity, as well as nonanalytic conditions, for example, the requirement that the candidate *be* in analysis for a certain length of time or the analyst's reporting on the candidate's analysis to the training committee of the institute. I return to the question of such contextual factors in detail later in this book.

While psychoanalysts have not welcomed lower socioeconomic-status patients and have shunned public clinic settings for their work, the rejection has been a two-way street. As a labor-intensive, non-symptom-focused mode of treatment, psychoanalysis appears inefficient, if not irrelevant, to medical doctors and bureaucrats alike. Psychoanalysts have, in fact, had to find ways to work with patients once or twice a week. They have also found ways to address insurance companies that want symptom-focused progress reports. Analysts tend to feel they have stepped out of the analytic role when they do such things. I argue later that one could expand the scope of psychoanalytic inquiry to include a consideration of the entire context in which the work is done, including such "nonanalytic" activities.

Marie Langer: From Vienna to Managua

Marie Langer was a prominent psychoanalyst, feminist, and Marxist who, like Fromm, refused to disassociate her psychoanalysis from her politics. Rather than develop a comfortable private practice, she was committed to working with the politically oppressed and the economically underprivileged. Rather than keeping psychoanalytic theory in a separate world from political theory, she interrogated the ways in which the psychoanalytic theoretical and technical model bore the imprint of an oppressive economic and political system. In her therapeutic work, she was willing to be flexible technically in the service of making treatment available on a democratic basis, in a way that would be relevant to human suffering which she saw as having social and political roots.

In her book *From Vienna to Managua: Journey of a Psychoanalyst*, Langer (1989) describes her training as a psychoanalyst in Vienna, at the Werner Vereinigung, Freud's institute. In the early 1930s her Social Democratic Party was banned by the Nazi government, along with most other political parties. The administration of the institute met with Freud and decided that none of their analysts would be allowed to be active in any clandestine party or to treat members of those parties. Langer continued with her political activities and received reprimands from Bibring and Federn, but she had meanwhile decided to give psychoanalysis a lower priority in the context of the political events that were then occurring. In 1936 she left to join the Republic in the Spanish civil war. When her cause appeared doomed, she left for Argentina. When a rightist dictatorship took power in Argentina, and Langer felt her life threatened there by death squads, she fled again to Mexico, in 1974. After the Sandinistas took power in Nicaragua, Langer joined an international group that devoted itself to helping the Nicaraguan government develop a mental health system that would be accessible to all.

Langer had long been critical of Freudian psychoanalysis from a Marxist and feminist point of view. She developed a perspective on psychoanalysis that integrated the political and the historical. In her introduction to Langer's book, Nancy Caro Hollander writes, "She

[Langer] asserted that psychoanalysis is a science of human subjectivity in which the psychoanalyst attempts to clarify the relationship between immediate subjective experience and the objective conditions that belong to the general conditions of society" (p. 11). This definition of psychoanalysis goes beyond the interpersonal to the societal; it is a definition with which Fromm and Sullivan might well have been in sympathy.

Langer criticized Freud for failing to take account of the political and historical context of his theory. Like the Frankfurt school theorists, she thought that his view of women, for example, was embedded in the social prejudices of his time and that the Oedipus complex was specific to patriarchal society. She noted that Freud took account of society in his account of superego formation but that he failed to place his particular society in historical context.

Langer saw work in Nicaragua as the opportunity to develop a practice, based on psychoanalytic principles, in a historical context in which an attempt was being made to develop a socialist and democratic alternative to the traditional patriarchal and elitist order. For Langer, one implication was a shift to brief therapy and group therapy. Langer saw protracted psychoanalytic therapy as elitist insofar as few people could thereby be served. The patriarchal, capitalist order would thus be built into the psychoanalytic situation. She favored group therapy as consistent with socialist aims in the sense that it encouraged people to view their pain in social terms and because it encouraged group effort to alleviate suffering. For Langer, such group therapy constituted the pure gold of psychoanalysis, defined as a historically situated science of subjectivity. Yet, there is much in this approach that many, if not most, psychoanalysts would regard as heavily alloyed with base metal, if not nonanalytic altogether. Can one conceive of a brief, group-based psychoanalysis, in which people are taught to view their pain in social terms?

Teaching people how to view their pain, or anything else, smacks of suggestion. Freud probably would have objected on this basis. Yet, one might claim that Freudian interpretations also teach people how to view their pain, in the guise of scientifically objective statements of fact. Langer undoubtedly would have been equally convinced of the objective validity of her view of her patients' pain, from her own Marxist and feminist viewpoint. She, at least, is more open about her wish to teach her patients. Many contemporary analysts, particularly those influenced by Irwin Hoffman's (1991, 1992) social constructivism, are more skeptical about the truth claims of any psychoanalytic discourse or interpretation. These analysts would resonate with Freud's wariness about indoctrinating patients with his own point of view, though with an expanded view of what might constitute indoctrination. In her sense of surety of her knowledge of the source of her patients' suffering, one might view Langer as having inadvertently reintroduced the very authoritarian attitude that she was so effective at critiquing.

In doing group therapy, Langer was seeking efficiency, in the service of reaching greater numbers of people. She was also being consistent with her own field theory, which viewed the cure, like the cause of suffering, in social phenomena. If alienation and exploitation were at the root of personal suffering, then social solidarity and support were the antidote. Is this a psychoanalytic approach to human suffering?

On one hand, one might argue that just as interpersonalists have redefined the psychoanalytic situation to include two people,[4] an approach that includes broader social factors naturally would lead to a practice involving groups of people. There is, indeed, a literature on "group analysis" (Bion, 1961). Langer's approach, further, seems parallel to the "corrective emotional experience" (Alexander, 1956) in individual psychoanalysis. That is, if society has exploited and oppressed the individual, the therapy group is to provide a support-ive counterexperience. Contemporary, especially relational, analysts do tend to believe that a new experience in the analytic situation has important mutative effects (e.g., Winnicott, 1958b; Greenberg, 1986; Mitchell, 1988; Fosshage, 1992). They emphasize, however, the patient's resistance to the new experience, as well as the patient's tendency to reproduce or hold onto the old object relationship. In the focus on repetition of the old experience and conflict about having a new experience, many contemporary analysts would locate the specifically analytic element. Both Alexander and Langer believed, evidently, that the analyst could know what new experience the patient needed and could provide such an experience to a receptive patient. To say that the patient has conflict about

---

[4]The classical view of the analytic situation is that the field includes only one mind, that of the patient. The analyst, standing outside the field, observes and comments. The two-person, interpersonal view is that the analytic field includes two people, the patient and analyst. The object of observation is the interaction between the two, not solely the mental activity of one of them. I expand on this point in the theoretical section of this chapter.

giving up repetition of oppressive and exploitative relational patterns is to say that the patient has the oppressor within himself. Such a viewpoint is quite consistent with a contemporary Kleinian analytic model (described and elaborated on later in this chapter), which emphasizes projective and introjective processes. This view of the victim as containing the oppressor, however, is not consistent with a social analysis that views the working-class individual as the victim of an oppressive ruling or capital-owning class. To be fully psychoanalytic, then, one might say that Langer's approach would have to include some consideration of how oppressive and exploitative social relationships get reproduced within the group.

Last, Langer's psychoanalysis was brief. Freud's analyses were also brief. From a classical point of view, analysis takes time for two reasons: it takes an extended period of time for the free associative process to overcome resistance, and it takes time to "work through" insight, once achieved. Contemporary, analytically oriented brief therapists (e.g., Malan, 1963; Mann, 1973) have sought to shorten this process by taking a more confrontational approach to resistance, by settling on a focal issue rather than trying to cover all bases comprehensively, and by setting a termination date in advance. These approaches would certainly appear to have at least some analytic guiding principles, insofar as they rely on an analytic model for understanding the patient's problems and on the concept of resistance.

Relational psychoanalysis takes time not so much because it takes time to develop insight but because it takes time for the analytic pair to work their way into the kind of relational pattern that has proven problematic for the patient and to work their way out. The only form of brief therapy that seems to focus on these relational issues is that of Mann (1973), who believes that in a time-limited therapy the central issue must be separation. The focus is thus on separation from the beginning of the treatment. Mann believes that this narrow focus is not an impediment, however, in that he thinks separation issues are at the core of neurotic problems in general. Thus was conceived an analytic brief therapy.

It is unclear whether Langer developed a comparable analytic rationale for her brief approach. Perhaps she relied solely on a more directive, confrontational technique to overcome resistance and "teach" her patients about what she saw as the reality of their lives and the socioeconomic system that shaped their experience.

The Community Mental Health Movement in the United States

In 1963 the U.S. federal government, as part of John F. Kennedy's "New Frontier" program, initiated a community mental health movement. Funding was provided for the development of community mental health centers to provide service to every area of the country. These centers were to provide therapeutic services, as well as research, training, evaluation, consultation, and preventive services. The community was to be involved in program planning and oversight of the centers. People from the community to be served, paraprofessionals, were to be trained to provide culturally sensitive services, with professional oversight. Federal funding was to be provided for eight years and to decrease each year, with the balance to be picked up by local governments or private funding sources. As a result of this initiative, 540 clinics (out of a planned total of 2,000) were opened around the country by 1974 to provide the opportunity for psychotherapy to thousands of low- and moderate-income Americans.

The early and mid-1960s were a time of a heightened sense of social responsibility for many Americans. The civil rights movement, in particular, raised the consciousness of many Americans about social inequities. There was confidence, naive, perhaps, to the contemporary sensibility, that government could act to remedy many of these inequities. There was also a greater confidence than many people could muster today in the efficacy of mental health treatments. Jobs were created by the thousands for graduates of training programs in the mental health disciplines, who were emerging in increasingly large numbers from federally funded programs. There were scholarships from the federal government, particularly for minority-group students who would work, it was assumed, in the new community mental health centers in underserved areas.

From the beginning, three fairly distinct currents flowed within the community mental health movement. One was composed of those who emphasized the "community" aspect. These people stressed the role of oppressive social conditions in the genesis of mental illness, much as Langer and Fromm did, but usually without the Marxist ideological framework. These community-minded professionals stressed the role of the community mental health center in initiating political action for social change, in community organizing, advocacy for individuals with social service agencies, the training of indigenous paraprofessionals to prepare the community to take care of itself, preventive interventions, and consultation to community groups and agencies. A second group was composed of psychiatrists, for the most part, who emphasized the use of the new psychoactive medications. One of the major sources of impetus for the community mental health movement was the desire on the part of government to save money on the hospital treatment of the mentally ill. The development of the major tranquilizers in the 1950s allowed for the deinstitutionalization of large numbers of mentally ill people, with the hope that medication would keep them out of the hospital. Medication offered the promise of a very cost-efficient form of treatment. The community "activists" and the medication dispensers often failed to see eye-to-eye, with the activists accusing the psychiatrists of enforcing social control with chemical strait-jackets (e.g., see Kupers, 1981) and the psychiatrists accusing the activists of being naive and uninformed about the medical dimension of mental illness.

The third current was composed of therapists, for the most part, who were more or less influenced by psychoanalysis. Insofar as the theory of psychotherapy was derived from psychoanalytic theory, therapists from all the mental health disciplines brought a psychoanalytic sensibility to their work in community mental health centers. These psychoanalytically informed therapists came into conflict with both of the groups previously noted. Community-oriented people saw psychoanalytically based treatment as elitist, requiring too much time and money per person, thus not widely applicable. The emphasis on verbalization and the intrapsychic, as opposed to the social, realm was incompatible with the guiding principles of the community-oriented worker. Psychoanalytically oriented practitioners tended to see the community-oriented as insufficiently concerned and caring about the individual, about people's emotional lives.

The medically oriented workers saw these therapists as overemphasizing the psychological at the expense of the biological. Therapists saw the psychiatrists as having a mechanistic and reductionistic view of human suffering. Underlying many of these differences in theory and practice were power struggles. Until the 1970s psychiatrists were at the top of most community mental health center hierarchies. Psychologists tended to be psychoanalytically (sometimes behaviorally) oriented, while social workers tended to have a community (sometimes family systems) orientation. The arguments about which approach would prevail were sometimes actually arguments about who was in charge. (See Shaw and Eagle, 1971, about a struggle between paraprofessionals and psychiatrists over the direction to be taken by one of the pioneering inner-city community mental health centers.)

These alignments were shaken up, to some degree, by new developments in the late 1960s and 1970s. Family therapists appeared, integrating the systems approach implicit in the orientation of the community activist with the therapist's sensitivity to interpersonal relationships. Second, with budgets tightening, bureaucrats came increasingly to control the centers. Control of the budget was control of the institution. The bureaucrat's primary concern, especially in hard times, was cost-effectiveness. In these terms, the psychiatric approach won hands down. The community approach, with its intangible goals, its lack of focus on concrete symptoms, was quite vulnerable. Prevention and consultative activities were often the first to be cut when the belt was tightened. The psychoanalytic therapist, with her long-term, labor-intensive approach, was not likely to see eye-to-eye with the administrator.

The community mental health movement made it possible for psychoanalytically oriented clinicians to encounter the inner city in the United States. This contact both isolated psychoanalysts to some degree, as just described, and also stimulated a renewal of thinking about how psychoanalysis could become more broadly applicable across social class, racial, and cultural lines. One of the major manifestations of this renewal were the Union Project at the William Alanson White Institute and another at New York University.

"Union Projects" at the William Alanson White Institute and the New York University Postdoctoral Program

In 1963, the William Alanson White Institute of Psychiatry, Psychology, and Psychoanalysis, an interpersonally oriented psychoanalytic training institute, embarked on a collaboration with a local of the United Auto Workers Union. The union was interested in developing a liaison with the White Institute and its clinic in the interest of providing easy access to psychotherapists for its members. In return for a lump sum grant from the union welfare fund, the clinic would provide free service to union members. The White Institute was interested in the opportunity to provide services to a working class population and to study the characteristics of working-class people and the therapy approaches that would work, or not work, with them (Grey, Ortmeyer, and Caligor, 1972). With a theoretical background derived from Sullivan's interpersonal and social psychiatric point of view and Fromm's Marxist analysis of the interaction of character and socioeconomic environment, the White Institute found this project compelling. Over five years, 266 patients were seen from the union. At the height of the project, 40 therapists were seeing 43 patients in evening and Saturday appointments. The average number of sessions was 16 per patient, with a range from less than three sessions to four years of treatment. The majority of patients were seen in some form of family treatment, even in this psychoanalytic institute. Whether by design or necessity, then, the White Institute therapists, like Marie Langer, ended up seeing their patients for a relatively short time and usually in some form of group. The White Institute group also gave presentations in the community to educate union members about mental health issues and to reduce the sense of stigma in seeking therapy. In summarizing what they had learned from their experience, Caligor et al. (1971) highlight the action orientation of "blue-collar" patients, their focus on symptom relief, and their disinclination to make a long-term commitment to therapy. The therapist must be flexible, must be willing to "hear" actions as communications, and must be willing to take a directive, authoritative stance and to focus on symptoms within a short-term model, according to these authors.

Late in the 1960s the New York University Postdoctoral Program in Psychotherapy and Psychoanalysis attempted to develop a similar liaison with the Union of Hospital and Health Care Workers. The national parent of this New York-based union, however, was not interested in the project. In the early 1990s, this idea was revived at the initiative of a committee of the postdoctoral program concerned with multicultural issues in psychoanalysis. A group of candidates, graduates, and faculty of the program met through 1990 and 1991 to develop a liaison with the union and to formulate goals for the project and policies that would advance these goals. The group decided that the focus would be on countertransference, that is, on the therapist's own experiences in psychoanalytically oriented therapy with working-class and minority patients. Interest was directed toward how our personal attitudes and technical procedures would develop with patients from socioeconomic backgrounds different from that of the typical private practice patient. In that sense, the focus was different from that of the White Institute group, which had been mainly interested in patient characteristics. Like the William Alanson White project, the postdoctoral project included a case seminar in which participants could process their experiences. The postdoctoral project also built low-fee supervision into the project. Unlike the White project, only individual therapy was offered, on a twice-weekly basis. The fee was the amount paid by the union benefit fund for psychotherapy, plus a low-to-moderate copayment based on income. The project aimed to replicate a private practice context so far as possible, while limiting participation to patients who would otherwise not have access to the private practice network.

Compared with the White Institute project, the New York University group had much less success attracting patients from the Union and in finding therapists to see them. At its peak, three patients were being seen by three therapists. Several other patients were referred from the union who could not be assigned to therapists. Although more than 20 people from the postdoctoral community volunteered to work in the project, only 9 volunteered to see patients. (The rest volunteered to supervise.) Of those who were willing to see patients at a low fee, few were volunteering "prime" evening hours. Most referred patients requested evening hours, so they could not be placed with therapists.[5]

Theoretical Considerations

Freudian drive theory tends to be skewed toward a one-person model. Within a one-person model, pathogenesis involves conflict within one person over instinctual impulses. Other people attain significance as stimuli for, and objects of, drive-derived impulses. Freud's theory was intended to provide a general psychology, not only an explanation of psychopathology. Thus, all human behavior was to be derived from the vicissitudes of sex and aggression. With concepts such as sublimation and displacement available, one could fully explain the entire range of human behavior by specifying the underlying drive(s), its vicissitudes, and the defenses with which it interacts.

The implications of a one-person theoretical model for psychoanalytic technique are far-reaching. If the entire basis of a patient's neurosis is to be found intrapsychically, the analyst must be careful not to contaminate the intrapsychic situation by influencing the patient. Hence the classical prescription that the analyst remain

---

[5]In the 1960s at the White Institute, as noted, 40 therapists evidently were willing to volunteer evening or Saturday hours to see a low-fee patient. One wonders whether the 1990s therapists were feeling more financially strapped or were less willing to sacrifice for other reasons.

anonymous, nongratifying of the patient's wishes, reserved as far as possible, refraining from all interventions except the imparting of information to the patient through interpretation. Classical Freudians also believe that an anonymous analytic stance frustrates the patient and thus facilitates the emergence and expression of underlying transference wishes. Interpretation is not regarded as an interpersonal act, but rather as the conveyance of information about the patient's unconscious. Transference, the patient's feelings and ideas about the analyst, is regarded as a manifestation of the patient's unconscious, not related in any real way to the person of the analyst. The very word "transference" implies that these feelings and ideas are transferred from elsewhere, that is, the past, from parents. Transference, then, by definition, distorts. By demonstrating to the patient that his feelings and ideas about the analyst are distorted, the analyst shows the patient the reality of his unconscious impulses and conflicts. Herein lies another reason it is important for the analyst to remain anonymous, for if she were to reveal herself, she might inadvertently stimulate patient reactions other than those based on a preexisting transference. Even worse, the analyst might provide some external justification for the patient's transference expectations and thus preclude an interpretation of transference as a distorted perception carried over from the past.[6]

This classical analytic stance is consistent with the 19th-century scientific ethos within which Sigmund Freud was embedded. Objectivity, the scientist's standing outside the field being observed, was the hallmark of a scientific procedure. The scientist's subjectivity was to be set aside or controlled for, so as not to contaminate observation. The patient's mind was to be observed objectively like any phenomenon within the natural sciences. In accord with the Enlightenment's valorization of reason,[7] knowledge about the

---

[6]From my own two-person perspective, one is tempted to ask whether or not the patient is being mystified by an interpretation of transference as distortion. Gill (1982) argues that there generally is a plausible basis for a patient's transference perceptions and that transference ought to be interpreted without reference to distortion. Instead transference should be viewed as bias or selective attention or inattention, thus emphasizing both the complexity and ambiguity of the analyst's behavior, and the patient's active role and investment in seeing the analyst a particular way.

[7]See Mitchell (1993) for a comprehensive discussion of the intellectual context in which Freud thought and wrote.

unconscious, the rendering conscious of unconscious impulses and conflicts, would set the patient free.

In the mid- and late-20th century, a two-person psychoanalysis emerged. From this point of view, pathogenesis takes place within interpersonal relationships. Sullivan's (1953) interpersonal approach, for example, emphasized the pathogenic role of anxiety transmitted from parent to child and the mystification of children by parents. Whereas Freud's developmental psychology emphasized drive development (e.g., the development of libido from the oral to the anal to the phallic mode), Sullivan's developmental psychology emphasized the vicissitudes of interpersonal relationships.

A two-person psychoanalytic perspective views the treatment situation as likewise involving two people. The analyst is seen as inevitably a full participant in an interaction, whether he is silent, talkative, frustrating, or gratifying. Transference does not emerge in isolation from the influence of the analyst even when the analyst is reserved, since that very reserve has an impact on the patient. Anonymity and nongratification are no longer psychoanalytic imperatives; in fact, such a stance tends to be seen as impossible to achieve. The analyst's subjectivity being inevitably revealed in the interaction, transference is viewed as reflecting not only the biases, preconceptions, and organizing principles that the patient brings to the interaction but also his more or less plausible perceptions of the analyst. The analytic goal is less to impart insight than to facilitate a collaborative inquiry into the nature of the analytic interaction, to develop awareness of the patient's active role in creating interpersonal patterns, without denying the analyst's contribution, and to foster flexibility where there was rigidity.

This two-person model focuses on individuals in the context of their interaction. Just as the dyadic perspective enriches one's understanding of the individuals involved, so a larger social perspective can enrich our understanding at the level of both individual and dyad. I term a model that includes such a larger perspective a "three-person model," the third "person" representing the social context. (See Lacan, 1977, Greenberg, 1991, and Cushman, 1994, for such models in the literature.) I employ a three-person model in this book in the sense that I emphasize the analytic significance of the racial, cultural, and social class status of patient and analyst, as well as the institutional context of their work.

Contemporary relational theory seeks an integration of one- and two-person models, of intrapsychic and interpersonal dimensions of the analytic situation. An effort is made to understand the organizing principles, or transference predispositions, that the patient brings *to* the analytic situation and to keep in mind that the manifestation of the patient's psychic life bears the imprint of the context provided by the analyst and his participation, as well as the nature of the analytic situation. In terms of development, relational theory adopts a two-person model by viewing the child's psyche as structured, to a degree, by interaction with parents. At the same time, a one-person perspective is accommodated in the acknowledgment that there is no one-to-one correspondence between what happens in the interpersonal field and what the child internalizes (Mitchell, 1994, personal communication). Similarly, in the analytic situation, the patient is regarded as influenced by what happens with the analyst in the interpersonal field, and vice versa. At the same time, the patient's perception of the analyst, as well as the analyst's view of the patient, has no exact correspondence to what happens between them. The principle that the patient and analyst influence each other has been discussed in terms of "mutuality" in the analytic relationship (Aron, 1991); nonetheless, the focus of analytic work on the patient's transference predispositions is discussed in terms of the "asymmetry" of the analytic relationship (Burke, 1992).

All theories, from Freud's to Sullivan's, in fact, integrate one- and two-person models in some fashion. Although Freud moved from a (two-person) emphasis on the actual sexual molestation of children to a (one-person) emphasis on the sexual wishes and fantasies of children, he never denied that the external world had an impact on development. For example, his concept of the "complemental series" (Freud, 1916–17) seeks to develop a model for the interaction of fantasy and external reality. Sullivan, for his part, had a concept of "personification," which sounds remarkably like internalized objects. Sullivan's concept of parataxic distortion acknowledges a gap between psychic experience and what takes place in the external world.

Contemporary relational theorists such as Hoffman (1991) go so far as to question the polarity of fantasy and reality altogether and thus call into question the distinction between the intrapsychic and the interpersonal. Hoffman and other social constructivists believe that "fantasy" always accommodates "reality" and that there is no perception of "reality" that is not filtered through, if not enhanced by, "fantasy" (Greenberg, 1991). In discussing theoretical models as they are actually used, I call attention in later chapters to what I regard as the clinical consequences of skews, in a one-person

direction, for the most part, in the context of an untenable polarization of fantasy and reality, of intrapsychic and interpersonal.

Two-or three-person field-theoretical models are essential to any
consideration of socioeconomic difference in psychoanalysis and to
any consideration of psychoanalysis that occurs in a clinic or
community context. If one adopts a one-person model, race, culture,
and social class, when they appear as patient concerns, must be
reducible to an intrapsychic phenomenon such as a drive-defense
conflict. A two-person model allows one to take account of analyst
as well as patient concerns, feelings, and attitudes about race,
culture, and social class and the interaction between the two subjectivities around these issues. A three-person model frames both analyst
and patient attitudes about socioeconomic issues in the context of
the society of which both are socialized members. A three-person
model further allows us to take account of a public clinic context for
psychoanalytic work as an analytic issue, rather than solely as a
potential interference with the ideal analytic setup of two people
conceived of in isolation from the social and institutional arrangements around them.

A Kleinian projective-introjective model adds depth and richness
to the ways in which one can think about issues such as race in
psychoanalysis. Before elaborating on this statement, I will review the
theoretical underpinnings of that model.

Melanie Klein made heavy use of the concept of projection as a
defense mechanism in her theoretical studies of early psychic life.
Klein thought that infants deal with intolerable levels of aggression
by disowning their aggressive impulses and, in fantasy, projecting
them onto other people. This defensive process creates a sense of a
persecutory outer world, to which the infant reacts with fear and
rage, completing a projective-introjective vicious circle. Klein
(1975a,b,c) called this state of affairs the paranoid-schizoid position:
paranoid because of the persecutory outer world thus created and
schizoid because of the psychic split created when the "bad," that is,
the aggressive, is split off and disowned. Klein thus created a model
of the mind in which people split the psychic world in order to rid
themselves of certain contents. With her concept of "projective
identification," Klein (1975a) emphasized that people unconsciously
retain their identification with the split off psychic contents even
after they have been "placed" into other people.

Bion (1988a) and Racker (1968) expanded on Klein's view of
projective identification by proposing an interpersonal dimension to
what, for Klein, had been a fantasy, an intrapsychic process. Racker,

for example, claimed that the recipient of a projection could identify with the projected psychic content and thus actualize the projector's fantasy. Bion discussed the "containing" function of the recipient of a projection, that is, that person's role in "detoxicating" the projected psychic content, so that it could be returned to the projector in more assimilable form. For Bion and Racker and for contemporary Kleinians in general, projective identification could serve a communicative function as well as a defensive function. The induced experience of the analyst can provide important clues about the experiences that the patient, unable to tolerate or contain, projects onto the analyst. (Bollas, 1987, adding a Winnicottian perspective, makes a similar point.)

The projective-introjective model can illuminate the psychic functions served by societal conceptions of race, social class, gender, and social orientation. Race, like these other phenomena, is a construction, an abstraction: as pointed out by Fish (1995), our racial categories are created by isolating certain physical characteristics and creating constellations that do not mirror observed invariances. For example, nose width, lip thickness, type of hair, and skin color are part of how Americans construct racial categories, but these physical characteristics do not necessarily go together. North Americans deal with this complexity by categorizing as black anyone with one parent categorized as black. Other cultures construct racial categories differently. To complicate matters further, the physical characteristics regarded as relevant to racial categories are continua, yet we treat them as dichotomies in the service of fitting our dichotomous racial categories. So we have a dichotomy (black-white) constructed out of arbitrary constellations of physical characteristics that are continua. We do so in the service of creating a focus for projection and introjection. The "opposite" race creates a category of people who are "not me" into which we can project unwanted psychic content. Such contents can have a negative valence: aggression, exploitativeness, criminality, sloth. Or the projected contents can have a positive valence: intelligence, spontaneity, sexuality in its positive aspects. To complete the analogy, I think it useful to conceive of projective identification that can take place on a societal level. Consider an example. White people in our society commonly attribute aggression to black people. Meanwhile, whites routinely exclude blacks from more affluent neighborhoods with better schools and from higher-paying jobs with more status. Lack of opportunity, poverty, and poor education create anger, thereby actualizing the preconception. Blacks may introject the aggressive image projected on them by whites and establish a projective-introjective vicious circle. Whites are enabled to feel comfortably benign and virtuous, despite evidence of white police brutality, wars in the Caucasian world, and so on. In the psychoanalytic situation, patient and analyst can similarly use race as a focus for projection and introjection.

Projective identification and other defense mechanisms that seek to disown aspects of self inevitably impoverish or distort the person and his psychic life. This outcome is easy to discern when psychic functions that are useful are disowned, for example, when a patient idealizes his analyst by attributing to her the capacity for analytic insight and understanding in a way that makes him feel inadequate, unable to perform the self-analytic function in her presence. Societally devalued minority group members may disown and project onto the dominant group qualities such as intelligence and competence and feel depleted of such characteristics themselves. Freud, with his concept of reaction formation as a defense, further demonstrated that people may pay a price for the repression of even seemingly negative impulses like destructive aggression. An excessive passivity or inability to assert oneself may result. Sublimation (Loewald, 1988), in contrast to repression, transforms an impulse, rather than disowning it, in a way that fractures the psyche and puts one out of touch with oneself. Klein's followers (e.g., Alford, 1989) without using the concept of sublimation, tend to derive from primitive aggression the entire range of ways in which we human beings "force" nature to fit into our man-made categories and influence the human and inanimate world so as to further our wills and purposes. The disowning of primitive aggression, then, may disable us in terms of a wide range of constructive, as well as destructive, activities.

I want to take this analysis a step further to suggest that when "mainstream" members of a society create a devalued "other," both the mainstream and the marginalized citizen pay a psychic price. Here I use Paul Wachtel's (1989) conceptual framework in his aptly titled *The Poverty of Affluence.* Wachtel maintains that Americans have become addicted to economic growth. Late capitalist, consumer society depends on the constant stimulation of needs and desires in the population. If we were to become satisfied with what we have, the engine of economic growth would lose much of its fuel. Wachtel argues that Americans have come to feel deprived if they do not have more than their parents had or more than they had last year. As a result, there is a preoccupation with avoiding a sense of deprivation and stagnation even in this, the richest society on the face of the earth in this, or any other, historical period.

I agree with Wachtel's analysis of this phenomenon in terms of the influence of the late capitalist economic system. Further, one may understand this preoccupation with growth in the psychic terms I have been using in this book. That is, a sense of deprivation and stagnation derives from depressive experiences that are a widespread, if not universal, human reaction to the existential conditions of life, that is, the impossibility of complete fulfillment. One of the unconscious functions of the creation of a devalued and marginalized "other" might be conceived of in terms of the localization of these depressive experiences "out there." Poverty and affluence are relative terms, defined with reference to each other. It would not be possible to feel affluent except in relation to someone else defined as poor, and vice versa.[8] Given the existence of a poverty-stricken group of people "out there," our ignoring of them may reflect our wish not to know about our own potential sense of deprivation; our attribution of their neediness to laziness, exploitativeness, and so on may reinforce the disowning of our own sense of need and entitlement. Projective identification, however, always results in a tenuous sense of freedom from what is disowned. So, returning to Wachtel's observation, we pay a price for our attempt to avoid feeling deprived. That price entails a sort of manic denial, a ceaseless pursuit of more and better, an inability to rest content with what we have.

In concluding, I suggest that in co-opting a great deal of marginalized minority cultures, white, middle-class Americans seem to reintroject some of what they have externalized. This is especially evident in the realm of music and clothing styles, where adolescents (members of mainstream society who are relegated to, and often seek out, marginal status) serve as the conduit from the ghetto to the suburb. As noted later, Cornel West (1993a) points out that the drug culture of the ghetto embodies and caricatures the consumer, feel-good culture in which we all live. It should not surprise us, then, that when drug busts are conducted in ghetto "drug supermarkets," the customers' cars that are confiscated often turn out to be from the suburbs. In summary, I have argued for the advantages of a two-person, projective-introjective psychoanalytic model in taking account of race, social class, and culture in the treatment situation.

---

[8]Under conditions of starvation or homelessness, of course, the sense of deprivation is rooted in the threat to life, rather than in a comparison with other people. The omnipresence of fear of deprivation in even a relatively affluent society may be due to infantile experiences of even temporary deprivation, which may be experienced by the infant as catastrophic before the development of a sense of time.

I conclude this section with a discussion of analyzability and the applicability of psychoanalysis from the perspectives of various theoretical models.

I noted that Freud, as well as subsequent classical authors, saw various potential obstacles to the psychoanalytic treatment of the poor or the culturally different. In addition, there are various problematic aspects of a public clinic context for psychoanalytic work. The problems may be summarized as follows: such patients may require a more directive approach, raising the dangers associated with suggestion; material help may be required, precluding abstinence; abstinence may be further precluded by the multiple roles that therapists in public clinics are required to fill; poor or culturally different patients may not have the same educational background and verbal orientation, being more action-oriented, compared with more affluent patients. My argument here is that all of these issues become problematic from the perspective of a classical or ego psychological treatment model; when considered from a relational perspective, the treatment process is reformulated in a way that makes work with the poor and the culturally nonmainstream and work in public clinics far less problematic.

Recall that the classical/ego psychological treatment model emphasizes insight as the mechanism for change, while anonymity and nongratification on the analyst's part are considered essential to both the emergence and resolution of transference. The emphasis on insight makes a verbal orientation essential, while framing action, or "acting out," as resistance. If we assume that the patients in question are more action-oriented and less verbally oriented than "mainstream" patients, then their treatment is necessarily relatively fraught with obstacles and resistance. Given their assumed preoccupation with material deprivation, an abstinent stance on the part of the analyst becomes less feasible.

From a relational perspective, the mechanism of change is located in the relationship rather than in the insight of the patient. Accordingly, verbalization is likely to be seen as one among many modalities of relating, rather than as the privileged modality for conveyance of information from analyst to patient. The distinction between verbal communication and enactment breaks down when verbalization is regarded as an act that defines a relationship as well as a disembodied transfer of information.[9] Even silence is a relational act, from this point of view, so that any conception of anonymity becomes untenable. Further, nongratification becomes more difficult to conceive of when the possibility of non-action is no longer conceivable.

The distinction between verbalization and action having been undermined, then, there is less reason to question the analyzability of the so-called action-oriented patient. There is less reason to assume that the analyst must assume a directive stance for lack of a capacity for insight on the patient's part, since enactments can be analytically valuable. Even if the analyst decided to take a directive or gratifying stance with a particular patient, there is no reason to assume, a priori, that the analytic work is thereby compromised. The analytic work might equally well be compromised by failure to take directive or gratifying action with a patient who is especially sensitive to deprivation, whose transference sensitivities have to do with remoteness, say, with significant others. The practical realities of a patient's life may require that the therapist get involved with approval of carfare money in a clinic, writing a letter for a patient who needs documentation of a mental disability for Social Security benefits, or even providing emergency food or money. There are times when it would be inhuman not to get involved with impoverished patients in such ways. From a relational point of view, such gratifying actions do not necessarily compromise an analytic stance, mitigate against the development of transference, or render the transference unanalyzable. Failure to respond to a patient's need may, with certain patients and in certain circumstances, also contribute to the development of an analytic impasse. One does not escape such dilemmas with even well-to-do patients. They, too, express needs and wishes, and the analyst often has to decide whether to attempt to gratify or meet these needs or refrain from doing so. (See Mitchell, 1993, for an extended discussion of these dilemmas with nonimpoverished patients.)

Patients with Third World origins often have expectations that caregivers will be directive, gratifying, and interactive. The abstinent,

---

[9]Levenson (1982) discusses the "pragmatics" or the "metacommunicational" aspect of verbalization. That is, he focuses on how speech acts convey both a message and a message about the message that defines the relationship between speaker and listener.

anonymous analytic stance may be even more difficult for them to adapt to than is the case with the middle-class North American. Relational psychoanalysis provides for the possibility of adapting to these expectations without departing from an analytic position. Relational analysts are not *necessarily* directive, gratifying, or relatively active with their patients (Greenberg 1991). Relational psychoanalysis does take the position, however, that interaction is inevitable; thus, such forms of interaction do not necessarily break the analytic frame.

There are innumerable ways in which a public clinic, its administration, its policies, other staff members, and so on impinge upon the therapist and his work with his patients. There are demands put upon the staff for productivity; more than one staff member is involved in making treatment decisions; the clinic may require staff therapists to approve various requests on the part of patients that are not inherently treatment decisions; patients may interact with various other staff members who do not have a therapeutic relationship with them and thus split the transference in various ways. Recall some of the cases from Chapter 1 in these connections: the therapist who *was* grateful that her patient came that day and my unsuccessful attempts to work with administrators and other clinicians to continue the treatment of my patient José. In the clinic where I worked, patients would often spend time visiting with clerical staff, whom they knew from the community. My impression was often that these people could give the patients an informal and supportive forum that the therapists could not or did not give. It was not uncommon for patients to complain about their therapists to clerical staff (and for the clerical staff to sympathize, if not agree, with the patients about certain staff!). In any case, clearly, any psychoanalytic point of view that takes on the task of understanding treatment in such a setting must be a field theory. It must be capable of taking account of, and thinking psychoanalytically about, not only what happens between patient and analyst but what happens in the clinic as a whole.

In summarizing this part of my discussion, then, I am arguing that relational psychoanalysis provides for a more democratic approach to the treatment of inner-city patients, with its less restrictive views on analyzability and its potential for accommodating technical flexibility. A field theory, further, can accommodate the complex clinic context in which therapy in the inner city takes place.

Postmodernism

The word postmodern is often applied to our historical moment, as well as to intellectual, aesthetic, and cultural characteristics of our time. "Modernity," with reference to which postmodernism is defined, is associated with the 18th-century Enlightenment. Enlightenment philosophy, associated with Locke in England, Voltaire in France, and others, emphasized rationality as the royal road to truth, as opposed to religion, faith, tradition. Within the Enlightenment tradition, there was a split between the British empiricists, such as Locke, Berkeley, and Hume, and continental rationalists, such as Diderot and Voltaire (see Greenberg, 1991, for a more complete discussion of these philosophical traditions in terms of their relevance for psychoanalysis). The empiricists took the position that what we know of the world derives directly from sense impressions; rationalists took the contrasting position that we cannot know the world directly, but only as mediated by our minds.

Nineteenth-century science represents the flowering of the empiricist tradition within the Enlightenment with its emphasis on objectivity, the splitting of the subject from the object in the belief that by removing the observer, one could obtain an unbiased view of the object. The attempt to objectify and master nature in the Industrial Revolution, by embodying the Enlightenment-based project of application of scientific rationality to practical problems, is at the heart of modernity. The idea of "progress" is characteristic of modernity, along with a tendency to view less technologically developed people or people who live more by faith, emotion, intuition, and religion than by rationality as "primitive." This framework was consistent with, and justified, European colonialism. People in nonindustrialized societies were objectified and subjugated throughout the world, as was nature in its pristine state. Modernity has brought us the megalopolis, modern transportation, agribusiness, nuclear power and nuclear weapons, and our standards of objectivity in science. In psychoanalysis, the idea of the objective, blank-screen analyst derives from the modernist worldview, as well as from concepts of progress and development and the triumph of rationality over the irrational associated with ego psychology. Therapeutic aspirations associated with the psychoanalytic medical model are also associated with modernism, as is modern medicine itself. The concept of the self as a defined entity, with sharply limited borders, what Mitchell (1993) has termed the "spatial metaphor" of the self, derives from the self of the subject-object split. Modernity thus informs what have come to be experienced as commonsense notions of self and other, our sense of individuality and individualism, our ideas of what makes life worthwhile in terms of progress and achievement, and the polarities and categories we use in defining ourselves and other people.

Enlightenment empiricism tends to eliminate personal subjectivity or to pathologize it as an interference with objectivity. The modern ideal is of the detached scientist or the technocrat, the objective, controlled, and in-control man. I say "man" rather than person here because the modern masculine ideal approximates, much more than the modern female ideal, the human qualities of value within this worldview.

Postmodernism can be seen as a swing of the pendulum, a reaction to modern objectivism and individualism. The return is not to religion and faith, however; rather, the postmodern "mood" (Bernstein, 1993) is one of skepticism and critique, of exposing the hidden, contingent assumptions behind categories and ways of thinking that have come to be taken for granted and thus part of what is considered rationality itself. Deconstructionism, a quintessentially postmodern enterprise (Derrida, 1976, 1978), aims to expose the hidden contradictions within a system of thought and the ways in which the seemingly opposite terms of a polarity contain and implicate each other. Derrida points out the mutual dependence of mainstream "discourse," that is, ways of thinking and categorizing, and the discourses of marginalized others. Foucault's (1980) work addresses how social power arrangements are created and reinforced by categories related to gender and sexuality; polarities, such as male-female, for example, tend to establish a hierarchy. Butler (1990) and other postmodern feminists point out the discrepancy between the characteristics of actual human beings, which are quite complex and ambiguous with respect to traditional gender categories, and the simplistic, bipolar nature of those categories themselves. The same could be said about racial categories. In the face of the obvious fact that race exists on a continuum, our categories force us to draw a line between black and white, a line that serves as the basis of a power differential. More fundamentally, one could ask on what basis we pay attention to skin color and the other physical factors associated with race at all. Postmodern, deconstructionist thinking of this sort tends to contextualize knowledge, make it local and political, and undermine any pretense of universality. Knowledge is seen as always relative to the categories and ways of thinking, or discursive practices, we are using. These categories and ways of thinking are chosen on the basis of political ends or tradition, rather than on grounds that are inherently rational or true to nature. In this way, postmodernism constitutes a critique of Enlightenment epistemology.

A crucial feature of postmodern critique of modernity is a radically different view of the nature of the relationship between the individual and society. Where the modern view was of a split between the individual and society, in a postmodern view, the individual is a creation of society. This point of view had its roots in the priority that Marx gave to the capitalist socioeconomic setup in determining the course of individual lives and in structuralism (e.g., Piaget, 1954; Levi-Strauss, 1963; Chomsky, 1968) which views human mental life as derivable from socially shared deep structures. Lacan (1977) adopted this point of view in claiming that the unconscious is structured like a language. Language, the symbolic order that constitutes society, is, for Lacan, at the very heart of the individual psyche. Postmodern intellectuals emphasize the structuring impact of our discursive practices, that is, the categories in terms of which we speak and think, the concepts available to us, the organizing principles given to us for structuring our experience. Even the self, the very core of our individuality, can be seen as constituted by the way language is structured, by our cultural individualism and the value we place on separateness. Where modernity saw society as created by essentially free individuals, postmodernism sees society, in the form of language and discursive practices, as creating the individual. We have here a critique, a deconstruction of modern Western individualism.

What are the implications for psychoanalysis and for the psychoanalytic consideration of the issues discussed in this book of the postmodern point of view? Sigmund Freud in many ways was a postmodern pioneer (Barratt, 1993); that is, his line of thinking led him to call into question the unity and transparency, even the knowability, of our selves. Yet he and Melanie Klein following him tried to explain this multiplicity and discontinuity of self in ways that did not disturb the Western assumption of a unitary self. The idea of defensive projection and introjection provided the way to picture a unitary self that, in pathology, split itself, taking in pieces of other selves or putting pieces of self into others.

As often happens in the development of psychoanalytic theory, a fundamentally new way of looking at the human psyche was introduced as a way of understanding pathological phenomena. Self-multiplicity and discontinuity were seen as extraordinary, as products of excessive aggression and splitting. More recently, some contemporary Kleinians have moved away from describing projective identification in terms that are essentially pathological. For example, Bion (1988a) emphasizes the communicative, even transformative, function of projective identification. Depathologizing projective-introjective mechanisms, making them part of ordinary life, goes some way toward the view that multiplicity, instability, and discontinuity (coexisting dialectically with stability, coherence, and continuity) are inherent in human mental life (see Mitchell, 1993, for an elaboration of this position).

In contemporary psychoanalysis, generally speaking, there has been a move away from a conception of the patient as a separate, bounded individual, distinct from the analyst. Concepts such as projective identification and the transference-countertransference matrix (Ogden, 1994) constitute the dyad, rather than the individual, as our unit of analysis. In relational psychoanalysis, in dialectical fashion, the patient and analyst are thought to be constituted by the dyad, insofar as each discovers a version of self within the dyad that, in many respects, has not existed before. Yet, it is equally valid to say that each individual constitutes the dyad. Each individual brings a unique history, personality, and set of behaviors to the interaction and sees the interaction through the lens of his or her own perspective.

Influenced by postmodernism, many psychoanalysts have recently become skeptical about any conception of absolute truth, or rationality, generated within the psychoanalytic interaction. As Mitchell (1993) has pointed out, we have shifted from a search for truth, to a search for meaning in psychoanalysis. Hoffman (1991, 1992), taking a position he calls "social constructivist," points out how reality and conceptions of that reality are constructed within the analytic interaction. Here again we have a dialectical point of view, as Hoffman insists that social constructivism does not imply that anything goes. He believes that there is a reality external to our constructions that constrains us, that our constructions may fit more or less well, but that is fundamentally ambiguous and thus susceptible of being apprehended validly in more than one way. Hoffman also points out that social constructivism need not rob the analyst of his or her sense of conviction. Rather, the sense of conviction comes from within one's perspective, rather than being thought of as deriving from God-given (or Freud-given) truth.

Psychoanalysis has moved in a postmodern direction, then, as it has become more of a field theory and as absolutist epistemology has given way to perspectivism.

What are the implications of a postmodern point of view for our understanding of culture, class, and race? Taking race as an example, a postmodern view would consider race as a category derived from the conceptual and language network in which it is embedded. This network gives us our categories for classifying and understanding people, including ourselves. Thus, from this point of view, our identities are defined and created in terms of these and other categories; in this sense, we are constituted by race, culture, and class, among other categories. The categories are "out there" in the discourse, the social meaning-making system, and we become individuals as we assume a position within that system, for example, as white or black, upper class or lower class, Jewish or WASP or Irish, male or female, and so on. One regards race, from this perspective, as a socially constructed category, as particular to a certain time, place, and cultural context. The significance of race is something created within a discourse, thus contingent, that is, not inevitable or fully given by any "objective" reality. We focus on skin color and other physical characteristics, among the myriad of potential human characteristics, as significant because our social language/conceptual network makes this a salient quality of people; further, we assign meaning to various physical characteristics in line with the culturally specific associative network attached to race. As contingent categories, these elements of our social discourse are open to scrutiny, interrogation, reflection.

The postmodern emphasis on the social discourse is a valuable corrective to an unreflective acceptance of these categories as simply objective qualities of the world. The postmodern perspective also broadens our focus beyond individual meaning-making associated with race, culture, and class. However, on its own, the postmodern point of view is one-sided, contains its own internal contradictions, and thus is susceptible of, requiring, deconstruction. Postmodernism, for example, sets up questionable polarities between social construction of categories and categories constituted by objectively given characteristics and between social constitution of categories and individual, idiosyncratic constitution of categories. I find it most useful to think that the individual and society constitute each other, that each exists in a dialectical relationship to the other. Let me elaborate, first using postmodernism's own deconstructive method.

How would it be possible critically to interrogate a category within a social discourse, if that category were fully constituted within that discourse? Our thinking would be entirely constrained by the conceptual/language network of our society; we could never gain outside perspective on the categories within that network. In order to think critically about our own discourse, there would have to be multiple discourses that are not fully consistent with each other. Or there would have to be potential for individuals to constitute these categories in idiosyncratic ways that would be potentially at variance with the socially given discourse. These two possibilities dovetail: the socially given discourse is multifaceted, not monolithic, and thus individuals can and must create their own networks of meaning from among the possibilities that are socially given. In addition, individuals can and do create new categories or redefine old categories in ways that have not existed before.

Consider Lacan's treatment of the relationship between language and the individual as an example in this connection, I believe that Lacan does not take sufficient account of the ways in which the individual creates language. Not only may an individual use words in an idiosyncratic way or even coin a new word, but words in combination, in the contexts created by other words, create virtually infinite creative possibilities. Poetry or poetic interludes in prose speech or writing provide a prime example of this use of language. Even in prose, however, words are symbols and, as such, occur in "transitional space." That is, like the transitional object, words exist "out there" in the socially shared world, while simultaneously being the product of individual creative activity. Harris (1992) puts it this way: "symbols have elasticity and infinite playfulness" (p. 132). Drawing on the work of Vygotsky (1963, 1975) and Bakhtin (1981), Harris presents a model of language as the medium through which meaning making is negotiated between parent and infant. As two subjectivities encounter each other, words provide a crucial arena in which communication takes place, understanding occurs or fails to occur, and a creative intermingling of experience can take place. Dialogue between people, for Harris, creates a transitional space in which two minds meet, modifying and transforming each other, often creating experience that had not existed before. In short, I argue that Lacan overemphasized the fixed, societally structured aspects of language and underemphasized language as a vehicle for individual creativity and intersubjective encounter.

An account of the individual as essentially constituted by language or other social phenomena would seem not to have a place for individual human agency and will. Such a one-dimensional view of the human being is not in accord with the commonplace human experience of being the author of one's actions and thoughts. It poses a particular problem for therapists for whom the human potential to take responsibility for personal change is essential and for people with political agendas that rest on the human capacity to take a critical stance with respect to society. The effort to demonstrate the primacy of the social itself represents a critical response to Western individualism. It would be ironic if the outcome of this line of thinking would be to portray the individual as so much a creature of preexisting discourses as to be helpless to challenge them. The only way out from this absurd position is to posit some form of interaction between the personal and the social.

Thus, we must think in terms of a dialectic between the social constitution of categories, such as race, culture, and class, and individual creation of these categories and their meaning. In line with this point of view, throughout this book I consider culture, class, and race as categories that both constitute us and are constituted by us. The constitution of race by projection and introjection is the mechanism through which the social construction of identity occurs, while also serving uniquely individual defensive and self-defining purposes.

Consider now the issues raised by constructivism. The problem here is finding a way to think about the dialectic between and among the following factors: (1) the existence of a reality external to our minds and perceptual apparatus; (2) the ambiguity of that reality, that is, the potential to perceive and understand that reality plausibly in more than one way, so that the filtering and interpreting functions of our minds and senses are an inextricable part of our apprehension of reality; and (3) the ways in which we may be "hard-wired," that is, preprogrammed to attend to, and organize, reality in certain ways. Clearly, most of us arrive in the world predisposed to organize stimuli into the pattern, the gestalt, we know as the human face and to attend to that stimulus. It is a valuable contribution of postmodernism to call our attention to the ways in which our apprehension of reality is structured by ways of organizing experience, for example, language and conceptual categories that are socialized into the child. Nothing in this point of view, however, necessarily excludes an external reality, or hard-wired tendencies to organize that reality in particular ways, which constrain our constructions, whether those constructions be idiosyncratic or socially shared. A postmodern point of view becomes one-sided if it denies these elements that constrain discourse.

When our conceptual and language categories are essentially arbitrary but have become reified, the postmodern point of view is especially valuable. An example here is race. I pointed out before how racial categories are formed through the postulating of arbitrary constellations of physical characteristics. The linking of racial categories to psychological characteristics of people placed in the various categories is also arbitrary. Nonetheless, such categories take on a life of their own as people reify them and use them as the basis for a sense of identity and solidarity with other people. Racial categories come to be regarded in essentialist terms, as referring to inherent attributes of persons, rather than as categories that are socially constructed on an arbitrary basis. Interrogation of such categories, in the postmodern manner, transforms what had seemed given, commonsensical, into preconceptions that are specific to a time, a place, a particular social context.

Finally, I address my own critique of postmodernism to the question of values. Postmodernism has consistently attempted to subvert the universalist pretensions of the Enlightenment. Postmodern philosophers have convincingly argued that the foundations of Enlightenment rationality are historically contingent and local. In their effort to eschew absolutist foundational beliefs, however, postmodern philosophers and social critics have sometimes failed to recognize that they, too, along with the rest of humanity, must have some foundational beliefs and values that form the perspective from which they mobilize critique. Bernstein (1993) writes:

> Habermas accuses Foucault of sliding down the slippery slope of "totalizing critique." Critique . . . must preserve at least one standard by which we engage in the critique of the present. Yet when critique is *totalized*, when critique is turned against itself so that all rational standards are called into question, then one is caught in a performative contradiction [p. 151].

Derrida (quoted in Bernstein, 1993) makes the same point when he says, "I cannot conceive of a radical critique which would not be ultimately motivated by some sort of affirmation, acknowledged or not" (p. 317). It appears that if we are to maintain a critical attitude toward what is given in our society, based on the historical contingency of *all* foundational beliefs and values, we cannot do so without ourselves adopting some such foundational belief or value. Is this a problem? The key here is what Bernstein calls "fallibilism," the recognition that we are, at every point, adopting a fallible position as we engage in critique and analysis. We then become both the deconstructors and the deconstructed, in the best tradition of postmodern deconstruction of polar opposites. The challenge, then, is to believe strongly and deeply, without the assurance of an unquestionable foundation. This position amounts to taking personal responsibility for our moral commitments, as opposed to making appeals to universal validity. Bernstein puts it this way: "We engage in critique as second person 'participants' and not as third person neutral observers. As participants our critiques and affirmations are always tentative, fallible, open to further questioning" (p. 319).

Let me then make a statement about my own values, as expressed in this book. A postmodern sensibility runs throughout this work. I often found a projective-introjective psychoanalytic model useful because of its consistency with postmodern skepticism about bipolar categories, rigid self-definition, and the marginalization of the "other," whether it be in the form of nature or disfranchised and devalued people. That is, the projective-introjective model tends to undermine rigid distinctions between self and other and to destabilize the self. The model allows for understanding the function of categories based on class, culture, and race, in constituting and maintaining a self and a disowned other.

Postmodern writing tends to speak from the margins of society, from the point of view of minorities, of the disfranchised. Listening to marginalized voices tends to reveal the often invisible bases on which the mainstream point of view is constituted, as well as the bases on which other points of view are rejected. This book speaks from the margins of psychoanalysis. It is about patients, contexts, and types of work that have been avoided in our theory and our practice. My aim is to develop a perspective that highlights aspects of the psychoanalytic model that may not be visible from the mainstream. In the tradition of Foucault and Derrida, my effort is subversive, skeptical, democratic, antiauthoritarian, and antielitist. In a sense, these values place me squarely within another mainstream, that of Western—specifically, American—individualism and the democratic political vision. There is also a traditionally Jewish (but not only Jewish) preoccupation with otherness and with oppression. These values are capable of involving me in a new form of elitism as I distance myself from the psychoanalytic mainstream and thus engage in my own effort at creation of a marginalized other. Here enters a final value: dialogue, finding some balance between recognizing the otherness of one's "opponent's" point of view and recognizing, in Hegelian fashion, the ways in which these seeming opposites create, negate, and preserve each other.

3 / RACE, CULTURE, AND SOCIAL CLASS

Therapists working in the public sector (as well as many in private practice) inevitably confront social class, race, and culture as issues in their relationships with patients. Inner-city public clinics, in particular, involve work in neighborhoods that are generally poor, with people from a variety of racial minority groups, representing varied national and cultural backgrounds. It becomes vital to think about these factors psychoanalytically. I argued earlier for the utility, indeed, the necessity, of a relational and a projective-introjective theoretical model in a psychoanalytic approach to these issues. In this chapter, I demonstrate in depth the application of this theoretical model to class, culture, and race. All of these concepts have to do with categories that create an "other" that can serve as the focus for self-definition and projection. In this sense the discourses of race, class, and culture (and gender and sexual orientation) have a common, deep structure. One commonly hears that the "real issue" is class in many discussions of race, that is, that black and white middle-class people are more alike than black middle-class and black poor people, or white middle-class and white poor people. There is truth to this statement. There may also be truth to the statement that the "real" issue is race when class appears to be at issue. On a deeper level, these categories are interchangeable, simply different surface manifestations of the process whereby a denigrated or demonized or simply disowned "other" is created.

In her paper entitled, "Race, Class, and Psychoanalysis? Opening Questions," Elizabeth Abel (1990), writing with feminist, as well as broader, social concerns, comments on the "tendency of psychoanalysis to insulate subjectivity from social practices and discourses" (p. 184). She says that this tendency runs "contrary to a feminism increasingly attuned to the power of social exigencies and differences in the constitution of subjectivity" (p. 184). She then goes on to wonder whether psychoanalysis can encompass the "social" in the sense of "the role of race and class in a diversified construction of subjectivity" (p. 184). Her fundamental question in this essay is posed as

74

whether the resistance of psychoanalysis to the social is adventitious or intrinsic—how labile psychoanalysis is, how far its boundaries can expand to incorporate issues of social difference into a discourse useful, if not for changing the social order, at least for theorizing this order's intervention in the production of diversely gendered subjects [pp. 184–5].

And, I would add, diversely classed, raced, and cultured subjects.

Abel finds that object relations theories in psychoanalysis, insofar as they view the self as "inexorably social" and "constructed in a relational matrix" (p. 185), have the potential to accommodate the social in a psychoanalytic framework. This is what I hope to demonstrate in this chapter as well. For those with social concerns, a psychoanalysis that does not accommodate the social arguably makes, thereby, a statement of indifference to social issues or of collusion with the established order. Speaking from a relational perspective, psychoanalysis can no more be a "blank screen" with respect to the impact of the social order on individual subjectivity than the analyst can be a "blank screen" by virtue of his silence.

Social Class

I was once referred a patient, Mr. A, by a colleague who has a practice in a posh section of Manhattan's Upper East Side. My office at the time was in a far less posh section of the West Side. I met with this man, who, at some point, mentioned his family background. Mr. A was from one of this country's most prominent and wealthy families. He mentioned his family background ostensibly incidentally to describing how oppressive his family was. His parents wanted nothing to do with him; they left his care to servants. He always had to be on good behavior; he felt as if he were an ornamental object in his parents' home.

As he was talking to me, I was having a multitude of reactions. I became acutely aware of the furnishings in my office, which were not lavish, to say the least. I wondered what he could be making of these humble surroundings and of my appearance and clothing. I felt a sense of importance at having been referred such a prominent patient. I found myself curiously unable to empathize with the childhood distress he was describing. I was envying him. I was thinking how nice it would be not to have to worry about money. With Mr. A, I could not summon up a sense of how it must feel to have parents who appeared not to care about one. In fact, I thought that perhaps this man was actually trying to impress me with his social status, while hiding behind the pretense that it was really a burden to be so rich. I now see that, like his parents as he described them, I was regarding the patient as an ornamental object, and I was not caring for him or about him. In addition, as I worried about my clothes and office furnishings, I was feeling inadequate as an ornamental object myself.

Some weeks later, Mr. A had still not paid my first bill, given to him five weeks earlier. I was very much aware of the impact on my personal finances of his failure to pay me; I was quite furious and increasingly envious of his comfortable financial situation. I felt supremely disregarded, as if he just assumed that since money was not an issue for him, it must not be for me either. When I brought up that I had not been paid, Mr. A said that he would have to call his accountant to find out what happened. He could not recall what had happened to my bills; he thought he had given them to the accountant, but he would call to make sure. Perhaps, he said, things would work more smoothly if I simply sent my bills directly to his accountant. I began to say that I would prefer not to have an accountant between him and me in financial matters, when it occurred to me that *this* is how he felt neglected by his parents. I was to be fed by the accountant, if at all. I felt uncared for, neglected, ignored, by a person who had so much to give if he only would.

The hierarchy was reversed, but many of the issues were similar in my work with patients in the public clinic. I was then the one with status and money. Aside from my personal social status, I was, in the eyes of many of the patients, a representative of the entire social welfare system, including not only the hospital I worked for but also welfare, Medicaid, Social Security, and so on. As such, I believe I was often seen as the guardian of enormous resources. This perception fed into many requests from patients that I advocate for them in their quest for one form of benefits or another. Sometimes, patients enacted their sense of deprivation in relation to me in the way they asked for, or demanded, carfare or food. For example, there were several instances in which I became aware that clinic patients who were receiving tokens, authorized by me as therapist, were actually traveling in their cars. Recall the child patients I described in Chapter 1 who routinely provoked conflicts with their therapists around the snacks that the clinic kept on hand for them. If the therapist offered a child a packet of cookies and a pint of milk, the child would request, demand, beg for juice, too, or more cookies, and so on. Often much of the session time was spent negotiating with children about the amount of food they would get. One might see this sort of interaction as a manifestation of oral neediness or a defensive acting out. But then again, one might see it as an emotionally powerful enactment of social class issues in the therapeutic space, encoded in action and thus unavailable for analytic understanding unless one is attuned to these matters. These patients were, perhaps, feeling far more deprived, envious, angry, and needy, in relation to me, than I was in relation to my upper-class patient. How can one pretend to be analyzing the transference or countertransference if these issues are not considered, engaged, and understood as meaningful aspects of the experience between patient and analyst?

One patient I saw in the Bronx, Ms. B, came from a working-class family with considerable pathology, including alcoholism and physical and sexual abuse. She had obtained a scholarship to an Ivy League university but had dropped out after two years. Ms. B benefited enormously from therapy and became aware of powerful self-defeating tendencies based on her conflict about succeeding in life, which would mean surpassing her parents and the rest of her family. Having obtained a good job and gone back to school, Ms. B one day told me that she had decided to quit her job and do some ill-defined freelance work. Until money began coming in, she would go back on welfare. At first I was impressed with the hostility I felt in such an undermining of self, as well as of me and our work together. As we discussed her decision over many weeks, I also learned that having a good job made Ms. B feel isolated. In particular, she felt she could not connect with me unless she were "down and out." I was a professional who helped people with problems, so she would risk losing me, along with her connection with her family, unless she had problems. Being upwardly mobile socially meant losing one's vital sources of support. My experience with other patients in such interactions has been that they can feel they support the therapist, as well, by holding on to a subordinate status. They believe that they need to help the therapist feel useful by their being helpless and dependent. There was some truth, from my point of view, to my patients' beliefs about what makes me feel useful. I can feel a sense of security and usefulness in an effective and dominant position. It was also true with Ms. B that I felt gratified to see my patient's socioeconomic success and that the success of the therapy felt undermined when she retreated from her ambitions. The social class structure that formed part of the context of our work thus organized the transference and countertransference configurations in important ways.

Social class issues have been ignored by psychoanalysts, for the most part (but see Grey, 1966; Speigel, 1970; Whitson, 1990; Dimen, 1993, for exceptions to this neglect). One might surmise that psychoanalysis, having developed as a treatment for the well-to-do, had little reason to concern itself with issues that come up around socioeconomic diversity. Another reason concerns the impact on the therapeutic situation of one's theoretical framework. Social class, as an inherently relational phenomenon, cannot be accommodated as worthy of analytic attention in its own right within the one-person psychology of classical psychoanalytic theory. A one-person drive theory can regard the analyst's social class, for example, as only an incidental trigger to a fundamentally drive-related mental process within the patient. The analyst's social class, along with all his or her other personal characteristics, is, from this point of view, analogous to the day residue that triggers a dream. For example, if the analyst's relatively high social status triggers envy in the patient, the patient's aggression comes under analytic scrutiny. Any feelings or attitudes that the analyst may have based on the social class differential between him or her and the patient and the patient's perceptions or speculations about those feelings and attitudes are to be set aside or, at most, used as sources of hypotheses about the patient's inner world.

In a two-person model, a social class differential, along with the feelings that both patient and analyst have about this differential, becomes an inherently important part of the analysis. Put another way, the difference between a drive-based, one-person theory and an interpersonal/relational, two-person theory may be stated as follows: the former must regard analytic material referring to social class as "manifest content," that is, to be reduced to, or translated into, drive-defense terms, while the latter may regard social class as "bedrock" analytic material to be considered as one element of equal status with other elements in a broadening inquiry that examines the relational experience of both participants. An integrated relational point of view may regard material that is manifestly about drive issues as a displaced commentary on a social class differential, as well as the reverse. For example, a patient's anger at the analyst may be seen as secondary to his plausible attribution of a condescending attitude to his higher-class analyst. Alternatively, the patient's attribution of contempt to his analyst on social class grounds may be seen as derivative of a more basic aggressive or competitive attitude toward the analyst.

A three-person point of view further calls our attention not only to the analytic dyad but also to the patient's and the analyst's relationship to the social context within which the analytic dyad functions. This context includes the social class setup of the society of which patient and analyst are members and the taken-for-granted attitudes about social class within that society that condition both patient's and analyst's assumptions about self and each other.

Let us now return to the case of Ms. B. On one level, her anxiety about transcending her social class status can be seen as a reflection of a transference predisposition based on her experience with her parents and her assumptions about how best to maintain her contact with them. On this level, one can account for her maintenance of her dependent status with me simply in terms of the internal world that she brings to the interaction. On another level, one might regard her assumption that she could best maintain her connection with me by remaining subordinate as based on plausible, if not accurate, perceptions of me and our situation together, powerfully shaped by the values of the society in which we both developed our personalities. I *do* derive a kind of security from my relatively high social status, and I *did* feel useful when she was in trouble and I could be of assistance. To conceive of the transference situation as entirely her creation means to deny plausible, well-founded assumptions and perceptions she has of me, of my personal and socially derived attitudes toward her, in part, a function of the social class differential between us. Taking this point of view in my work with Ms. B facilitated my deepening grasp of the nature of the experience between us as I became more acutely conscious of, and interested in, how our discussions proceeded, particularly when I was inclined to pick up on her weaknesses. I paid careful attention to my responses to her initiating discussions of her strengths. I focused more attention on exploring conclusions she might be drawing about how best to engage me, how I seemed to be engaging her, and how we each perceived the social class issues between us. Our inquiry into this transference-countertransference arena was not always easy, but through it we were able to engage deeply and work through crucial issues that had thwarted the development of this talented young woman.

From the point of view provided by the projective-introjective model, Ms. B and I were disowning and attributing to each other helplessnesss and dependence, as well as strength and resources. Before proceeding further with the use of this projective-introjective model in discussing social class, I must give some attention to what social class means in our society.

Academic sociology tends to discuss social class in terms of income, occupation, and residential address (Hollingshead and Redlich, 1958). These characteristics do not always function as a unit and so lead to a degree of ambiguity in the class system. For example, a plumber or electrician may make more money than a college professor, but the professor is generally considered to be of higher social class based on occupation, given that intellectual work has higher status than manual work in our society. In this case, the status of the work outweighs the status of income. An upper-class person may not work at all, with his or her status being higher, if anything, for the lack of occupation. Different societies give differing weight to these factors in assigning social status. In India, for example, where the caste system has religious as well as social class significance, the highest class of all is the priests (Brahmins), who support themselves by teaching and performing ritual functions and receiving the donations of the people they serve. Unlike the Brahmins, commercial people, who set out to make money, are toward the bottom of the hierarchy, below priests and politicians. The relatively greater significance given to money in the United States is related to the Protestant ethic (Weber, 1958), according to which one's virtue is measured by one's worldly success. The high valuation given to money also suits a capitalist economic system.

The meaning of social class is quite different within a Marxist framework. Here, social class refers to one's relationship to capital, the means of production. The ruling class has ownership of capital, with rights to the profits therefrom. The working-class does not own capital and has no access to the surplus value attached to goods in a market economy. The relationship of the working-class to its work is one of alienation, in that work becomes a commodity; the worker loses his or her personal relationship to the product or the process of working itself. Social class also refers to the relationships between people in a market economy. The working-class is exploited by the ruling class. Social class, from a Marxist point of view, emphasizes the power structure of society and the relationships people have to their labor and the profits thereof.

For Dimen (1993, 1994), the class structure of society shows up in the psychoanalytic situation in a variety of ways. For example, Dimen associates a good deal of countertransferential anxiety with the social location of psychoanalysts, in the "professional-managerial" class (Ehrenreich and Ehrenreich, 1979). This class, Dimen points out, following Ehrenreich (1989), is a very insecure class. The dominant status of this class in society makes its members subject to envy and resentment, and they have nothing more tangible by way of capital to hold onto than their knowledge and expertise. "Rooted in the very work of professionals, then, this anxiety about felt fraudulence and looming loss is actually built into the role of analyst in a class-structured society" (Dimen, 1994, p. 79). Dimen goes on to argue that the alienation inherent in capitalist society is reflected on the individual level, in psychic alienation, as well as alienation within the psychoanalytic relationship. On the psychic level, alienation refers to the alienation of the individual from himself, that is, the basic problem with which psychoanalysis attempts to deal. In the analytic relationship, alienation, for Dimen, refers to the way in which money, which makes analysis possible, also dehumanizes the process and turns what is, in one aspect, the most intimate, loving, and personal of encounters into a commercial transaction. Dimen regards this state of affairs as an inevitable concomitant, a reflection, of our class structure. Money symbolizes, according to Dimen (1993), the societal "fault lines" (p. 7) in terms of race, class, and gender, that create difference and hierarchy among people. At the same time, money comes to stand for love and hate within the analytic relationship. The anxiety that appears around billing and payment policies, the amount of the fee, or paying for missed appointments reflects anxiety about an alienation that is as much derivative and reflective of the social system as of individual history and psychology. Dimen (1994) argues for an acceptance of the paradoxical nature of the analytic relationship in terms of being both loving and hating, both intimate and commercial, making possible a "temporary, reparative resolution" (p. 98) of the contradictions between money and love, between love and hate.

Dimen implies that the social class structure, interpersonal conflict and alienation, and intrapsychic alienation are transforms, or analogues, of one another. What exists on the social level cannot but find reflection in the individual psyche, and vice versa. Dimen (1993) puts it this way: "At the heart of psychoanalysis, this most private of encounters, lies society, just as at the heart of public life lies the alienation psychoanalysis tries to cure" (p. 11). I espouse a similar, systemic point of view elsewhere in this book, for example, when I argue that social structure, the structure of a public clinic, and the events that take place in therapeutic dyads within such a clinic reflect one another. Since society and the psyche are not clearly delineable, it follows that psychoanalysis cannot define its field of inquiry as the individual mind, or even the dyad, without reference to the broader social and political surround.

In the United States, we are uncomfortable with acknowledging that we have a social class system. Such a system does not fit with our democratic ideals and illusions. Perhaps this ideal and illusion are our birthright from the American Revolution; we define ourselves in contrast to the hierarchical British, from whom we differentiated. We tend to deny that we have a social class system at all, sometimes by extending the term "middle-class" to include almost the entire population. Another manifestation of this denial is to overemphasize the degree to which people can be upwardly mobile. We tend to deny the degree to which class status tends to stick to one. The result is that Americans tend to take lower social class status as evidence of personal failure or deficiency, a point made by Sennett and Cobb (1972) in their book, *The Hidden Injuries of Class*. This feeling of deficiency in relation to lower-class status is also a legacy of the Protestant ethic. Low self-esteem and self-blame are the hidden injuries of class.

The word "class," notwithstanding our denial, means category or type. Such words imply a fixed quality to one's class status. One's class membership becomes a part of one's relatively stable sense of identity, of one's sense of the type of person one is. The class status of one's parents is hard to outgrow, even for the upwardly mobile. Changes in class status occur imperceptibly slowly, if at all. One's preconceptions and stereotypes about social classes thus become important factors determining one's self-image and the images one has of other people. We do tend to assume that there are defined "types" of people, and class status is an important marker for the distinctions that we make.

Postmodern social theory tends to see class categories, along with gender, racial, and cultural categories, as constructions, rather than as categories reflecting some "natural," that is, prediscursive, divisions among people. Our perceptions of other people are organized and structured by the categories we use, and vice versa. The question arises, then, On what basis, to what ends, are social categories constructed in the way that they are? One answer is that gender, racial, and class categories may be constructed to serve political ends; that is, they may serve to create a polarity that lays the groundwork for a power differential. For example, some contemporary feminist authors have argued that the categories "male" and "female" are constructed in the service of establishing a power differential between the two groups. One might say similarly that, although race, as constructed, forms a continuum, the categories "white" and "black" are polarized in the service of maintaining a power relationship. The social class system, likewise, can be seen to establish categories in the context of a hierarchical social organization. The self-image or self-esteem or lack thereof that attends one's class status depends, to a great degree, on the position of one's class in the social hierarchy. The hidden injuries of class, the low self-esteem and the self-contempt, are illuminated when one holds in view the powerlessness and the exploitation that attend lower-class social status.

Social class categories, then, are constructed on a social level, serving social functions. They are also constructed on a personal, psychological level to serve psychic functions. Consider, in particular, how social class differences can serve as a basis for projecting psychic qualities onto or into other people and for constructing an acceptable self-image. Recall commonplace examples from Chapter 2: how aggression, sexuality, criminality, exploitativeness are often disowned by people of relatively high social status and projected onto, or into, those of lower social status. People of lower social status may disown intelligence and ambition and project these qualities onto those of higher social status, in another version of the hidden injuries of class. Recall how projective identification on a large social scale can take place. For example, the failure to provide adequate schooling and job opportunities to neighborhoods of lower socioeconomic-status people makes it likely that educational motivation will suffer. Such an outcome then actualizes the preconception that lower socioeconomic-status people are poorly motivated, bent on exploiting the system. This vicious circle can lead to an internalization of this self-image by poor people and further reinforces the vicious circle. Meanwhile, higher-status people, having disowned their own inclination to exploit the system, can feel virtuously diligent and honest. A blatant example would be the owner of a so-called cash business whose proceeds are in cash so no taxes can be paid without leaving a paper trail, who has strongly judgmental attitudes about "welfare cheats." As another example, as described in chapter 2, relatively high social status people commonly attribute aggression and violence to relatively low social status people. Various forms of social oppression, poverty, and so on create widespread anger among poor people. Our failure to pass strict and effective gun control laws further contributes to making street violence likely. Violence in ghetto neighborhoods then reinforces the preconception. Meanwhile, our own violence, or violence on our behalf in the form of police brutality, gets put in another category.[1]

In the clinical psychoanalytic situation, social class differences can provide the focus for projection and introjection by both patient and analyst. Preconceptions about people based on social class can form the nucleus of an attribution that serves projective and introjective functions. For example, in the case of Ms. B cited earlier, her relatively low social class position contributed to my seeing her as helpless and needy. This experience made me less aware of such qualities and feelings in myself and contributed to my feeling more the helper, the one with resources, the one whose life is all together. Ms. B downplayed her own resources and competence and became the needy one in her search for caring and nurturance. What we each disowned in ourselves, the flip side of our conscious self-images, reappeared in the transference in the sense that Ms. B felt that she was taking care of me by being helpless. By helping me to feel useful and strong, she nurtured me. Our roles were reversed. When it comes to projective and introjective processes, what goes around comes around. A one-person focus on Ms. B's mind in isolation runs the risk of colluding with her willingness to play the "sick" role and makes it more difficult to analyze this aspect of her psyche and our interaction.

Discussions of analyzability, in which lower-class patients often end up on the unanalyzable side, may reflect the analyst's psychic defensive operations. I have just illustrated a clinical situation in which what might be considered ego deficits in the patient turn out to be, in part, reflective of the patient's perception that the analyst is quite fragile and needs support. The danger in an ego psychological approach to such a situation is of reification of what amounts to a strategy for maintaining a personal connection. Even Pine (1985), who develops an inclusive approach by giving full psychoanalytic

---

[1]Employing a two-person Kleinian framework helps explicate the vicious circle that arises as the "recipient" of a projection is transformed in a way that actualizes the projector's expectation. Klein herself initially developed a one-person concept of projective identification. That is, projective identification was seen as simply a fantasy of ridding oneself of psychic contents by placing them into another person. Bion (1988a) and Racker (1968) developed the idea that the recipient could actually receive and identify with the projection. Levenson (1972) has moved in the same theoretical direction by pointing out how analysts are "transformed" by their patients.

status to "supportive" elements in the interpretive process, locates the need for support entirely in the patient. In this way, the analyst may collude with the patient to overlook the patient's investment in keeping him in the "strong" position. Reifying the patient's helplessness can also serve the function of disowning the analyst's own sense of needing support from the patient. We need to be alert to who is being supported in so-called supportive therapy.

Another example in this connection concerns the inner-city clinic that provides food to child patients, as previously mentioned. Recall how our clinic's magnanimity cloaked a more self-interested attempt to maximize our Medicaid payments. Or recall the therapist who, low on visits that week, *was* so glad her patient showed up. Taking a one-person point of view, one might regard the patient's saying, "You're lucky I came today" as resistance-born disavowal of the patient's dependence or perhaps as transference born of a caretaking response to a parent. Such a point of view may indeed be valuable. If one does not consider, however, that the patient may have picked up, in some fashion, the therapist's dependence on the patient within the context of the clinic and its administration, the therapist herself may be disavowing an important aspect of their interaction.

Aside from projective-introjective processes, these vignettes illustrate the use of a three-person psychoanalytic perspective in looking at the role of social class in public clinic work. I intend them to illustrate my point that one cannot fully understand the dyadic interaction in the therapy room without taking account of the context, in terms of the community in which the clinic is located, as well as the internal structure and politics of the clinic itself.

Race

Racial prejudice has been a central element in American history from the very beginning, with the subjugation of Native Americans and the enslavement of African people as particularly dramatic examples. White Americans could eventually tolerate or even welcome the emancipation of the slaves but could not so easily free themselves of the preconceptions about, and attitudes toward, black people that had served to justify slavery as an institution. Afro-Americans became a quintessential "other" for our society. Cornel West (1993b) describes the outcome: "We were 3/5 human, we were monkeys or rapists. Now we are crack addicts and criminals" (p. 15). West (1993a) brings an antiessentialist critique to bear on the black identity-formation process in this country; that is, he emphasizes the ways in which the black–white polarity has been constructed in the service of power and economic arrangements. To make his point that blackness and whiteness are constructs that come into existence only in relation to one another, West (1993a) writes:

> Those who came to the United States didn't realize they were white until they got here. . . . They had to be told they were white. An Irish peasant coming from British imperial abuse in Ireland during the potato famine in the 1840s, arrives in the States. You ask him or her what they are. They say "I am Irish." No, you're white. "What do you mean I am white?" And they point me out. Oh, I see what you mean [p. 11].

West (1993b, p. 121) points out that the concept "Europe," so intertwined with our concept of "whiteness," did not exist until 1458, when Pius II introduced the category after the Turks took over Constantinople. The threat of an outside force had created a unity among those who were threatened. A boundary was drawn, a polarity created. West, determined not to accept this polarity uncritically himself, warns against the demonization of whites. He believes that the psychic processes which result in racism are universal: "Hatred of those who are cast as degraded 'other' will always be with any human society" (p. 9). He writes: "In a democratic society, you cannot demonize, because demonizing means you have lost contact with the humanity of your foes. . . . once you demonize, then you are calling into question the possibility of dialogue or further engagement down the line" (1993a, p. 35). Further: "It's legitimate to abhor and hate oppression and exploitation, but we cannot lose sight of the humanity of those who are perpetuating it" (p. 107).[2] West opposes black nationalism on the grounds that this movement accepts uncritically an essentialist view of blacks that is simply the reverse of the usual polarity. He advocates: "Demystify the categories in order to stay tuned in to the complexity of the realities" (p. 20).

There is a multifaceted inquiry into the construction of blackness/whiteness in West's writing. Considering the integration of the slaves into America, West points out how they lost, over time, their

---

[2]Kleinian interrogation of all forms of splitting comes together with Christian love for one's oppressor in West's work!

sense of identity as Africans with their own culture. In place of that sense of identity was a degraded and demonized identity, for the most part. There were remnants of the African identity and culture, to be sure, for example, in the form of jazz music, which found acceptance and admiration among both blacks and whites.[3]

West's analysis portrays contemporary black identities as carrying, burdened with, the underside of our late capitalist, postmodern culture. In common with the working-class member of any race, black identity is forged in the context of a capitalist economic order in which workers are needed to be exploited. West (1993b) discusses "the construction of the Negro subject . . . the degree to which you understand yourself as degraded, inferior, and subordinate, precludes and forecloses political possibilities for how you will act" (p. 191). The degraded black identity is seen as part of a larger social process by which a docile group of slaves, later a working class, was created. Black is cognate with working class.

West (1993a) views contemporary culture as, in part, an extension of the capitalist order. That is, insofar as the late capitalist system thrives on consumption, the individual is led to need ever-increasing levels of stimulation: "One sees an addiction to stimulation as the requisite for the consumerism which helps keep the economy going" (p. 148). The black "underclass" gives a kind of ultimate expression to this postmodern addiction: "Crack is indeed the postmodern drug because it is the highest level of stimulation known to the human brain" (p. 148). On another aspect of this phenomenon: "Roughly between 1964 and 1967 black neighborhoods underwent qualitative transformation and the qualitative transformation that they underwent had much to do with the invasion of a particular kind of commodification, namely the buying and selling of a particular kind of commodity—drugs" (p. 149). West (1993b) similarly views the indifference to human life in the drug culture as reflective of the alienation and dehumanization inherent in an economic order in which labor and, thus, laborers, become commodities (p. 104). West shows how the demonized "other," the black "underclass," can be seen as showing us the disowned face of our own selves, the face of the culture in which we are all embedded.

---

[3]There were also positive images of nurturance associated with the black woman "mammy," at least among whites. In Faulkner's *Sound and the Fury*, the black slave woman emerges as the stable, sane character in the context of a degenerating white family. Faulkner, not flinching from his perception of degradation in the white world, is perhaps free from the need to degrade the black.

West puts the matter in terms more familiar to psychoanalysts when he writes of "the crucial role that blackness plays as a metaphor, be it a signifier of the id, or of chaos, or whatever" (p. 129). He summarizes, on the situation of the black "underclass" (and, therefore, of us all) in America today: "people with no roots, no cultural armor to deal with the traumas of life—of death, disease, disappointment, and despair—we find ourselves caught up in a market culture that provides us not with the values but with hedonistic self indulgence and upward mobility" (p. 149).

Sigmund Freud is generally considered to have neglected considerations of race, but, according to Gilman (1993), race is at the core of Freud's work. Gilman maintains that in fin de siècle Vienna, Jews were regarded as a race, often, in fact, as black. The Jewish race was regarded as diseased, as the carriers of disease, and as deficient, especially intellectually. Gilman marshals evidence that Freud himself accepted the idea of the Jews as a diseased and deficient race, in a way common to German Jews of the time: he projected this image onto East European Jews. But Freud himself, as he was well aware, had roots in East European Jewry. Gilman's analysis puts Freud's aspirations in the Viennese medical world in a new light: the Jewish physician inevitably was trying to cure himself. Freud became both analyst and patient. Gilman maintains that Freud, nonetheless, disowned the sense of himself and of his race as diseased and deficient. He projected these qualities onto women, according to Gilman, who finds therein the source of Freud's denigration of femininity.

Psychoanalytic Literature on Race

The following vignette illustrates the advantages of two- and three-person perspectives when race is a clinical issue. The material is from Holmes (1992), a prominent Afro-American analyst, in an article on race and transference:

> As a new psychology intern, Holmes was assigned a Black woman who had gone through intake with a white female psychiatrist. In her first interview with Holmes, she was sullen and withdrawn. In the second interview, Holmes explored the patient's evident anger, as she had been encouraged to do by her supervisor. The patient explained her disappointment with having been assigned to Holmes by saying: "You're black, you're a woman, and you're a psychologist!" Holmes, in reporting this vignette, emphasized how the patient exacerbated her own sense of insecurity as a new intern. She reported, however, that her supervisor focused on

the patient's low self-esteem as a black woman, her anger, and her defensive contempt of Holmes [p. 3].

The supervisor in this vignette, a black man, adopted a one-person point of view; that is, he emphasized how the patient's contempt for Holmes revealed the patient's mind. In drive terms, the patient's contempt was derivative of aggression, perhaps self-directed, then secondarily projected onto the therapist, using race, along with gender and professional status, as a focus.

If one considers this vignette from a two-person perspective, other issues arise. For example, we note that Holmes's self-esteem was shaky in this situation. Did the patient notice Holmes's vulnerability or infer it from her status as a psychology intern? How did the patient react if she did notice? Was she perhaps testing her *therapist's* self-esteem, her survivability in the face of attack? Was the patient interested in how Holmes felt about being black, a woman, a psychologist? What conclusions might she have drawn about Holmes if she challenged the patient's denigration of their race and gender, or if she did not challenge her? Once Holmes began to focus on the patient's anger and self-contempt, did the patient feel that Holmes was counterattacking, or, perhaps, was she reassured to feel that Holmes had survived her attack and had maintained her analytic stance? All these questions, and more, are raised when one begins to consider the presence of Holmes in the room as a person, a separate center of subjectivity. From a one-person perspective, such questions could also be raised, but in terms of the patient's projections. That is, one could wonder if the patient were projecting onto Holmes her own sense of vulnerability, as opposed to wondering whether the patient plausibly, if not accurately, construed some of Holmes' behavior as reflecting vulnerability and insecurity. In the former case, one sees the patient as engaged in defensive activity; the analyst's interpretations focus on the patient's conflicts. In the latter case, one is tracking an interaction between two people, two subjectivities.[4] Interpretations are commentaries on the state of the interaction and the contributions to it of both participants.

A three-person perspective also calls our attention to Holmes's status as a new intern and how she felt about this position, her

---

[4]The concept of projective identification can provide a bridge between intrapsychic and interpersonal processes. That is, the analyst may identify with the patient's projections in a way that sets an interpersonal process in motion.

relationship with her supervisor, her supervisor's relationship to the patient (in his own mind and in terms of how Holmes views this relationship), his racial attitudes, his relationship to the psychoanalytic community, and so on. Holmes took on herself the task of challenging the traditional psychoanalytic neglect of race as a useful aspect of the psychoanalytic process. How did she feel about this role? What was her internalized model of the traditional psychoanalytic community and her relationship to it? How might these factors have affected her relationship with her supervisor and her patient? Did she take a compliant or rebellious stance, or both, in relationship to her supervisor, let us say, as a black man who had adopted a fairly traditional psychoanalytic posture? Was her work with her patient affected by her desire to please him, to try on his way of working, to be able to depend on his experience and expertise, to defy him? How might such factors have impacted upon, and been interpreted by, the patient?

There are important implications of these theoretical choices for the psychoanalytic consideration of race. If the analyst operates with a thoroughgoing one-person drive theory, the patient's concern with race is seen as reducible to a drive issue. An analyst with this point of view might see race as an important issue, but not an inherently *analytic* issue, by definition. Analysts with a classical sensibility, such as Holmes, who write about race tend to stress its value as an *entrée* into transference material. From a two-person point of view, by contrast, race is seen as a potential focus of interaction, in which the feelings, attitudes, biases, preconceptions, and prejudices of both parties form part of the field. From this perspective, race can be seen as important analytic material in its own right. Aggression, for example, can be seen as derivative of racial issues in the dyad, as well as vice versa. The analyst working with a two-person model might also regard a concern with racial issues on the part of patient (or analyst) as defensive or otherwise derivative of nonracial concerns. On the other hand, such an analyst would not, prima facie, regard such material as superficial or nonanalytic solely on the basis of its pertaining to the interpersonal or sociocultural matrix in which the analysis takes place. To regard a patient's concerns around racial, cultural, or class issues in the analytic relationship as nonanalytic material may constitute dismissal of the patient's feelings. In some cases, the one-person model may be maintained at the cost of failing to address the patient's feelings about the analyst and his stance with respect to race. In such cases, the operation might be a success, but the patient could be dead.

A classic psychoanalytic paper on race in psychoanalysis is by Schachter and Butts (1971). This paper attempts to find a place for race within a one-person, classical psychoanalytic model. Yet, the authors appear to be aware of two-person factors, including the analyst's subjectivity, in the cases they present. Unable to find a place for these factors, given their theoretical commitments, they can do no more than mention the feelings of the analyst as an interesting side issue. I argue that the analyst's experience of the interaction around race, as described, could be seen as a crucially important element in the analysis. If the analyst's experience is taken account of as an important piece of the transference-countertransference matrix, the door is opened to a consideration of the patient's perception and fantasies about the analyst's subjectivity (Aron, 1991) around race. Our understanding of the discourse of the patient around race is enriched by a consideration of how it may include a commentary on the analyst's participation.

In their first clinical example, Schachter and Butts present a white male patient in analysis with a black male analyst. The patient had difficulty sexually and in relationships with women. He felt insecure on his job and in his relationships. His sense of insecurity seemed to crystallize in a sense that his penis was too small. From his dreams, Schachter and Butts conclude that his image of the black man was as "physically assaultive, drunk, and debased . . . the patient feared his analyst's aggression and sexual exploitation" (p. 796).

Some months into the analysis, the patient "triumphantly" reported having been able to have sex with a woman. Schachter and Butts report that the analyst responded with "mild disbelief in the therapeutic significance of the patient's achievement [which] in part reinforced the patient's stereotyped perception of the Negro as a virtual sexual superman" (p. 797). Schachter and Butts also comment on the analyst's "need to disclaim his therapeutic power to achieve such a great effect with the patient" (p. 797). The analyst, it seems, both diminished himself and asserted his superiority with respect to the patient in this interaction.

In the other case presented by Schachter and Butts, the patient is a black male, and the analyst is a white female. The patient presents himself in a negative light, that is, as irresponsible, indiscriminately sexual, and aggressive, in accord with some negative stereotypes. He openly discusses his own prejudice against blacks, his belief that whites are more controlled than blacks. He claims that the analyst is more accepting of him and of black people in general than he is. Schachter and Butts point out that the analyst chose this patient to work with in an analytic clinic because she thought that, as a black man, he would have fewer options and would thus be less likely to move in the course of the analysis and leave treatment! The analyst also had a rescue fantasy in relation to a prospective patient likely to be rejected by other analytic candidates and an identification with the underdog, which was also expressed in her involvement in the civil rights movement.

In elaborating the theoretical framework within which they view these clinical interactions, Schachter and Butts state:

> The catalytic effect of the analyst's race upon the development of the transference occurs when the racial stereotypes are concerned with the same affects and conflicts as the transference. These stereotypes do not reflect a transferring of feelings from earlier significant figures onto the therapist. They provide a structure upon which a problem can be hung, and much of the transference can be worked out around the racial issues that are brought up early in the treatment. If the stereotype and the developing transference are both reflections of the analysand's personal difficulties, this confluence of transference and stereotype will facilitate the analysis [p. 803].

Schachter and Butts's formulation about the white patient was that he held a stereotype about black men as sexual athletes. This stereotype served to catalyze his feelings of inadequacy and his fantasies of magical repair. With regard to the black patient, the authors state that he held a stereotype of white women as sexually cold and remote. This stereotype catalyzed feelings about his mother and her exclusion and rejection of him. The authors believe he fended off the analyst by a recital of behaviors that he thought would activate her negative stereotypes about black men. Thus, in both cases, Schachter and Butts believe that racial stereotypes served to catalyze transference configurations that existed independently of the stereotypes per se.

Note the duality in Schachter and Butts's formulation: racial stereotype on one side, transference on the other. The authors appear to be saying that when a preexisting racial stereotype fits a preexisting transference disposition, the analysis is catalyzed in that the analysis of the racial material is, in itself, the analysis of the transference. But how could it be otherwise? Why would a patient hold to a particular racial stereotype about the analyst unless it fit with the patient's transference predisposition?[5] Is a racial stereotype applied to one's analyst not in itself transference? I believe that Schachter and Butts make this distinction here because they are having difficulty fitting a racial stereotype into the mold of transference as defined in a classical psychoanalytic model, that is, as drive-derived perceptions of the analyst transferred from the past. They are going to pains not to be open to the charge that they are taking "superficial" social factors as ultimate psychoanalytic material. Yet, they wish to argue that racial issues need to be taken account of in psychoanalysis. The solution, then, is to regard racial material as a potentially royal road to the unconscious. Sometimes, they seem to be saying, a racial stereotype is available felicitously in the environment that facilitates symbolic expression of drive-defense transference. One might say, analogously, that the analysis is facilitated when the day presents residue that fits with the transference to produce a dream. Schachter and Butts thereby inadvertently adopt a reductionistic approach to racial issues. An alternative would be to consider that transference and racial stereotypes as they appear between analyst and patient inevitably drive one another or are actually inseparable. That is, racial stereotypes arise as expressions of preexisting transference, or preexisting transference material is produced to express a racial stereotype that has arisen in the mind of the patient, perhaps in response to the behavior of the analyst, in a circular, self-perpetuating cycle, or both occur. Schachter and Butts are constrained by their theory to distinguish racial stereotypes from transference in a way that diminishes or actually removes, race as a psychoanalytic issue.

In their clinical presentation, nonetheless, Schachter and Butts note aspects of the analyst's subjectivity in both cases that potentially enrich our understanding of the analytic interactions. Without a relational theoretical framework, however, they cannot maximize the psychoanalytic yield from their astute clinical observations.

Consider the interpretive possibilities opened up by such a shift in the theoretical frame. With respect to the white patient with the black analyst, one might regard the interaction as an example of projective identification, in which the patient's own sense of

---

[5]There are two possible answers to this question. First, the analyst's behavior in itself can be plausibly seen as fitting the racial stereotype. Second, the patient is interested in the analyst's response to being stereotyped in that particular way. These two answers to my question make sense only within a two-person psychoanalytic framework, so I ignore them for the moment.

deficiency and powerful aggression are disowned and projected into the analyst. The racial stereotype, as Schachter and Butts suggest, might "carry" the projection in this case. The analyst, with his own racial stereotypes, his own rivalry with the patient, and his own sense of inadequacy, may be quite receptive to being "projected into" in just this way. Schachter and Butts seem to note this aspect of the situation without elaborating on its psychoanalytic significance or usefulness. From a relational point of view, however, we now have a circular process, in which one can focus either on the patient's awareness of the analyst's subjectivity and his response to this awareness or on the patient's preexisting transferences. For example, one might ask, Does the patient take a subservient, weak stance because he thinks this is what the analyst wants? Does he think the analyst needs or wants to feel like the powerful black sexual superman? One might also view the racial basis for such speculations as being on an equal footing with the preexisting transferential bases. An integrated relational perspective that accommodates the intrapsychic as well as the interpersonal provides a framework for inquiry into all aspects of this analytic process. I include here inquiry into the impact of the racial difference without implicitly dismissing the significance of this difference by reducing it to some intrapsychic factor.

With respect to the second case of a black patient with a white analyst, Schachter and Butts have again given us all the data we need to construct an interactive, intersubjective view of this clinical situation. Their commentary on the analyst's subjectivity suggests that the analyst's "tolerance" and "acceptance," her identification with the underdog, concealed an exploitativeness on her part. Did the patient believe he needed to take a degraded role in order to afford his analyst the opportunity to be "tolerant"? Was he presenting himself as exploitative in order to support her denial of such a characteristic in herself? Was there an element of mockery in his so doing? Did the patient believe that the analyst's accepting attitude concealed more negative feelings about himself as a black person? Was the patient introjecting an image of himself that he thought the analyst was disavowing? The analyst in this case is strikingly self-aware, only a step away from a fully intersubjective view of her interaction with this patient. I believe that her ability to take this final step is impeded by her theoretical model, which does not give her a framework for thinking about her own contribution to the interaction.

Schachter and Butts, again, have given us a great deal of important information about both patient and analyst, the ingredients

for an in-depth understanding of this interaction. It is as if their level
of clinical awareness has outstripped what their theoretical model
can contain, as if they need or seek a new paradigm. They are a
black and a white analyst writing about (presumably with respect to
their own experience as analysts) interracial analytic dyads. Perhaps
the "parallel process" in the writing attuned them to the mutuality of
each interaction and made it more difficult for them to dismiss the
analyst's subjectivity, including racial preconceptions, as pathological
countertransference. To hold out the ideal of a countertransference-
free analytic stance, when race is an issue, is to believe in the
possibility of transcendence of racism. Race would then be only the
patient's issue. Such a stance would be at variance with the tenor of
our times, the prevailing sentiment in liberal circles, at least, in favor
of self-examination around racial matters.

Culture, Ethnicity, and Psychoanalysis

The word "culture" has a variety of related meanings. Kluckhohn
(1949, cited in Geertz, 1973, pp. 4–5) gives 11 different meanings of
the word, from "the total way of life of a people," to the "social
legacy the individual acquires from his group," to "an abstraction
from behavior," to a "theory on the part of the anthropologist about
the way in which a group of people in fact behave." In the most
general terms, Herkovits (1948, quoted in Betancourt and Lopez,
1993) defines culture as the "human made part of the environment"
(p. 630). Traiandis et al. (1980, cited in Betancourt and Lopez, 1993)
elaborates on this definition by distinguishing the physical elements
of culture, such as buildings and tools, from the "subjective"
elements of culture, such as social norms, roles, beliefs, and values.
Rohmer (1984, cited in Betancourt and Lopez, 1993) defines culture
as "'a highly variable system of meanings' which are 'learned' and
'shared by a people or an identifiable segment of a population.' It
represents 'designs and ways of life' that are normally 'transmitted
from one generation to another'" (p. 630).

The related word "ethnic" is derived from the Greek *ethnikos*,
which means "national" or "gentile," according to Webster.[6] It also
means pertaining to "races or large groups of people classed

---

[6] As with the Hebrew word *goy*, which means both "nation" and "non-Jewish,"
there is an implicit ethnocentrism. That is, the nations are defined by their divergence
from the standard, from God's people.

according to common traits or customs." Betancourt and Lopez (1993) define ethnicity in relation to "groups that are characterized in terms of a common nationality, culture, or language" (p. 631).

The concept of culture as a "system of meanings" makes it possible to locate this concept within a psychoanalytic frame of reference, within psychoanalytic culture, as it were. The central feature of culture by this definition is that it refers to the process of assigning meaning to things, behavior, feelings, and ideas, as this meaning-making is influenced by processes of socialization. It refers to the categories and meanings available within a particular community. While there are inevitable idiosyncratic variations in meaning assignment, it is also possible to speak of general trends in a particular society, and it is to these general trends that the word "culture" speaks. Schweder (1991), an anthropologist, proposes a "cultural psychology" and speaks of a dialectical relationship between the individual psyche and culture:

> Human beings starting at birth (and perhaps earlier) are highly motivated to seek meanings and resources out of a sociocultural environment that has been arranged to provide them with meanings and resources to seize and to use. . . .no sociocultural environment exists or has identity independently of the way human beings seize meaning and resources from it, while, on the other hand, every human being's subjectivity and mental life are altered through the process of seizing meanings and resources from some sociocultural environment and using them [p. 74].

From Schweder's point of view, then, psyche and culture fully interpenetrate each other. The aim of Schweder's "cultural psychology" is "to find ways to talk about culture and psyche and culture[7] so that neither is by nature intrinsic or extrinsic to the other" (p. 100). Geertz (1973) has a similar conception of the relationship between culture and the mind:

---

[7]Schweder's definition of culture seems consistent with Rendon's (1993) statements that "culture is a historical accretion of a group's creative activity" (p. 112) and that "ethnicity is the history of our identifications, including the identifications of those we identified with" (p. 111). Rendon, from his point of view, understands the central role of food in common understanding of culture or ethnicity as referring symbolically to culture as identification or internalization. (His heading of the section in which he speaks of food is "We are what we eat.") Rendon points out how language is a central element of culture, insofar as language structures our meaning-making. In Lacanian terms, culture is the symbolic realm. From other points of view, culture is the superego or the patriarchal order.

The concept of culture I espouse . . . is essentially a semiotic one. Believing, with Max Weber, that man is an animal suspended in webs of significance he himself has spun, I take culture to be those webs, and the analysis of it to be therefore not an experimental science in search of laws, but an interpretive one in search of meanings [p. 5].

Elaborating on his perspective, Schweder (1991) delineates a concept of "intentional worlds" (p. 76). The intentional world is made up of "intentional objects" (p. 76), defined as things that "have no natural reality or identity separate from human understanding and activities" (p. 75). For example:

A weed is an intentional thing. It is an intrusive, interfering or improper plant that you do not want growing in your garden. Consequently, a daisy, sunflower, a foxglove, or perhaps even a thorny rose that turns up in your vegetable patch might be plucked out as a weed, while one can find intentional worlds in which crabgrass, marijuana, or dandelions are not constituted as weeds at all. Instead they are cultivated as cash crops [p. 75].

An intentional object can include not only concrete things but also the entire realm of human behavior, speech acts, and so on. Geertz (1973, pp. 6-7) cites Ryle's (1949) similar concept of "thick description," contrasted to "thin description." "Consider" (Geertz writes, paraphrasing Ryle) "two boys rapidly contracting the eyelids of their right eyes. In one, this is an involuntary twitch; in the other a conspiratorial signal to a friend." A third boy, he adds later, performs the identical physical movement, but this time it is a parody of the second boy's "amateurish, clumsy" wink. The description of the physical action by itself constitutes thin description. The description of the action in terms of its meaning to human beings constitutes thick description. Geertz (1973) writes:

Between what Ryle calls the "thin description" of what the rehearser (parodist, winker, twitcher) is doing ("rapidly contracting his right eyelid") and the "thick description" of what he is doing ("practicing a burlesque of a friend faking a wink to deceive an innocent into thinking a conspiracy is in motion") lies the object of ethnography: a stratified hierarchy of meaningful structures in terms of which twitches, winks, fake winks, parodies, rehearsals of parodies are produced, perceived, and interpreted, and without which they would not . . . in fact exist, no matter what anyone did or didn't do with his eyelids [p. 7].

In this vivid way, Geertz develops the same concept as Schweder with his idea of "intentional worlds."

For Schweder, then, an intentional world is a particular world of meaning in which a human being lives. Schweder (1991) then redefines a sociocultural environment as an intentional world. From this point of view, he derives his definition of culture:

> Culture is the constituted scheme of things for intending persons, or at least that part of the scheme that is inherited or received from the past. Culture refers to persons, society, and nature as lit up and made possible by some already there intentional world, an intentional world composed of conceptions, evaluations, judgments, goals, and other mental representations already embodied in socially inherited institutions, practices, artifacts, technologies, art forms, texts, and modes of discourse [p. 101].

Cultural anthropologists like Schweder, then, in common with psychoanalysts, seek to study the intentional worlds of people.[8] Schweder's anthropological focus puts the emphasis on shared, "already there" intentional worlds, what we call culture and what Lacan and other postmodernists call language.

When the cultural psychologist approaches a new culture, he encounters dilemmas like that of the relational psychoanalyst: how to understand the intentional world of another person. Schweder, consistent with much contemporary psychoanalytic thinking, recognizes that there is no neutral place from which to study someone else's world. One can strive to make sense of the other only from the vantage point of one's own intentional world. Geertz (1973) puts it in this way:

> What we call our data are really our constructions of other people's constructions of what they and their compatriots are up to. . . . Right down at the factual base, the hard rock, insofar as there is any, of the whole enterprise, we are already explicating: and worse, explicating explications. Winks upon winks upon winks. Analysis, then, is sorting out the structures of signification [p. 9].

Schweder (1991) calls this process of explicating other people's explications "thinking through others" (pp. 108–110); he outlines four aspects to this process: one aspect has to do with thinking through others as a "situated perspectival observer thinking *while*

---

[8]Other cultural anthropologists, for example, those with a Marxist orientation, put the focus on socioeconomic factors.

there in an alien land or with an alien other, trying to make sense of context specific experiences" (p. 110). From this point of view, for Schweder, "the process of representing the other goes hand in hand with a process of portraying one's own self as part of the process of representing the other, thereby encouraging an open-ended self-reflexive dialogic turn of mind" (p. 110). In this statement, Schweder elegantly portrays the situation of the postpositivistic participant observer in a way that is quite analogous to the psychoanalytic process as conceived relationally. The second aspect of thinking through others Schweder calls "getting the other straight," that is, "providing a systematic account of the internal logic of the intentional world constructed by the other" (p. 109). Schweder cites Freud's concern with representing the other's psychic reality as a model for this aspect of the process.

The third aspect of thinking through others Schweder links with deconstructive processes. He calls this "thinking one's way out of or beyond the other . . . intellectually transforming him or her or it into something else—perhaps its negation—by revealing what the life and intentional world of the other has dogmatically hidden away, namely its own incompleteness" (p. 109). The psychoanalytic analogy here is to interpretation where the analyst points out what is obscured or denied by the patient, the internal illogic of the patient's intentional world, or the assertion that implies its opposite.

The final aspect of the process of thinking through others is like the previous aspect, but now with reference to the observer. Schweder refers to this aspect as "'thinking through others' in the sense of using the intentionality . . . of another culture or person . . . as a means to heighten awareness of our own less conscious selves" (p. 108). Schweder cites examples of cultural "virtuosity" in particular realms of experience; for example, the Indian culture specializes in a sense of personal sanctity, often missing from our more pragmatic Western outlook. The psychoanalytic analogy here is to heightened awareness of countertransference based on interaction with the patient, to ways in which analysts learn about themselves based on interaction with their patients. All these aspects of the process of "thinking through others," taken together, refer to a process in which both participants construct, then deconstruct, a self and an other within the interaction.

Geertz (1973), in his conceptualization of culture, challenges what he calls the "stratigraphic" (p. 37) conception of the human being. This view sees people as composed of layers, (physical/biological, psychological, cultural), with each layer in some hierarchical relation to the other, according to one's notion of what is primary and what is secondary in human nature. At "bottom" is some conception of basic human nature, in relation to which all the other levels are an overlay. Geertz, by contrast, sees human nature as inseparable from all these layers. In relation to culture, in particular, Geertz contests the notion that culture is an overlay. He conceives of human beings as organisms that require a cultural surround, which cannot be conceived of in isolation from some sort of cultural context. Thus, Geertz maintains, there is no way to know human beings except relationally, that is, within their culture. Geertz's point of view undermines any attempt to create a hierarchy of cultures based on some ideal human nature that can be degraded by any particular culture. There has been an evolution in anthropology analogous to what has occurred in psychoanalysis. Classical anthropology postulated a dichotomy between human beings and their relational context in the form of culture, as classical psychoanalysis postulated a dichotomy between the individual and the social surround. Contemporary developments in both fields seek to undermine such dichotomies. No concept of a patient can be developed independently of the specific context in which one has come to know the patient, just as no human being can be known externally to her culture. To this Schweder would add: and except within the interaction with the anthropologist-observer, who has his own cultural context.

Historically, psychoanalysis has been slow to recognize the specifically cultural context of psychoanalytic work. Freud may have been invested in presenting his theory as universal, that is, transcendent of culture, in order to counter the anticipated assumption in his milieu that, as he was a Jew, his theory would reflect only Jewish psychology (Javier, 1994, citing Bruner). Freud's view of the analyst as objective and anonymous also made it difficult to accommodate the analyst's cultural embeddedness, as well as the cultural embeddedness of his theory. A "narcissism of the theoretical/cultural kind" (Foster, 1994) develops, however, when the analyst and his theory are regarded as somehow beyond culture.

Thus, the points made by Geertz and Schweder are useful to analysts in reinforcing the awareness that when we speak of a patient's culture, we are always speaking of that culture from the point of view of our own culture. There is no way to speak about a patient or his culture from a culture-free point of view; this point may seem obvious, yet it is too often forgotten in ostensibly objective descriptions of a patient whose culture is foreign to us. Davidson

(1987) aptly makes the point as follows: "Cross-cultural therapy begins with a state of unfamiliarity, mistrust, and confusion. The therapist and the patient are an enigma to each other at the outset. They must of necessity become participant-observers and ethnographers of each others' cultures" (p. 663). Vaughns (1994) points out that taking such an attitude as Davidson describes requires the analyst to "see himself as the cultural alien from the other's point of view." Doing so without losing a sense of rootedness and commitment to one's own vantage point is a special case of sustaining the tension between being a subject and an object, as described by Benjamin (1988).

The analyst's culture includes an intertwined personal culture and an "analytic culture" (Whitson, 1990), which includes the particular qualities we analysts value or require in order to work the way we do. Judgments about a patient's "analyzability" reflect assessments made from the vantage point of analytic culture. Analytic elitism and exclusivity result from failure to acknowledge the particularity of the analytic viewpoint. From the perspective I am adopting here, one would reframe situations that traditionally led analysts to question a patient's suitability for analytic work as reflecting a two-person or two-culture conflict or dissonance, rather than a statement made about one person (the patient) from any sort of absolute, culture-free vantage point.

Lombardi (1994) considers how variations within psychoanalytic theory reflect the culture of a particular time and place. Freud's one-person, closed system model, according to Lombardi, is consistent with patriarchal, colonial society in which one people were thought to be able to take over and dominate another people without being affected and transformed by the subjugated people. Lombardi sees the Kleinian emphasis on destruction and reparation as reflecting a cultural response to World War I. She sees British object relations theory with its emphasis on human connection as a later response to the alienation of postindustrial society.

Nationhood

Closely related to the concepts of culture and race is that of nationhood, that is, the concept of a defined people. Postmodern approaches to nationhood focus on the ways in which a nation is constituted. Culture and race are two of the parameters commonly used in the construction of the concept of a particular nation. My own interest centers, as well, on the ways in which a sense of nationality forms part of the process of individual identity formation through projective-introjective mechanisms. In this section, I review some literature on the processes by which nations are constructed, as well as the psychic implications.

One major polarity in terms of which modern nations are defined relates to the split between the West and the Third World. The origins of this split are to be found in European colonialism, within which the modern West and the "developing" world arose in relation to each other. Frantz Fanon (1963) saw the essence of colonialism as the European attempt to dominate, enslave, and exploit Third World peoples. The idea of progress, along with belief in the superiority of the Christian religion, served to rationalize this domination by portraying the subjugated people as primitive or unsaved, in need of European civilizing influence or Christian salvation. The potential aggression that European domination might provoke in subjugated peoples was channeled into ecstatic religious practices and inhibited by Christian beliefs in the virtue of turning the other cheek. In a capitalist context, however, the masses of Third World people became more valuable as markets than as slaves. This factor led the colonial powers to grant more freedom to the colonized peoples in the service of stimulating a vigorous economy. Thus began a process of liberation that led inevitably to decolonization and the creation of modern Third World nation-states.

Fanon (1963) describes the devastating effects of colonial ideology on the self-images of Third World people:

> The total result looked for by colonial domination was to convince the natives that colonialism came to lighten their darkness. The effect consciously sought by colonialism was to drive into the natives' heads the idea that if the settlers were to leave, they would at once fall back into barbarism, degradation, and bestiality [pp. 210–211].

The colonizing people sought to be considered as a

> mother who unceasingly restrains her fundamentally perverse offspring from managing to commit suicide and from giving free rein to its evil instincts. The colonial mother protects her child from itself, from its ego, and from its physiology, its biology, and its own unhappiness which is its very essence [p. 211].

The anger stimulated by colonial domination, according to Fanon, fed this feeling on the part of colonized people that they needed to be protected from themselves. Psychiatry as it developed in Third World countries (Fanon himself was a psychiatrist) furthered colonialist aims by defining reactive aggression as mental illness, as the reflection of an inherent badness or deficiency in the colonized people. Fanon says that psychiatrists-in-training in colonial Algeria were taught that Algerians were inherently violent and criminal, impulsive, immature, and incapable of introspection and articulate verbal expression. Fanon cites Carothers, of the World Health Organization, who wrote, "The African makes very little use of his frontal lobes." The normal African is like a "lobotomized European" (p. 302). Fanon quotes a Professor Porot, who wrote: "The Algerian has no cortex: or, more precisely, he is dominated, like the inferior vertebrates, by the diencephalon. The cortical functions, if they exist at all, are very feeble, and are practically unintegrated into the dynamic of existence" (p. 301). Thus, colonial Europeans could tell themselves, "The hesitation of the colonist in giving responsibility to the native is not racism nor paternalism, but quite simply a scientific appreciation of the biologically limited possibilities of the native" (p. 301).

Fanon shows how the concept of the Algerian, as representative of colonized peoples, served to rationalize and justify colonial practices. In addition, it created a disowned other for the European, a context for European projective identification.

Homi Bhabha (1990) writes about culture and nationalism from a Lacanian and Kleinian point of view that integrates the political with the psychological, the psychoanalytic. For Bhabha, the nation, culture, or community is the "social imaginary" (p. 304), and the nation is "imagined community" (p. 310). From a Lacanian perspective on the "imaginary," the nation is like the illusory, unified image of the self that an infant gets in the "mirror stage" (Lacan, 1977) upon seeing the body reflected in a mirror. The infant's unintegrated experiences confront the unified mirror image of self and gives birth to the "imaginary," the self as entity. Similarly, the nation, the unified people, sets aside diversity and difference in the formation of a coherent image of identity as a people. "The social imaginary—nation, culture, community—become subjects of discourse and objects of psychic identification" (p. 304). The supposed characteristics of a people are raised "to the status of essence" (Lefort, quoted in Bhabha, 1990, p. 298). Bhabha goes on to discuss the psychic functions served by this creation of the imaginary nation. The nation is a "differentiating sign of Self, distinct from the Other or the Outside" (p. 299). The concept of the nation establishes a space in which one can own certain psychic qualities, by identifying with a nation defined in a certain way, and establish an "Other," other

nations, peoples, and cultures that are, in Sullivan's terms, "not me."
Bhabha quotes Freud: "'It is always possible to bind together a
considerable number of people in love, so long as there are other
people left to receive the manifestation of their aggression'" (p. 300).
But such a splitting process is inherently unstable; the disowned
returns to haunt the projector as persecutory images: "The ambiva-
lent identifications of love and hate occupy the same psychic space;
and paranoid projections 'outwards' return to haunt and split the
space from which they are made" (p. 300). Bhabha writes of "racist
fantasies of purity and persecution that must always return from the
Outside" (p. 317). Alluding to his own experience as an immigrant
in England, he writes of weather: "The English weather also revives
memories of its daemonic double: the heat and dust of India; the
dark emptiness of Africa; the tropical chaos that was deemed
despotic and ungovernable and therefore worthy of the civilizing
mission" (p. 319). Ultimately, in Kleinian terms, what is disowned,
projected onto the Other, must return, the projector must identify
with the recipient of the projection, and the split psyche tends
toward reunification. In Lacanian terms, there is a "gap" between the
unified, imaginary image of self and self-experience. The creation of
stable images of nationhood is undermined by the necessity continually to re-create them. The knowledge of national culture "cannot be
a knowledge that is stabilized in its enunciation: 'it is always
contemporaneous with the act of recitation'" (p. 303, internal quote
from Franz Fanon). On the national-identity level: "The threat of
cultural difference is no longer a problem of 'other' people. It
becomes a question of the otherness of the people as one" (p. 301).
Bhabha sees cultural and national stereotypes, the reification and
essentialization of cultural difference, as the attempt to stabilize this
process of psychic identity formation through projection. The Other
is like the personal unconscious, the container for what Bhabha,
quoting Levi-Strauss, characterizes as "at once ours and other" (p.
313).

   Bhabha's perspective recalls my own experience as a child
studying American history. In the 1950s through the early 1960s I got
the distinct impression from my history classes that the United States
of America was a uniquely virtuous country. Whenever evil appeared
in the world, the United States would intervene, like the proverbial
white knight (the choice of color is not accidental) and save the day.
There was no complexity here, no sense that killing of other human
beings was involved in saving the day, no sense that moral dilemmas
might be posed or that in the heat of battle it might not always be

clear who was good and who was evil, who was victim and who murderer. Even more dramatically, I never thought about the implications of what white Americans had done to Native Americans, even though I had all the information to draw the conclusion that Europeans had stolen this territory from its inhabitants and shed much blood along the way. Cowboy and Indian movies of my childhood portrayed the "Indians" as the treacherous, dangerous, and evil ones (although there were exceptions like Tonto on the "Lone Ranger," the equivalent of the black person in the phrase "Some of my best friends are black"). In retrospect, to portray cowboys and Indians in this way was quite a feat of selective inattention and tendentious history writing. In any case, for many in my generation, the civil rights movement and the anti-Vietnam War movement were experiences in which this national self-image was transformed. We became able to contemplate the "badness" in the United States. At first, we tried to hold on to the splitting process by simply reversing the valence and idealizing Ho Chi Minh, for example, while finding malevolence in most official American motives and actions. The counterculture's slogan "Make love, not war" implied that we (the "new generation") were loving, while our elders were the misguided, if not evil, force. Now we turned our selective inattention to the degree to which the prosperity on which our generation depended rested on the exploitative practices we condemned; we ignored the self-destructiveness of many in our own generation, lives ruined by drugs, and so on. The maturity of our generation has been marked by a more complex, less polarized view of good and evil and of where it resides. I find a striking example of this complex-mindedness in Cornel West (1993a) with his exhortation to resist the temptation to demonize whites, to acknowledge the advantages of American democracy, for example, while not losing sight of the oppressive forces at play.

Examples of the ways in which national, racial, or generational identity has been used to create an Other in the service of splitting processes could be multiplied endlessly. The Jews, along with Gypsies, perhaps, as people with Asian roots and a resistance to assimilation, have been the quintessential Other for Europeans. When Jews sought to cast off the role of degraded and victimized Other in reclaiming their ancient homeland in Israel, the psychic situation was reproduced between Jews and Arabs. Each having become Other to the other, there was little acknowledgment of the other side's legitimate claims, little recognition of the other people's humanity. At this writing, as political realities force Jews and Arabs in the

Mideast to talk with each other with a settlement in mind, we have
the opportunity to observe and participate in a fascinating exercise
in psychic realignment. Something similar happened over the last few
years as East European countries and Russia were dedemonized in
American minds. Have we moved on to a stage of greater tolerance
for complexity in the nuclear age, in which demonization leads
sooner or later only to self-destruction? Or are we in a less stable
interim period between demons? A more complex possibility is that
we are living in an age in which the way we draw boundaries around
and between peoples has been undermined. The economy is now
global; the "age of information," of computer, transportation, and
media networks, transcends national boundaries. Perhaps the very
concepts of boundary, of nation, of people are obsolete, to be
replaced by concepts of which we, as yet, have little inkling. Parallel
changes may well be going on with respect to concepts such as
ethnic and racial identity. The title of the series in which some of
Cornel West's (1993a, b) writings are published is *Beyond Eurocen-
trism and Multi-Culturalism*. The implication is that we have gone
beyond taken-for-granted ethnocentrism, but we are also in a process
of transcendence of the very concept of ethnic identity; this process
occurs as we interrogate the process of identity formation and the
power (as well as psychic) arrangements that are served by the
drawing of boundaries in a particular way.

Culture in Clinical Work

Dan

In my private practice, I see Dan, a gay man in his 30s who grew up
in the American South. He had a professional career as a dancer;
currently, he is a freelance writer. Although he has never asked, he
assumes I am heterosexual. He generally expressed no concern about
my attitude toward, or feelings about, his sexual orientation. I asked
from time to time what he assumed about me in this respect, and he
would say that he saw no evidence of homophobia. At the time of
the vignette I am about to report, we were talking about this issue
somewhat more frequently than usual; Dan had recently had a dream
in which his lover's therapist was giving out reprints of an article he
had written that clearly revealed homophobia; Dan tried to warn his
friend about the danger he saw, but his friend resisted seeing that his
therapist's approach involved trying to change his patient's sexual
orientation. We talked about this dream in terms of both Dan's
fantasy that he might find me homophobic if he looked and his

reluctance to pay attention to my subjectivity in this respect. I felt, generally, that Dan was quite formal and compliant in our sessions in a way that made me want to loosen things up and be more playful and challenging. Bringing up, often clearly on my own initiative, the possibility that Dan might wonder about my subjectivity seemed to me part of this project of challenging his reserve and respect for me as the doctor. I noted that the therapist in the dream was passing out the reprints that revealed his homophobia and wondered if this was a reference to my having taken the initiative in exploring this issue with Dan.

One day Dan mentioned that he was contemplating finishing our work together at the end of the year, about nine months away. I commented, in our discussion, that I hoped Dan would feel more free to be spontaneous with me in our sessions before we terminated. He commented that he agreed that being able to be more spontaneous seemed like a worthwhile project and that he was rethinking his timetable. I was struck with the respectful and compliant way in which Dan adopted my recommendation that he become more spontaneous! Ruefully, I noted how my own "pushiness" was encouraging Dan's compliance. In the next session, Dan told me that, in thinking through our discussion, he had had the following thoughts. In the prior session itself he had first thought he could become more spontaneous, as I had said, but then he realized that he could not and further, did not want to. He thought, It makes me want to say "fuck you" to anyone who doesn't let me be me, and I'd want to say "fuck you" to you too—it may just be *me* to be polite and respectful of people who give me no reason not to. He thought one aspect of this interaction between us was that he was a southerner and that respect for authority and a degree of formality and reserve were culturally syntonic. I felt that Dan was asking me to respect his identity, including his culture, and that in doing so he was challenging me in his own way, not mine. This struggle over spontaneity and reserve had personal significance for me. I, in fact, grew up in the Midwest, as did my parents, in areas where the non-Jewish[9] majority culture emphasized good manners, respect, emotional reserve. My mother, I felt, had absorbed this ethos and was herself quite unexpressive emotionally. My father, on the other side of the spectrum, was quite flamboyantly and uninhibitedly expressive.

---

[9] I am Jewish, and Dan is not. Religious, cultural stereotypes were evoked here, although as of this writing we had not discussed our interaction in these terms.

He was also domineering, where my mother was (often resentfully) compliant. The contrast between my father and mother created a split within me, conflict over being "pushy," expressive, and spontaneous. So I had to ask myself, Had I made Dan into the container for that aspect of my own sense of self that was identified with my mother and the midwestern cultural way of being? Had I drawn Dan into my own internal struggle? Keeping in mind that Dan had been a performing artist, one has to wonder about our relationship's not mobilizing his more expressive side. Perhaps I had been more responsive to his reserve than to his expressiveness and thus had reinforced his tendency to emphasize this aspect of himself in our interaction. In articulating the ways in which I envisioned his changing, I may have been disowning my own more reserved self. In calling attention to who he was, he had helped me to reinternalize my own struggle.

From time to time my own more compliant side manifested itself in relation to Dan. As background, one needs to know that Dan's familial situation was similar to mine in certain respects. Dan's mother had been a performing artist before getting married and having children. Her personality was effusive and dramatic. Dan's father was more sober and reserved. He was given to long lectures to his children about proper behavior; Dan often felt his disapproval, especially when he allowed himself to be spontaneous and dramatic. Sometimes in our interaction, Dan seemed to be identifying with his father, while I identified with him in relation to his father. For example, once, early on in the therapy, I had reached for a drink out of a soda can I had near my chair. Dan had a strong reaction: he felt I was distracted from listening to him. At the time it seemed that Dan saw me as insufficiently attentive. Over time it came to feel to me as if I were on a rather tight leash. Especially on hot days or when I was thirsty, I sat there wishing I could allow myself to take a drink and feeling inhibited, as if I were pretending to be a good boy but secretly wanting to be defiant. One formulation of what had developed between us was that Dan had identified with his father and thus induced in me a feeling of inhibition and stifled rebellion such as he had felt in relation to his father. For my part, I was predisposed to react this way based on my identification with my mother, who seemed inhibited in relation to my father. There was a confluence of our inner worlds that facilitated this particular psychic division of labor.

Notwithstanding his defense of his integrity on a cultural basis, Dan seemed to use our interaction to challenge himself in his own way. Here is an example. One day, shortly after we had talked about him as a southerner, we were talking about some reading he had done that had introduced him to the concept of countertransference. This reading reminded him of our discussions of what he thought I felt about his sexual orientation. I encouraged him to speculate about my countertransference in this respect. After a pause, at one point, I asked about a dream he had alluded to in the previous session but had not told me about. Dan said, "Had enough of this talk of countertransference?" I was stunned, and we both laughed (nervously, on my part). He might have said: "You asked for spontaneity? Here it is!" Dan went on to say, after a moment, that he had felt flirtatious challenging me in this way. He had discovered something about his own capacity for spontaneity with me, his own ability to challenge me, and the associated sexual level of our interaction. Perhaps all the talk about homophobia, as difficult as it was, was easier than talking about sexual attraction between us. Since this discussion, sexual attraction between us has been more often and explicitly a focus for discussion.

In this case, taking a cultural perspective facilitated the analytic work by diminishing the authoritarian aspects of the analytic situation from Dan's point of view. In calling attention to the cultural difference between us, Dan put us on a more nearly equal level, that is, as two people with different cultures, as opposed to the hierarchical relationship we had established together, he with his compliance, me with my formulation of my own goal for him, all the while maintaining that I wanted him to be less compliant. My stated wish for him to be more spontaneous was taken by him at first, and not implausibly, as the directive of an authority. His initial superficial compliance was followed by an integration of my point of view on his own terms via defiance of me. The cultural perspective facilitated this integration by creating an interpersonal structure for defiance of me. Paradoxically, he was giving up the hierarchical perspective even as he defended it as part of his cultural worldview, just as I reinforced his compliance even as I stated my wish that he renounce it. I return later to other aspects of the value of a cultural perspective within the analytic relationship.

The Culture of Psychoanalysis, Culture in the Public Clinic, and My Experience in India

I believe that my experience as a Peace Corps volunteer in an Indian village provided me with an invaluable education about culture, which has been essential in my career as a psychoanalyst and as a clinician in the inner city. I have come to believe that Americans outside the polyglot, multiethnic, large cities are extraordinarily unaware of culture. The United States is such a large country, its suburban and rural areas so homogeneous, the melting pot operated so long and so well, that many Americans only rarely see, much less interact with, people who are unlike them culturally and ethnically.[10] I grew up in a midwestern suburban area with little heterogeneity. Among the Scandinavian and Irish Americans, I was part of a small Jewish community. One might expect that under these conditions I would be acutely aware of ethnicity and culture. I was not: to notice or mention difference in that midwestern community in the 1950s would not have been polite, and the culture of that time and place emphasized politeness.[11] Within my family, as noted earlier, my mother was much more acculturated to the non-Jewish world than my father. She was reserved and well mannered; he was brash, outspoken, bold in a stereotypically Eastern European Jewish style. While unaware of the cultural issues here, I believe growing up in this way made me preconsciously aware of culture; I was primed for what I was to discover in India.

Two images of India stand out for me as representative of much of my experience there. The first is of myself, or one of the other volunteers, stepping outdoors and being immediately surrounded by a crowd of people. In the United States, such an occurrence would be cause for alarm, a mugging, or injury. In India, what was happening was curiosity. The crowd, composed of people astonished to see a white-skinned person, gathered to stare. This kind of event was a lesson to me in how one has to start from scratch in one's meaning-making in a different culture.

The second image is of initially setting foot in India. Leaving the airplane at the Calcutta airport, I entered a small building, the terminal, in fact, where *no one was moving*. There were several

---

[10]This situation is fast changing. A recent article in the *New York Times* following the 1994 San Fernando Valley earthquake near Los Angeles mentioned the surprise many Americans, myself included, felt seeing large numbers of Latino Americans and Asian Americans on television in the area that had become a symbol of American suburban homogeneity.

[11]What I was acutely aware of was being short. Only in adult life did I make the connection, consciously, between my sense of being short and being Jewish in a largely Scandinavian and Irish environment.

maintenance men carrying small brooms, standing there, with big black eyes, staring at us as we got off the plane and approached the terminal. Ceiling fans rotated languidly in the humid air. There was a sense of having stepped outside time. Not only did nothing seem to be changing from moment to moment, but also there was a sense of continuity with other times produced in me by the slower pace and the absence of machines. In Indian villages, farming practices were not mechanized, for the most part, and cattle, buffalo, goats, donkeys, and pigs roamed the streets in even the biggest cities. It took a year for me to shed my American, culturally based feeling that I had to make something happen. The first year in India, I joined the ranks of "mad dogs and Englishmen" who are the only ones outdoors in the midday sun, as I rode my bicycle in determined search of work to do while everyone else slept. The second year, I relaxed and fully caught on to how one has to live in an Indian village. Since there were no telephones, I would often get up in the morning and ride my bicycle five miles, say, to meet a particular farmer. Arriving there, it was usual to find out that he was away or expected back soon, which might well mean the next day. By the second year, this state of affairs was no problem for me. I would sit in the local tea shop and meet some new people or simply stare at the animals, children, and other assorted passersby. Whatever work was going to get done would come to me. Another common occurrence was to go to the office of a government official to buy some vegetable seeds. Arriving in the office, I would find six or eight people who also had business with the official and who were sitting around his desk drinking tea. It would have been incongruous to say something like: "Excuse me, I hate to interrupt, but I just stopped by to get some seeds. I'm quite busy today. Perhaps I could just pick them up and be on my way?" I tried to do some such thing often during my first year, under the pressure of my residual American sense of urgency about getting things done. My urgency would be met with a tolerant invitation to have some tea first and meet the others who had gathered. By the second year, I had adjusted my expectations. India had gotten inside me.

I have used my internalized Indian self often as a psychoanalyst. In my experience, the psychoanalytic session has a culture of its own that is reminiscent of that of an Indian village. One has to enter a session with an openness to the unexpected. The expectations of patient and analyst, the attachment to any particular outcome get drawn into the process of the session. What is important is to be able to go with the flow of the session, to "be here now," undistracted, as far as possible, by the desire to have something happen other than what is happening. I believe this is something like what Wilfred Bion (1988b), who was born in India, meant when he advocated entering each session without memory and desire. Resistance, false self, negative transference, and countertransference are all expectable and part of the process in which one is inevitably immersed. They are not something to be overcome and done with, like so many roadblocks on the way to one's destination.[12]

On returning to New York after leaving India, my sense was of a place with as many complications as India, but with people who expected there not to be complications, with the result of frustration rather than acceptance. As I got to know New York better and especially after working in the inner city, it seemed to me that the city had many village people who had been uprooted and transplanted to a foreign, urban environment. I could imagine that they were far more disoriented than I had been on entering an Indian village. There were no guides or training programs, no language immersion experiences to help them, no sense that this was for two years, and then they would return to their old lives. I imagined recent immigrants in the inner city sitting in the tea shops of their native villages and embedded in a traditional culture where things moved more slowly, where one knew everybody, where roles were clearly delineated and understood. In the midst of the tenements of the Bronx, these people often tried to re-create their village community as best they could, staying near people from their own region and country, speaking their own language. In the city beyond the neighborhood there were a pace of life, a technological economy, an educational system, a language that were foreign. The children of these immigrants began to "get it" about this culture and create conflict between the generations. These children picked up American individualism and democracy, the American skepticism about authority, the emphasis on money and status, the desire to be unfettered, to do "one's own thing." To the parent, an immigrant from a Third World village, the child's challenging attitude was incomprehensible or meant only disrespect. Attempts to reassert parental control provoked further rebellion on the part of the

---

[12]There are times when I find myself trying to make something happen in a session, to change the direction of the flow in a way that feels productive. I am being deliberately one-sided here, because I want to emphasize a noninterventionist, non-goal-oriented aspect of psychoanalysis that is at variance with a strong current in North American culture.

children. I approached many clinical situations in the Bronx with this sort of background from my experience in India.

The Functions of a Cultural Perspective in the Analytic Relationship

As a meaning-making system, culture is inherent in the analytic field. Any attempt to understand how the interpersonal world looks to a patient or how meaning is created within a dyad must take account of the cultural meaning-making systems brought to the interaction by each participant. At some times, cultural considerations are in the background, as when the participants feel they share a common cultural framework.[13] At other times, cultural considerations come into the foreground, for example, when there is an obvious cultural difference or one that seems to be problematic in the interaction. There are times when clinical phenomena are susceptible of being viewed from a cultural perspective but could also be viewed diagnostically or as transferential phenomena or as resistance. I now discuss some of the functions of taking a cultural perspective in such contexts. My general point is that a one-person model of the psychoanalytic field can create a skewed view of the patient that is correctable with the two-person framework brought in with a cross-cultural perspective.

First, diagnosticians, in an effort to attain a certain kind of "objectivity," often make judgments based solely on the behavior of the patient, without understanding the meaning of the behavior in its social or cultural context. They may regard meaning as irrelevant, or they may simply assume that the meaning of a behavior is the same to the patient as it is to the diagnostician. In an effort to correct the biases introduced by this approach, some authors believe that it is important for therapists to think about culture in order not to misinterpret culturally syntonic behavior as psychopathology. For example, the *attaque* is an aggressive outburst that occurs in a dissociated state, commonly among traditional Latino women. From the point of view of a North American clinician, an *attaque* might look like a psychotic phenomenon or a manifestation of a severe dissociative disorder. A culturally informed perspective takes account of the fact that the direct expression of aggression is not consistent with the traditional female role in Latino cultures. The *attaque* then

---

[13]There may, of course, be unrecognized cultural differences creating impasses in the analytic work.

appears as a form of expression of aggression that is relatively acceptable since the woman is not considered to be in control of herself when it happens. From this point of view, the *attaque* might even be thought of as an ingenious way around the problems posed for women by the cultural prohibition of direct aggression. Nonetheless, not every traditional Latina woman has *attaques*, and one might wonder whether those who do are either characterologically overly compliant or constitutionally hyperaggressive, or perhaps whether these are the women with the most to be angry about. In any case, cultural understanding does not rule out understanding based on psychopathology, environmental pathology, or both. Rather, our understanding of the meaning and potentially adaptive functions of the behavior is enriched. Some authors also emphasize that a one-sided culturalist perspective may lead to *underestimation* of psychopathology or failure to take account of the depth of a patient's disturbance.

Psychoanalysts traditionally have assumed that the meaning of the frame to the patient was conditioned solely by a realistic working alliance, along with transferential factors. There has been little consideration given to what the frame might mean to the patient based on cultural factors. Some authors, therefore, try to introduce these concerns by urging clinicians to be aware of cultural norms in order best to establish rapport with patients or in order not to violate, unnecessarily, culturally syntonic expectations of how helping professionals work. For example, Vela and Bluestone (1982) point out that Latino patients expect a doctor to be authoritative. A nondirective or egalitarian approach is likely to be interpreted as a failure on the part of the therapist to do her job. From a traditional psychoanalytic perspective, the patient who feels this way is resistant or perhaps in the grip of a transference reaction based on a relationship with a withholding parental figure. The cultural perspective does not rule out these ways of looking at the patient's responses; rather, it enriches the variety of perspectives at our disposal and may therefore enrich and complicate our work.

The cultural perspective, with respect to the therapist's directiveness, entails a different theoretical framework from the traditional analytic framework. The cultural perspective calls our attention to the culturally derived template for a healer as, say, authoritative and directive. A discrepancy between this template and what the analyst provides provokes in the patient anger, disappointment, or a feeling of being deprived, which likely interferes with the establishment of rapport. The traditional analytic framework, by contrast, calls our attention to a different sort of template: a template of a parentlike figure who has certain characteristics (e.g., being depriving) based on personal history, drive factors, or both. The goal is to *elicit* this template through providing an ambience suitable for regression. If the patient responds with anger, disappointment, or a feeling of deprivation, then, the analyst believes that the patient's preconception has been revealed, not that the patient's culturally derived expectation has been disappointed.

Contemporary relational analysts have departed from the traditional prescription of a particular stance or type of behavior for the analyst (e.g., Greenberg, 1991a). Within this framework, then, there is room to have multiple concerns, for example, to be concerned about establishing rapport, about eliciting "old object" transferences, and about providing a new experience. These various concerns are conceived of as existing in dialectical relation to one another (e.g., see Greenberg's, 1986, discussion of how the analyst seeks a balance between providing "old object" and "new object" experiences to the patient). The relational framework thus can contain the kind of cultural issues raised by Vela and Bluestone, while not neglecting the more traditional psychoanalytic concerns.

A cultural perspective can be valuable in any kind of psychoanalytic work by providing an essential context of meaning within which to understand psychic phenomena such as conflict, transference, resistance, and so on. For example, consider how my understanding of Rosa's conflict about being in therapy (see chapter 1) was enhanced by my understanding of the cultural context. The background is that Rosa's mother was an immigrant from a small town in Puerto Rico. Partly because of my experience in India, I felt I could understand her failure, or refusal, to learn English in the light of her disorientation in New York. I imagined that it seemed quite daunting to her even to attempt to find a place for herself in the fast-moving, high-pressure society around her. Her husband, perhaps because men traditionally were more "out in the world," was more ready to learn the language and get a job. Rosa's conflict about going "downtown" to school, about succeeding in North America is understandable only if one takes account of the discordance between the society in which Rosa lived downtown and the rural Puerto Rican society that her mother was trying to maintain. The cultural conflict becomes part of the unformulated, unconscious backdrop to Rosa's behavior and her feelings. My understanding of Rosa and my empathy with her were enhanced by the depth of my own understanding of the cultural conflicts in which she was immersed. Without the cross-cultural background, I might have seen Rosa's conflicts about success downtown and loyalty to her mother as simply a separation problem, a conflict around differentiating herself from her mother, around growing up. From an intrapsychic point of view, indeed, Rosa did have such conflicts. One runs the risk of overemphasizing developmental failure and, perhaps, conflicts over aggression and dependence, if one understands and interprets without taking account of the cultural context. A psychoanalytic interpretive approach that does not take account of context, either interpersonal or societal, can be skewed or one-sided in its localization of a problem. An interpretive approach that emphasizes the intrapsychic locus of a problem in this way can result in an overpathologization of the individual (see previous diagnostic considerations) and result in iatrogenic resistance or compliance on the part of the patient.

Failure to consider the patient's cultural context of meaning may be coupled with the analyst's absolutism with respect to her own culture, that is, assuming that her culturally based views are universally valid. In the case of Rosa, from a cross-cultural point of view, the analyst's valuation of separation and independence might be thought to be skewed toward the independent side in relation to the patient's values; the analyst who neglects these considerations might take his own values as reflecting simply the natural outcome of successful development, in relation to which the patient's behavior might be seen as a deviation, a failure to achieve the norm or the mature state.

In terms of the projective-introjective model, one might reformulate the skew, or cross-cultural misunderstanding, that I am describing as a case of projection on the analyst's part. Just as Dan became for me the repository of my own midwestern reserve, Rosa might have become for me the locus of my disowned dependence and conflict over separation and independence. Cultural biases contribute to individual identity formation via the particular polarities, with privileged and denigrated poles, that structure the personality. When two people from different cultures meet, there is always the potential for the cultural difference to create the context for self-definition in opposition to the other. The ability to take the perspective of the other who is culturally different thus often coincides with a psychically integrative movement.

Many psychoanalytic authors have shown how resistance can generally be reformulated as transference (e.g., Friedman, 1987, 1988; Schafer, 1992) or as adaptive behavior, from the patient's point of view. Similarly, from a cultural point of view, what might appear resistant is often capable of being formulated as a culturally syntonic behavior. Many ethnic groups have jokes about their own "standard time"; for example, Jewish or Latino or Indian "standard time" might be half an hour late, implying that, usually in comparison to Northern Europeans, they tend to be late for appointments. Is lateness to appointments, then, to be considered resistance? Is the analyst who is annoyed about the lateness under the influence of Northern European rigidity? Is it a case of induced countertransference? Is it to be considered an indication that there is a conflict between the patient's and analyst's sense of what is felt to be late? Consideration of the cultural background of patient and analyst, along with the transference-countertransference configuration at a particular time, can enrich the potential field for analytic exploration.

Consider, as another example, the missed appointments encountered in the work with Rosa and Nancy (see Chapter 1). Here the possible meanings are numerous. Is one to view the missed appointments as resistant, in relation to some warded off drive or object relationship? As a sign of poor ego strength? As an enactment of an abandoning object relationship? As a culturally syntonic way of expressing difference or defiance with an authority figure? Is my expectation of consistency and continuity in this professional relationship a function of my personal culture, analytic culture, or both? Did Nancy and Rosa have entirely different expectations based on their cultures? Do people who grow up in extended family situations, for example, have less expectation of, and need for, consistency within a dyad? Do I dismiss our common humanity, in an overzealous cultural relativism, when I consider such possibilities? It seems to me that there are no a priori answers to these questions. Rather, understanding evolves as the analyst tries out various formulations, in keeping with her theoretical predispositions, her countertransference, and her understanding of the current transference-countertransference situation, and as she makes interventions based on them.

In Rosa's case, analytic exploration led us to an agreement that missed appointments reflected a wish to wind down or terminate the therapy that she did not feel free to express directly. I believe that her indirectness of expression has a cultural component; from this point of view, it is important to keep in mind that even as I sought to understand Rosa's behavior from her cultural point of view, I was implicitly challenging this framework and offering or imposing my own. In inquiring into the meaning of the missed appointments and in encouraging an exploration of what Rosa felt and wished to do, I was saying, You can speak directly to me about what you feel, even if it is in opposition to me. In so doing, I may have stimulated conflicts about deserting her tradition or part of her tradition, which may have needed analysis in its own right.

4 / A PSYCHOANALYTIC LOOK AT THE BIFURCATION OF PUBLIC AND PRIVATE PRACTICE

An ecological, open systems model, which I more fully describe in the next chapter, postulates mutual, circular influence among all parts of a system and between systems at various levels, from an individual mind to a large social system. On the mental level, subunits have value of various kinds: Freud's structural model posits a mental organization, a division of labor among id, ego, and superego. Yet, as Loewald (1988) points out, mental life is impoverished when these splits are too sharp, when the ego, for example, is cut off from the creativity and vitality of the id and its primary-process mode of thinking. Melanie Klein thought of the splitting of the good from the bad in mental life as essential in order to manage destructive aggression. Ogden (1994) further sees such splitting as contributing to intensity of experience. Yet, when splitting is too sharply maintained, it interferes with the ability to manage and contain complexity of experience. A rich and viable relationship, with oneself or another person, requires integration of diversity and contradiction within a framework of continuity. In short, there is a dialectic between unity and diversity, between boundaries and permeability, in mental life.

Moving to the social level, in this chapter I consider the split between the public sector and the private sector in contemporary American society. It would seem that our society requires a dialectic between an area of privacy and autonomy for individuals, a private sector and an area of community and shared concerns, a public sector. I argue in this chapter that the form of public-private splitting we have in the United States today is overly polarized. We are attempting to deny the basic unity and interdependence of all parts of our social system in an effort to rid ourselves of social phenomena we consider undesirable. This effort is akin, on a macrocosmic scale, to defensive forms of splitting on the individual level, which are ultimately self-defeating and untenable. We are forgetting how public and private reflect and interpenetrate each other in ways that I discuss later at more length.

After I had worked in the Bronx for a few years, I would occasionally be asked why I did not go into full-time private practice. The implication was that I could make more money but also that I was not following the expected career path, which led from the public sector to the private sector. A typical pattern was to take a job in the public sector upon finishing graduate training. Then, the successful career path was either to move up in the public sector into some sort of managerial job or into a position in which one trained junior people or else to move out into full-time private practice. To remain in the public sector, especially in a position in which one continued to see patients, made it seem as if one had failed to grow up or could not make it to the pinnacles of profession-al development. When I would interview for staff jobs, I myself was suspicious of people applying for such jobs who were not straight out of graduate school. Why were they still seeing patients in public clinics? Was something wrong that they could not make a go of private practice or get promoted out of clinical work in their public sector jobs?

I never stopped wanting to see patients in my public clinic job. To satisfy my needs for prestige and a feeling of having "made it," I wanted to be a manager, too, and I always enjoyed training junior people. It always seemed odd to me, however, that seeing patients in clinics should so quickly become something to outgrow. After all, my training had been devoted entirely to clinical work. Nothing in graduate school or my internship had led me to believe that I was being trained to be an administrator or a supervisor. If I was being trained to be a therapist, why was I to outgrow this function so quickly? Or was it the unspoken fact that I was being trained to work with *private* patients?

In fact, my graduate training did not prepare me to work in the public sector. Even though the director of my graduate training program was strongly admiring and encouraging of work in the public sector, nothing in the curriculum addressed such work. Our supervisors were private practitioners. Few, if any, of them had any experience in the public sector. We were supervised exclusively on work with university clinic patients, middle-class (and up) people like us. Few of us took any placements in the public sector before internship. On internship, supervision often focused on work with the occasional middle-class patient or one with whom one could work in the ideal private practice manner: more than once a week, no "acting out," missed appointments, concrete needs, and so on. There was a rare attempt to focus on work with the run-of-the-mill clinic patient. Even then, work with these patients was considered peripheral. I heard of the director of an inner-city hospital training program who ran a seminar called "The Other Patients" to focus on the impoverished, "multiproblem" cases that formed the bulk of the work there. It is as if it were an inconvenient fact that, in a program designed to train people for upper-middle-class private practice, the patients were an impoverished and multiethnic group of people with little sophistication about psychoanalytic therapy. These patients were the "others" with respect to the ideal private practice patient, but not with respect to who was being served in these inner-city hospital clinics. It is another odd aspect of this whole situation that most of the people who are involved in the devaluation of public sector work and the patients who are seen there are politically liberal people, with strong social commitments, at least on the level of political ideology. The biases built into psychoanalytic theory, in terms of considerations of analyzability, perhaps, make it possible to marginalize poor, multiethnic patients without this act seeming to be political.

All this is in the process of changing to some degree. Managed care has made private practice much more like public practice. The paperwork, the lower fees, the regulation of one's work—all this is familiar to practitioners in the public sector. University training programs now, routinely, send students into public clinics for their training experiences. My impression is that this is at least as much a function of the difficulty attracting patients to university clinics as it is a function of the desire to prepare students to work in inner-city settings. As the number of patients who can afford private practice fees shrinks, public sector jobs become more relevant, and multiethnic, multiclass practices become the norm. If there is a silver lining to this cloud, it is in the form of a renewed receptivity to working out ways to make psychoanalysis more flexible.

I now offer some thoughts on the basis for this traditional devaluation of public sector work and the idealization of private practice work. I argue that there is a confluence of cultural, socioeconomic, and psychic factors that in the North American context, lead us to bifurcate public from private practice in a particular way.

Western Individualism, Projective-Introjective Processes, and the Construction of Public and Private Sectors

Individualism, the Pursuit of Liberty, and the Rise of Capitalism and Protestantism

Hannah Arendt (1958) links our contemporary construction of public and private spheres to the rise of individualism in the modern West. Historically, public and private spheres were not always constructed in the way we construct them. Arendt points out the common roots of the words "private" and "privation." For the ancient Greeks and Romans, privacy implied a deprivation of the fulfillment of human potential possible in the public, communal life. For us 20th-century Americans, privacy implies intimacy, personal possessions, as well as that which is hidden, such as certain bodily functions. Arendt argues that this shift in connotative focus is linked to the rise of modern individualism and to the development and spread of Christianity. She traces the origin of individualism to the 18th-century Romantics, such as Rousseau, who extolled the individual in a rebellion against the pressures toward conformity inherent in social life. Individualism found expression in the capitalist economic system and in the Protestant ethic. Each of these developments contributed to the modern, American construction of the public and private spheres.

With respect to economics, Arendt writes that all ancient civilizations regarded private property, that is, land, with a house on it as the means by which one established one's presence in the world. Having property meant having a place, a connection to the earth, and thus a position in the body politic. It was not so much that there was a family, which then owned a piece of land. Rather, the family was constituted by the piece of land to which it was attached. In this sense, there was no distinction between public and private realms before modern times. With the rise of capitalism, private property came to be regarded as personal wealth. Thenceforth, "society . . . assumed the disguise of an organization of property owners who, instead of claiming access to the public realm because of their wealth, demanded protection from it for the accumulation of more wealth" (Arendt, 1958, p. 68). Individualism was reflected in the opposition thus set up between the individual and his wealth, on one hand, and the public sphere, on the other. Individualism was also reflected in the classical economic assumption that people acted primarily to further their self-interest. Thus, government came to be seen as existing primarily to protect the rights of individuals to pursue their self-interest, rather than to advance the public interest. Here we have the beginnings of the suspicion of the public sector, which reached an apogee in the late 20th-century United States.

With respect to the influence of Christianity, in *The Protestant Ethic and the Spirit of Capitalism*, Max Weber (1958) demonstrates a confluence between the ethics of Protestantism and the capitalist economic system. In Protestantism, one's virtue is demonstrated by one's worldly success. Material wealth is God's reward for righteousness. Therefore, material things attest to one's spiritual attainments. This ethic, Weber argues, leads people to work hard and to strive for material rewards, just the kind of activity that fuels the capitalist economic system. The accumulation of private wealth is encouraged in this setup; it follows inevitably from this confluence of economic and religious forces that the redistribution of resources through government taxation and benefit programs, insofar as they become obstacles to the accumulation of wealth, makes it more difficult to attain that state in which one's virtue is revealed. Thus, the enrichment and maintenance of the shared public sector are discouraged.[1]

Adam Smith (1776), in *The Wealth of Nations,* reinforced the individualistic slant of capitalism by arguing that the public good would be best achieved by each individual's striving for his or her own self-interest, so long as there is no restriction of competition. A market economy is fueled by each person's attempting to make as much money as possible; competition is presumed to keep prices fair. The marginalization of government, which has reached some sort of acme recently, follows from Smith's model, in which government intervention only disturbs the self-regulating market.

A somewhat different, though related, perspective on the public-private distinction is provided by Isaiah Berlin (1969) in his essay on "Two Concepts of Liberty," referring to what he calls "negative" and "positive" liberty. Negative liberty is defined by Berlin as freedom from interference. Positive liberty refers to the freedom inherent in pursuing a self-initiated and self-directed course of action. In both senses, the desire for liberty derives from the distinctly human capacity for free will. To be deprived of liberty, in either sense, is thus often experienced as being reduced to a status that is less than fully human. Negative liberty is "freedom from," while positive liberty

---

[1]It is ironic that the Protestant ethic leads to consequences so far removed from Jesus' advocacy of responsibility for one's fellow man and woman.

is "freedom to." The desire for negative liberty correlates with a belief in the inherent goodness of human beings and a faith that human interests will be harmonized if people are not interfered with; such belief and faith stand behind the positions previously referred to, that government interference can only disrupt the self-regulating processes of the capitalist marketplace. A belief in inherent human "badness" or destructiveness leads to a belief in the need for some sacrifice in negative liberty, in the service of other concerns, such as personal security. When crime is a major concern, for example, people are often willing to be taxed to pay for increased police protection and more prisons, even when they would otherwise oppose "big government" because of the interference with negative liberty.

Berlin emphasizes that positive liberty and negative liberty are often incompatible and that either or both of these may be in conflict with other liberal and humanitarian values, such as equality. Negative liberty, for example, may entail tax cuts leading to cutbacks in the resources for school systems, arts, and recreation programs, cutbacks that seriously restrict opportunities for self-development of large segments of the population, including the very people who vote for the tax cuts. The pursuit of negative liberty may entail abandonment of social programs, leading to increased inequality in a society. An increase in positive liberty for some people may lead to restrictions in the positive liberty of other people. Berlin points out that increased liberty for the wolf leads to decreased liberty for sheep. Berlin believes it very important to recognize and accept these inevitable conflicts, lest we pursue one goal and are blind to the trade-offs entailed. A single-minded pursuit of positive liberty on the part of one person or a group of people can lead to despotism. The determination to avoid despotism may require some sacrifice in positive liberty. Berlin points out the ambiguity of reason as a guide to negotiating these inherent conflicts: the person who pursues positive or negative liberty for himself or his group with the belief that he is guided by reason may thus be inclined to rationalize his denial of liberty in some form to other people. Such rationalization may take the form of the belief that one knows the best interests of other people better than they do. Colonialism, for example, was often justified by the idea that the colonized were benefiting by being modernized, civilized, rationalized, or economically developed by the colonizer.[2] For Berlin, the Enlightenment faith in reason thereby may lead to the most antiliberal, antihumanistic outcomes.

Berlin points out, with respect to colonization, how strongly people generally care that they be governed by people of their own group. To be governed by an "outsider" is perceived as interference, whereas to be governed by one's own group members is perceived as promoting self-determination. So powerful is this factor that people would often prefer an "in-group" despot to a democratic government sponsored from outside. This phenomenon is another example of how the pursuit of one form of liberty may lead to diminution of another form of liberty.

Adopting Berlin's perspective, I conceive of the private sphere as the area of negative liberty, in which one operates without interference from government and other influences from the public sphere. The public sphere may be conceived of as the sphere within which people are willing to accept a degree of restriction of negative liberty in the pursuit of positive liberty in one form or another. People collectively make trade-offs in terms of the balance between private and public sought in their society. The outcome in a given society is affected by such things as the degree to which people define themselves as individuals as opposed to members of a group and the heterogeneity of the society. At this moment in Western, particularly American, history, as I have pointed out, we belong to a strongly individualistic society that is heterogeneous. For people who perceive themselves as mainstream Americans, then, the public sphere seems to restrict their liberty in order to meet the needs of "out-group" people. The trade-offs required as such Americans seek to shrink the public sector, in terms of restriction of funds to school systems, arts, and recreation programs, an increase in social inequality, and suffering to certain people, are ignored or rationalized as ultimately beneficial.

---

[2]These considerations cast a disturbing light on the potential for authoritarianism in psychoanalysis, particularly when the concept of resistance is emphasized. In construing the patient's disagreement with the analyst, for example, as resistance, the analyst may believe that he knows what is in the best interest of the patient better than the patient does.

Developments in the United States

Individualism suited the conditions of life in the United States up until the Industrial Revolution. On the frontier, it was "every man for himself" as white people streamed out over a vast territory to carve out a homestead. People to whom the pursuit of Berlin's negative liberty was a high priority may have been predisposed to embark on such an adventure; at the very least, the idealization of negative liberty made a virtue of necessity. In any case, having a private home and a piece of property is still important to Americans, as compared to other, more urban societies. Contemporary suburban American life, with its houses each on a private piece of land and a private car for each adult and adolescent, is the ultimate expression of this style of life. Each individual or family appears almost self-contained and self-sufficient. The public sector, or government, appears necessary mostly for purposes of defense against external threats, which requires some pooling and organization of people and resources, and perhaps for the maintenance of the infrastructure and internal law and order. Otherwise, government regulation only interferes with the market economy; government benefit programs only encourage dependency and discourage the personal initiative that amounts to virtue in our society.

The flies in this ointment are urban life, the poor, and immigrants. Urban life requires a relatively large public sector. When people live in close proximity in apartment buildings, there is more need for public parks and playgrounds and public transportation. Cities also were, and are, the homes of immigrants who, not speaking English or lacking the requisite education, needed public support to enter the society and its economic system. The descendants of slaves, as well, eventually ended up in cities, where they often required public services and benefits. Urban politicians built their support by offering help to immigrants who did not know their way around American life. The public sector, in short, has become identified with the cities, the poor, the ethnically different immigrants and minorities.

In our pursuit of negative liberty, we Americans often appear to be trying to forget about our inner cities and the people who live there. It is a classic case of the type Berlin warned us about, in which we come to believe that the interests of all people can be harmonized through the pursuit of a certain form of liberty; the trade-offs and consequences of this pursuit are ignored. Our ability to do so is sustained by our belief in the rationality of the type of liberty that we are idealizing, as well as the disidentification of the white middle-class American with the inner-city dweller who tends to be poor, a person of color, a recent immigrant.

This attempt to shrink the public sector has occurred to the greatest extent in the United States; even our North American neighbors, the Canadians, have a much larger public sector than we do, which includes much more of the health care system, for example. European countries, even Protestant countries, have much higher rates of taxation than we are accustomed to and more highly developed public sectors. Socioeconomic homogeneity, in these cases, seems to correlate with a larger public sector and a less sharp dividing line between the public and private spheres of life. When people "out there" are experienced as "like me," there seems to be less tendency to draw such a sharp line. The privatization of life in the United States, whatever its historicocultural roots, creates a vicious circle of distancing between the middle-class white majority and those who are different racially, culturally, economically.

Projective-Introjective Processes

In psychic terms, one might note a parallel between the kind of bifurcation of the public from the private that I have been discussing and psychic splitting. The public sector becomes the repository, on the social level, for the "not me," for the disowned, the different, the degraded, the incomprehensible. The psyche, like a city or a society, has its "bad neighborhoods," populated by the aggressive, the dependent, the exploitative, the ruthless, the parts of ourselves that we define as bad or devalued. The psyche also has its idealized "good neighborhoods," which we try to protect and segregate. Our dreams sometimes make use of such analogies to portray the various sides of our psychic lives. We dream of muggers intruding into our private spaces, for example, of being on buses that end up on the wrong side of town and expose us to danger. The American struggle to shrink the public sector, to privatize everything, to reinforce our national borders, to bar languages that are not "standard" English—all this parallels our attempt to bar the return of the repressed or the dissociated. No wonder, then, that psychotherapeutic work in the public sector is often regarded as something to do and be done with on the way to private practice. Public practice is, in many ways, an excursion into uncomfortable psychic space, aside from the ways in which it goes against the grain of the capitalist entrepreneurial spirit.[3]

Experiences in the Public Sector

I noticed some of the ways in which my own devaluation of public practice found expression while I worked in the Bronx. To set the stage, I will describe the physical setting of the clinic in which I worked. On a side of the clinic was a one-block-long street that dead-ended into railroad tracks. That fairly isolated side street became the dumping ground for cars that had been stolen and stripped, used tires, washing machines, dryers, and other appliances that were expensive or inconvenient to dispose of in the proper way. In the part of Manhattan where I live, outraged residents would have seen to it that these carcasses were removed, if they had ever appeared. In the Bronx, these eyesores were allowed to collect, often for weeks. We came to take the situation for granted. The machines were removed only when our office manager, mobilizing her own outrage, called someone she knew in the mayor's office. The abandoned machines symbolized for me neglect and devaluation of that poverty-stricken neighborhood.[4]

As troubled as I occasionally was about this situation, I noticed from time to time the state of disrepair or neglect that I would allow in my Bronx office, compared to my private office. In my private office, I had framed pictures on my wall; in the Bronx I nailed up prints without frames. When my private office walls needed it, I got them painted at my own expense. In the Bronx, peeling plaster

---

[3] I am clearly critical of capitalism in this chapter. I believe, however, that the capitalism-socialism split in itself constitutes a kind of psychic splitting when capitalism is thought to embody our greed, acquisitiveness, ambition, desire to individuate while socialism is thought to embody our altruism, concern, caring, and desire to become part of a larger group. Socioeconomic ideology may thus contain within itself a psychic disowning of one or the other of these constellations.

[4] I am indebted to Richard Fulmer (1995, personal communication) for pointing out to me the latent socioeconomic aspects of this anecdote. The abandoned machines seem to me to condense representations of the capitalist system's waste and the use of the inner city as a psychic dumping ground, which is supposed to be invisible to most of society. It seems fitting that the situation was redressed only by means of a nonalienated, that is, personal, connection established between our office manager and the "system," in the form of the person she knew at the mayor's office.

would wait until the hospital, to impress auditors, would send the painters around. Although I am talking about appearances here, I believe there was a reflection of a deeper attitude toward my work in the two places that was not lost on my patients or, worse, was taken for granted.

Despite my pride in doing quality work in the public clinic, I noticed that I was less vigilant about pulling myself back when my mind wandered than when I was with my private patients; sometimes I ended sessions a bit early; I would say or do things without thinking them through as thoroughly as I would have in my private practice. I kept a game called Candy Land, a totally mindless board game, in my Bronx office. One child played this game every week. In my private practice I would have challenged myself to think through what was going on. In the Bronx, I welcomed the respite from the crush of paperwork and numbers of patients I had to deal with all day; I was heavily invested in the continuation of this mindless activity. I am being overly self-critical here to highlight the ways in which I colluded with endemic neglect in the Bronx. This child and I provided a respite for each other, and the treatment meant a great deal to both of us.

On an administrative level, the crush of work from which I needed a respite reflects another kind of devaluation of public sector work. Administrators in my hospital were overwhelmingly concerned with numbers, money, and regulatory compliance. The message to clinicians focused on seeing more patients and getting the paperwork done. It was suggested to clinicians that they double-book patients; if both showed up, they could each be seen for half the usual time. What do patients need 45 minutes for anyway? When audits approached, there were "paperwork days" on which we would cancel regularly scheduled appointments. In this bureaucratic approach to clinical work in the Bronx, patients were numbers or pieces of paper. The encroachment of managed care into private practice is often resisted on these grounds. Dehumanization of patients is an old story in public clinics.

The identification of the public sector with psychic qualities, including aggression, exploitativeness, and dependence, also colors the countertransferential attitudes often found in clinicians working in the public sector. Stereotypes about lower-class people, people of color, or those culturally different inevitably structure the countertransference reactions to which clinicians are prone in public practice.

From time to time I have had a taste of the kind of dehumanization I have been describing in the public sector. For two years, my
oldest daughter attended a large public high school after spending
her entire school career up to that point in small private schools. At
first, she was exhilarated to be "out in the world." She learned to find
her way in this school, to negotiate its bureaucracy, to get her classes
changed when necessary, and so on. I had had a harder time with
the school's bureaucracy; when we applied, the date on which the
school planned to mail out acceptances was after the date on which
private schools, to which we had also applied, required a commitment. I tried to get through to the assistant principal who handled
admissions to see if there was any way to find out earlier if our
daughter was accepted. I could not get through to him, and he did
not return my calls. I was outraged, felt I was being treated as a
nonentity, and had fantasies of calling the mayor's office, making
trouble, getting my needs noticed. I felt myself in the position of my
Bronx patients trying to deal with the welfare bureaucracy, for
example. Eventually, a secretary told me that one could come at a
certain time to the school to find out if one's child was accepted. I
thought that I had better cancel a couple of hours' worth of
appointments, since I would probably be made to wait, the required
person probably would be out to lunch at the time I arrived, there
might be a long line of parents, I would be a faceless member of that
line, and it would not matter to anyone that I had to get back to my
office.

This year my daughter began to feel dissatisfied in the public
school. She felt her teachers were often "putting in time," not
inspired or committed to their work. She began to see that it was
possible not to do her best and that no one would care. At that
point, she asked to apply to private schools. Respecting her
commitment to her own academic development, I felt obligated to
support her request, despite the sense that my effort to transcend the
elitist world of New York education had failed. When we went to our
first interview at a private school, after identifying ourselves to the
secretary at the front desk, a woman approached us who turned out
to be the admissions director and greeted us by name. I was stunned
by the contrast with the admissions process in the public school.
Here I felt recognized, attended to.

Does this sort of personal attention depend on having money, on
being able to buy one's way into a privileged situation? Perhaps in a
small town people can pay attention to one another as human beings.

In a large urban environment, are there simply too many people to treat each one as an individual? Given the overwhelming number of people, some degree of dehumanization seems inevitable. Human beings have a need to be recognized and attended to, however. Those who can afford to, then, will create smaller worlds, private schools, private practices, where personal attention can survive. This situation creates a vicious circle in which the "haves" need their money to maintain their private worlds; they resist taxation to finance the public sector. People in the public sector, poor, often people of color, get more and more dehumanized so that people in the private sector, often white, can avoid this process. In mental health clinics, staff are laid off, waiting lists grow, there are fewer and fewer resources available to give attention to the personal needs of people who show up at the door.

Psychoanalysis, par excellence, gives attention to the individual, to the unique needs of each person. Is it inevitable, then, that we can function only in a privileged private world? The answer must be yes, to the extent that we spend years, multiple times per week, on each person, at a high fee. Psychoanalysis has colluded with the bifurcation of public from private practice in developing criteria for analyzability and a definition of the "frame," which largely excludes public sector work from the psychoanalytic domain. We need to ask ourselves how we have ended up with a method that seems to work only with well-to-do patients in private practice.

If we can be adaptable, however, in terms of being willing to conceive of a psychoanalytic treatment that can take place at lower frequency, for a shorter time, in a clinic setting, we begin to bridge the gap between the public and the private as far as psychoanalysis is concerned. Psychoanalysis, further, can provide us with tools for gaining perspective on the psychic roots of the very elitism that psychoanalysis, as an institution and as a treatment method in the hands of purists, has helped perpetuate. Psychoanalysis provides the means to understand the psychic functions served by maintaining this public-private split, as well as the impact on ourselves and our patients, in the clinical situation, of the kind of demoralization and devaluation of our work that I described. All this, however, depends on an expanded use of psychoanalysis: an application of its analytic power to come to a deeper understanding of our relationships to the contexts in which we work and the ways in which these contexts frame our relationships with our patients.

5 / PSYCHOANALYZING THE CONTEXT: PSYCHOANALYSIS IN A PUBLIC CLINIC

I have argued that psychoanalytic work must take account of the social/historical, community, and institutional context in which it takes place. A conservative reading of this assertion is that a public clinic context, for example, is external to the psychoanalytic field per se but influences that field. For example, one might say that a long waiting list in a clinic and administrative pressure to take patients from that waiting list may lead a clinician to encourage his patients to terminate treatment earlier than would otherwise take place, in compliance with administrative mandates but also as a reflection of feeling overwhelmed by pressures emanating simultaneously from patients and clinic administration. Such developments may be conceived of as interference with the ideal course of treatment, which would run until it reaches an end point defined in relation to the treatment process itself. In this sense, the conservative reading is like the conservative point of view about countertransference, that it is, theoretically and ideally, outside the psychoanalytic field but may, when uncontrolled, adversely affect that field. In both cases there is a predisposition to view the influence of these "extraneous" factors as negative, as interference with a process that can be conceived of as existing in "pure" form aside from that influence.

A radical reading of my assertion would be that the context is an inextricable part of the psychoanalytic field, both in public clinics and in private practice. This perspective is parallel to a relational point of view about the psychoanalytic dyad according to which the analyst's countertransference is an intrinsic part of the field, even in the most skillfully conducted analysis. From the perspective of relational psychoanalysis, patient and analyst inevitably bring their own predispositions to the encounter. The interaction between the two psyches forms the transference-countertransference matrix. The patient's transference is fully understandable only in relation to the analyst's countertransference, and vice versa. In similar fashion, an institution, a clinic or a hospital ward, has its own dynamics that form the context for a dyad's work. This is a context in precisely the same sense that private practice provides a context for psychoanalytic work. From the more radical perspective that I am describing, the context would be thought inevitably to interact with the dynamics of both patient and analyst, as well as with the dynamics of the dyad as an entity. Patient transference and analyst countertransference are understandable only within the context provided by the institution, the community, and so on. Patient, analyst, and institutional context form a system, which can be thought about and understood psychoanalytically. From this point of view, it would not be possible to speak of patient and analyst in a public clinic without reference to the long waiting list and administrative pressure to do short-term treatment. Similarly, psychoanalysis in private practice is inevitably framed by the potential for open-ended, long-term treatment in that setting, as well as the payment arrangements typically made in that setting, and so on.

The point of view I am here describing as "radical" is what Kernberg (1992) describes as a "psychoanalytic-open-systems-theory approach." This model is nonlinear and ecological; that is, patient, analyst, and institutional context are considered to influence and define each other in circular fashion.One can take this model to a higher level by including the community and societal level, with the social system dynamics forming part of the context for the functioning of the dyad and the institution. As a reflection of the interaction of systems at multiple levels, one can often find analogous dynamics at various levels, for example, race relations in society paralleled within the analytic dyad. There can be a sense of finding "the world in a grain of sand, eternity in an hour" (William Blake, "Augueries of Innocence").

Bion's (1961) model of group dynamics reflects an open systems model. He argues that one cannot understand individuals without taking account of the groups of which they are members: "There are characteristics in the individual whose real significance cannot be understood unless it is realized that they are part of his equipment as a herd animal and their operation cannot be seen unless it is looked for in the intelligible field of study, which in this instance is the group" (p. 133). Bion noted how groups tend to develop constellations of anxieties and defensive styles analogous to individual anxieties and related defensive systems. He called groups that have adopted such anxiety-defense constellations "basic assumption" groups and categorized them under the headings of "dependency," "fight-flight," and "pairing." The dependency group seeks a leader on whom to depend, the fight-flight group tends to develop an enemy or an in-group/out-group mentality, and the pairing group fosters a relationship between a pair of members and leads, he thought, to the birth of a messiah. Bion's followers at the Tavistock clinic in London and the A. K. Rice Institute in the United States filled in the details, from this point of view, of how group and individual interact in particular institutional systems. The group is considered both to provoke primitive anxieties in its members and to offer them socially structured defense mechanisms (Jaques, 1955) for dealing with these anxieties.

Menzies (1975), for example, studied a hospital nursing service. She points out how a hospital, as an institution, stimulates the dependency wishes and needs of staff as well as patients and thus reactivates the anxiety situations of infancy and the defenses, splitting and projection, associated with these situations. Nurses have to deal with sickness and death, close bodily contact, attachment and loss. All this occurs in an institutional context in which the mission is to care. The nurses are thus led to expect that they will be cared for as well, yet such care is rarely forthcoming in a harassed, overworked, and crisis-ridden environment. Thus are stimulated infantile dependency and aggression and the associated primitive defenses. Menzies sees the operation of such defenses in the way work is divided up among nurses, for example. Nurses are given tasks to be responsible for, across many patients, rather than patients for whom to be responsible. In this way, nurses end up performing a particular task in a routinized and repetitive way, without forming a relationship with the people for whom she is performing the task. Patients come to be referred to by bed number. The detachment thus fostered serves to defend the nurses against the pain and loss inherent in caring for patients who are often destined to die. The hierarchy among nurses fosters splitting and projection. Feelings of incompetence and irresponsibility are projected onto those below one in the hierarchy, while harsh judgments of oneself are projected onto those above one. Vicious circles are thus set up that perpetuate distrust and resentment throughout the nursing hierarchy. The social defense system and the individual defense system reflect and reinforce each other as the individual tendency to detach, split, and project becomes structured into the worklife of the nurses.

Menzies points out that the social defense system actually perpetuates the anxieties of the nurses, insofar as it undermines the potential for caring and mutual support that might otherwise occur among the nurses and other staff. The social defense system also works against the ability of the nurses to become aware of what they feel and fear in connection with their work and thus makes it less likely that the individual will find constructive ways to process her anxiety as stimulated by the nature of her work. Social defense systems, in short, lead to an entrenchment of anxiety/defense systems that are even more recalcitrant than individual defense systems. Thus, individuals in groups tend to regress and to function at a lower level than they might be capable of in private life. Menzies provides a Kleinian/Bionian account of how individual and group processes reflect and reinforce each other and gives us one model for developing an open systems approach inclusive of individual and group levels. The concept of projective identification is the crucial mediating mechanism in a Kleinian open systems model, linking, as it does, the individual psyche with interpersonal occurrences. Those who have studied groups from this perspective add to the model with their consideration of how the group develops isomorphically with the psyche and of how the two levels mutually reinforce their structures and processes.

The patients and therapists I discuss in this book are members of multiple and overlapping groups, from clinic, to community, to society. In this chapter I work toward a psychoanalytic open systems model that is inclusive of public clinic and societal dynamics and that offers, thus, the broadest perspective for the understanding of systems and the individuals therein.

Clinical Illustrations from the Literature

Kernberg (1992), Gabbard (1986), Main (1957), and Stanton and Schwartz (1954) discuss psychoanalytic work within the context of hospital dynamics. Kernberg (1992), for example, presents two cases of inpatients from socially prominent and wealthy families. The VIP climate associated with these treatments attracted the attention of the hospital administration when there were complaints from the patient or family that engaged hospital dynamics in an especially obvious fashion. The first case, Lucia (pp. 175–179) was the daughter in a very wealthy and socially influential Latin American family. Kernberg was brought in to replace her previous hospital psychiatrist because the director of the hospital, presumably loath to offend the patient's parents in any way, thought her previous hospital psychiatrist was overly critical of the patient and her family. For example, the hospital director thought the patient's diagnosis was too severe. Kernberg was thus set up to be relatively lenient or tolerant of this patient, a setup that immediately placed him in opposition with much of the hospital ward staff, which thought certain psychiatrists and therapists were not firm enough with severely disturbed patients.

Lucia at first convinced Kernberg to exempt her from certain hospital activities and work, because she would instead take university correspondence courses. Several weeks later, Lucia was not participating in hospital activities and was also not studying and claimed not to have received course materials. When Kernberg looked into the matter, he found that course materials had indeed arrived. When Kernberg confronted her with his knowledge that course materials had arrived, Lucia at first became sexually seductive with him. Kernberg, with the help of one of his dreams in which Lucia puts her finger in his mouth, which calls to mind a Spanish colloquialism signifying exploitation, began to feel that she was manipulating him and confronted Lucia with his belief to that effect. Lucia soon made a complaint to the hospital administration about Kernberg's rigid attitude toward her, and she was again transferred to another hospital psychiatrist.

In discussing this case on the level of the dyad, Kernberg maintained that, in his lenient phase, he had identified "concordantly" (Racker, 1968) with the patient's "pathological grandiose self" (Kernberg, 1992, p. 179). He felt he had been "drawn into the role of an admiring and potentially corruptible as well as seductive father" (p. 179). Later, his attitude shifted to a "suspicious, persecutory" (p. 179) one, which he regarded as a "complementary" identification (Racker, 1968) with Lucia's "dissociated, sadistic, superego precursors" (p. 179). Kernberg felt that if he had had more tolerance for the activation of sexual impulses in himself toward Lucia, he might have recognized her seductive manipulativeness earlier.

Moving to the role of hospital and family dynamics in this case, Kernberg believed that the hospital director's assignment of him to replace the previous "bad" psychiatrist had seduced him into an "alliance with the patient's narcissistic defenses" (p. 180). Later, when he began to feel seduced and manipulated, he identified with "a rebellious ideology in the hospital" (p. 180), that is, the feeling that some psychiatrists and therapists were not firm enough with severely disturbed patients. Kernberg saw the hospital dynamics as reflecting the family's dynamics in which the mother controlled the father, who, in turn, was seductive, though basically unavailable emotionally, in relation to Lucia. Lucia's mother was able to use her social status and wealth to influence the hospital director to take any psychiatrist off the case who tried to set limits with Lucia. The hospital director and then Kernberg in the first phase of his work with her became the seductive and seduced father who was controlled by the mother. The pull to comply with Lucia's demands was so powerful that any psychiatrist who tried to oppose her had to be expelled from the system. An oppositional feeling with respect to Lucia and her internalized mother's omnipotent control was at first located within the "rebellious" hospital staff, later within Kernberg himself.

Discussion

Kernberg's analysis of this situation can be extended further. The hospital's own dynamics appear to reflect, on one level, the hospital's own needs for money and the support of socially influential people. In this sense, the hospital director was exploiting and manipulating Lucia and her family as much as they were with him. We might see here a reflection of capitalist dynamics, the commodification of Lucia's treatment. Thus, any action on Kernberg's part that threatened the hospital's ability to use Lucia's treatment to position itself better politically and economically could not be tolerated.

On another level, the split within the hospital staff about how to treat severely disturbed patients may be seen as reflecting a role split between therapists and those who have to live with patients on a daily basis. Therapists, from this point of view, are oriented toward understanding and empathy, because that is their job, but also, in part, because their contact with patients is limited. Ward staff are under more pressure from out-of-control behavior on the part of patients. There also appeared to be a split between those who had traditional psychoanalytic training, thus requiring limit setting as part of frame maintenance, and those who had less need for a strictly maintained frame. These splits were activated in Lucia's treatment.

Kernberg speaks of the "bridging function" of his countertransference:

> It was a response to both the patient's enactment, by means of projective identification, of a primitive internalized object relation and the hospital milieu's enactment, by means of a powerful though subtle role induction and/or facilitation in me, of a submission to [the hospital director] . . . as a defense against the underlying

rebellion against [him]. In other words, the patient's pathology of
internal object relations and the hospital's latent social conflicts
"clicked" in my internal reaction at the boundary between the
patient and the hospital system [p. 180]. . . . In my functions on the
boundary between the patient and the social system of the hospital
I unconsciously contributed to "switching on" the correspondence
between intrapsychic and social pathology [p. 188].

Kernberg's language here suggests that he is viewing himself, the
patient, the family, and the hospital system as discrete entities that
interact; projective identification and internalization are invoked as
mechanisms to explain the isomorphism between the dynamics at
various levels or sites. That is, the parallelism between the family
dynamic between mother and father, say, and Lucia's relationship
with Kernberg is explained by reference to Lucia's having internalized her mother and father, then by her having induced Kernberg,
for example, to play the part of the father through projective
identification. Lucia's relationship with the hospital director is
explained in similar fashion.

Additionally and without resort to such psychic mechanisms, one
could postulate that all participants are embedded in an overarching
system with its own dynamics. The behavior of Lucia, Kernberg, the
hospital director, and the others would then be understandable with
reference to this larger system, which could be characterized in
terms of the place of Lucia's family and the hospital in the capitalist
economic system and the alienating influence of this system in the
context of human relationships and work. Lucia and her parents,
accustomed to power and prestige associated with their wealth,
manipulate the hospital to their ends; the hospital reciprocally
manipulates the family and the patient in order to avail itself of the
benefits of their money and social position. On this level, the hospital
and family have found a way to scratch each other's backs. On
another level, however, this mutual manipulation is grotesquely self-
defeating for all parties. Lucia and her family are suffering, and her
treatment is being sacrificed in favor of considerations of money and
power. The setup is self-defeating for the hospital, too, since without
a commitment to put treatment first, the hospital has no reason to
exist. The commodification of Lucia's treatment results, on one hand,
in alienation (in the sense of dehumanization and objectification) of
Lucia's family and the hospital in relation to each other; on the other
hand, this process leads to the alienation of each individual involved
from himself or herself, in the sense that each person's need to help
or be helped is absent from the equation. As he becomes aware of

having colluded with Lucia's manipulation, Kernberg transcends this alienation, both within himself (in beginning to pay attention to his own sense of being manipulated) and in relation to Lucia. His efforts to give priority to Lucia's treatment needs founder as he runs up against the power of the hospital's commitment to exploit Lucia's family for the economic benefit of the hospital.

If one were to give priority to the dynamics of the socioeconomic system in which Lucia's treatment is embedded, one might regard the isomorphic individual and family dynamics as commentaries on the dynamics at the socioeconomic level. Lucia's seductiveness toward Kernberg, for example, could be seen as an enactment, a dramatic performance, reflecting the ways in which money and power are being used to seduce the hospital. The exploitation taking place within Lucia's family could be thought to reflect the structuring impact of the exploitation inherent in their social position. To give priority to the larger system dynamics in this way is consistent with the Marxist/structuralist tendency to give priority to sociocultural factors in the understanding of individual psychic life.

Clinically, however, I believe that giving priority in a one-sided way to dynamics at the macrocosmic level leads us to a dead end. A sociotherapy would follow, in which people's personal problems would be understood as inevitable, given their society. At the extreme, the outcome of therapy would be a commitment to political activity. I would not want to dismiss such a treatment outcome, but I would want to conceive of therapy in a way that allows for more flexibility in terms of focusing on the level of individual psychodynamics, family dynamics, or both. Thus, I believe it is preferable to conceive of the individual psyche and larger systems at all levels as mutually and circularly influential and interactive. Lucia's behavior is the final common pathway for forces and influences emanating from her as an individual, such as her temperament and her internal object world, and from her position within her family and within the hospital and larger socioeconomic systems. The analyst similarly brings his temperament and internal object world to a role within a larger system. Another individual might handle his place within the same system somewhat differently and thereby, perhaps, alter the larger system to some degree. On the other hand, the system is likely to elicit similar role-responsive behavior from a variety of individuals with different temperaments, histories, and internal object worlds. While the socioeconomic setup may predispose the participants to manipulation of each other, the specific form that the manipulation takes is determined by the psychic structure and needs of each participant. Lucia's need to seduce a father-figure to treat her as special both re-creates her early family situation and constitutes her way of enacting the alienation and manipulation that are part of her role within this system. Another patient might have done it differently. The analyst, for his part, finds himself induced into playing the part of the seductive father both by his role in relation to Lucia's internal world and by his role in relation to the hospital. One might assume that aspects of his own personality and internal world were activated, as well. Other aspects of the analyst's personality and role, however, are activated when he confronts Lucia on her manipulativeness. This action is framed as a persecutory one within Lucia's internal world and as obstructionistic to hospital interests, from the point of view of the hospital director.

What are the implications of the type of model one adopts in conceptualizing the relationship between individual and group processes at all levels? The implications are analogous to the implications of adopting a relational model, in contrast to a monadic model, when considering psychoanalytic work. That is, including the group context tends, first, to depathologize the patient or patient–analyst dyad. Second, doing so expands the area of psychoanalytic inquiry and understanding to include group processes. Third, having a broader view may lead the analyst—and patient, for that matter—to take action within the institution, for example, to further a psychoanalytic purpose. I consider these three implications in turn.

Adopting a monadic model in psychoanalysis is consistent with a medical model, which tends to find pathology in the patient. Since the analyst is not conceived of as part of the field, one must conceive of the source for whatever is wrong as residing within the patient. When one adopts a two-person model, disturbances are conceived of as residing simultaneously within each individual and in the interpersonal dynamic that they jointly establish. "Pathology" (if one continues to conceptualize a two-person disturbance in these terms) is thus no longer located solely within the patient.[1] Including larger-

---

[1] Analysts working within a two-person model vary with respect to the degree to which they believe pathology within the analytic dyad originates (typically, not only in poorly conducted analyses) within the analyst as well as within the patient. At one extreme on this continuum are some Kleinians (e.g., Joseph, 1989, as well as Fairbairn, 1958) who believe that the analyst is "press-ganged" by the patient into participation in a pathological process. At the other extreme, Aron (1991, 1992) and Hoffman (1983), following Ferenczi (1932), regard the analyst's personal participation as inevitably implicated in the structure of patient–analyst interaction. They thus advocate including the analyst's subjectivity as a primary object of inquiry within the analytic process.

system dynamics in one's perspective on the dyad would have a similar depathologizing effect.

The second implication of adopting an open systems model is that the field for psychoanalytic inquiry and understanding and thus the interpretive possibilities for the analyst are broadened. Kernberg, for example, mentions that if he had had more tolerance for his sexual feelings, he might have noticed more quickly how Lucia was manipulating him. I would add that if he had had more awareness of his role within the hospital system in relation to Lucia and her family, he might have noticed not only how he was being manipulated but also how he was manipulating Lucia as an agent of the hospital, as well as on his own behalf (e.g., to be seen as a "good" psychiatrist by both Lucia and the hospital director or perhaps to enact some of his own sexual fantasies in relation to her). A therapist in Kernberg's position might have been led to inquire into how Lucia understood his willingness to accommodate to her demands, what she imagined led him to do so. He might have become curious about how Lucia thought he came to be assigned to her in the light of the dismissal of the previous psychiatrist, what role her mother and the hospital director played, and so on. Broadening the psychoanalytic field to include large-group phenomena does not move us out of psychoanalysis into sociology; rather, it enriches our psychoanalytic inquiry by adding levels of meaning to our understanding of what occurs between our patients and us.

Finally, taking an open systems perspective broadens the field for psychoanalytic interventions. For example, a family systems model would lead one to note trouble in Lucia's parents' marital relationship. The mother's controlling behavior toward the father and the father's submissive retreat, coupled with a seductive alliance with Lucia, may indicate a bypassing of marital conflict. Would it be possible to have marital sessions as part of the treatment plan? Might it be possible to meet with both parents around limit-setting issues with Lucia, in an effort to find some basis for cooperation? With a similar aim, might it be possible to have meetings about Lucia's treatment with hospital staff from both sides of the split around firmness/leniency? Kernberg might have been led early on in the treatment to see if some way could be worked out to address Lucia's treatment needs while maintaining positive relations with the family. Perhaps a way could be found to transcend the polarization that typically takes place in institutions around the priority given to clinical versus administrative considerations. (I take up these issues in depth later in this chapter.) These efforts would be typical of systems interventions, but they are also psychoanalytically informed interventions. They flow from an attempt to avoid replication of the patient's internal object world in the surrounding hospital-family system, they attempt to break through the replication of those systemic conditions that led to, and reinforced, Lucia's internal world, or both. Such interventions, further, may be necessary to establish and protect a supportive environment for dyadic psychoanalytic work.

Historically, little attention has been devoted to the impact of systemic dynamics on psychoanalytic work. Freud's (1921) study of group psychology, for example, deemphasized systemic factors. That is, Freud viewed group processes as evolving from individual dynamics. Freud conceived of a group as forming when the relationship between a number of individuals and a leader is characterized by a regression from "object choice" (p. 48) to identification, and the object is put in the place of the ego ideal. "A primary group . . . is a number of individuals who have put one and the same object in the place of their ego ideal and have consequently identified themselves with one another in their ego" (p. 61). Individuals thus constitute a group by virtue of a common psychic function served by the group.

Bion (1961) is the exception as a psychoanalyst who took account of systemic factors. He offered a view more consistent with my own model in which individual and group processes are mutually interactive and influential. Bion writes as follows with respect to the group leader:

> The leader . . . does not create the group by virtue of his fanatical adherence to an idea, but is rather an individual whose personality renders him peculiarly susceptible to the obliteration of individuality by the . . . group's leadership requirements. . . . The leader has no greater freedom to be himself than any other member of the group [p. 177].

Bion thus outlines the interaction of the group "requirements" and the individual personality, and the interaction results in a person's taking the leadership role, the leadership role's being filled, or both.

Large Systems Dynamics
in Public Clinic Therapy

In this section I offer an example of the ways in which our understanding of interactions between patient and therapist in inner-city public clinics may be enriched by consideration of group processes. Recall the patient I cited earlier who told her "numbers-starved" therapist "You're lucky I came today." A therapist operating with a one-person model might focus on the resistant attitude implied in the patient's comment: she almost did not come to the session that day, and she seems to deny that she benefits from coming to the sessions. The therapist might then listen for anxiety stimulated in the last session or anxiety active in the transference. A therapist operating with a two-person model might focus on the defensive interpersonal functions served by such a provocative comment. Or, taking the patient's comment literally, even though it is spoken tongue in cheek, the therapist might become interested in the patient's possible (and plausible) speculation that the therapist is invested in her attending the session. The therapist might inquire as to whether the patient may perceive or speculate that the therapist is prone to feeling rejected or anxious about professional or personal adequacy or that this particular patient is especially important to her. The therapist may choose to process these matters silently or to inquire more actively as to the patient's perceptions and speculations. Patient and analyst may be led to consider the interaction of the therapist's participation with the patient's that creates a dynamic in which the therapist comes to be anxious about the patient's attendance at sessions or eager to see the patient, while the patient becomes reluctant.

A three-person, or group-process, perspective, has a different focus. Here the focus is not so much on the interaction of what the two people bring to the clinical situation, as on the way in which each person's subjectivity is constituted by the situation in which each finds himself. From this point of view, patient and analyst are creating an enactment that reflects an aspect of what is happening on the macrocosmic level. On that level, the institution is being supported with government funds with the cooperation of those patients who choose to attend sessions. This perspective informs us that such an interaction, whether overt, as in this example, or covert, cannot *not* happen, given the setup at the institutional level. At the level of the dyad, the therapist who takes this perspective has an expanded interpretive range, both within herself and in what she chooses to say to the patient. She may choose to address the intrapsychic, or she may choose to ask the patient what she has noticed or thought about that makes her think the therapist would feel lucky she came that day. The analyst will have the further possibility in mind that the patient may be consciously or preconsciously aware of the pressures on the therapist to see large numbers of patients or of the ways in which the institution and its employees, including her therapist, are supported with the cooperation of patients such as herself. The patient's resistance or the analyst's insecurity about the patient's cooperation assumes new and different meanings when the context is taken account of in this way. The here-and-now situation is more likely to be seen as contributory to the transference and countertransference, compared with the influence of preexisting dispositions, when one contextualizes the feelings of patient and analyst. There is a concomitant depathologization of the transference and countertransference. Taking account of the context may contribute to illuminating the nature of the transference even within a one- or two-person model. For example, the patient's resistance may be seen as reflecting a sense of being exploited; this aspect may not be as salient without an awareness of the institutional situation. Aspects of the meaning of the patient for the analyst may be inaccessible without knowledge that the patient's cooperation makes the analyst look good to her superiors, for example.

A perspective that takes account of one-, two-, and three-person factors provides the maximum interpretive flexibility in dealing with situations such as the one we are considering here. Such a perspective requires consideration of the ways in which the context interacts with the predispositions of each person. That is, the insecurity of the therapist in the public clinic may be called forth by the situation, but it is called forth in different ways and in more or less greater measure in some people than in others. The patient may react to the therapist's insecurity with anger, withdrawal, or support. The interaction of patient and analyst, within the context provided by the institution, constitutes the analytic field.

Taking account of the social and community context, further, allows one, or forces one, to keep in mind the typical and likely psychic impact of ghetto life. As demonstrated by Brown and Harris (1978), for example, inner-city life tends to breed depression. The women they studied in inner-city London were more likely than rural women and middle-class women to suffer both acute and chronic depression. The vulnerability to depression was found to be correlated with the absence of a supportive relationship and with unemployment, both of which were found to be relatively common among inner-city residents. The clinical symptomatology of depression may not be distinguishable from the depression of a middle-class person; nonetheless, surely, a clinician wishing to understand the psychic life of an inner-city patient and wishing to make a meaningful personal and professional relationship with such a person would want to bear in mind the conditions of that person's life that may contribute to her mental state. The consequences of inner-city depression can hardly be overstated. Particularly when parents are depressed and thus emotionally unavailable to their children, the impact on the children's emotional lives can be lasting and severe. A cross-generational pattern of depression and emotional inaccessibility, contributing to the abuse and neglect of children, may result (Lyons-Ruth and Zeanah, 1993). Such clinical phenomena also occur, not uncommonly, in higher social class environments; nonetheless, a "feel" for such developments in the inner city is essential for the clinician working there. Imagine how it would feel to have a young child, or two or three young children, when you have no support from their father(s) and no job. You are trying to find a baby-sitter for them so you can go down to the welfare office to try to get recertified as a welfare recipient; or you have no baby-sitter and you are trying to get them all onto a bus to take to the welfare center. Middle-class parents, with support from a partner and a stable job, find child rearing stressful enough; can a middle-class therapist begin to imagine what life is like for the inner-city parents and children we see in our clinics? An attempt to do so, at any rate, is a precondition for an informed and empathic approach to such patients.

Interstaff and Interdisciplinary Relationships

One source of interdisciplinary tension revolves around power in relation to the role of medical doctors vis-á-vis nonmedical therapists in public clinics. Medical schools or hospitals sponsor many community mental health centers; medical control is likely to be quite entrenched in such a setting. The Community Mental Health Act's insistence on a degree of community, thus nonmedical, control set up a tension between medical doctors and other staff, including nonmedical clinicians and bureaucrats. Interdisciplinary conflict on the state or national level, for example, around hospital admitting privileges for psychologists, further feeds such interdisciplinary tension on the clinic level.

Administrative issues assume added prominence when government funds are cut, as they have been often in recent years, and so stimulate governmental and hospital bureaucracies to ever increasing focus on cost-effectiveness calculations, units of service, and the amount of revenue generated. Quantity of service, along with documentation of that service, takes center stage; the quality of service provided or the experience of the "providers" is often ignored within the bureaucracy. As the performance of administrators and heads of service comes to be judged increasingly in terms of numbers of patient visits, the psychoanalytic orientation of many clinicians becomes a growing problem and source of tension. Clinicians who work with families and groups fit better with this administrative situation, since such staff see more patients per hour.

Given these tensions, multiple polarizations often occur in clinics, with each discipline or function emphasizing, in a one-sided way, a piece of the puzzle. The administrator represents the pragmatic, the bottom line, the financial point of view about the work, while clinicians focus on quality and integrity of the work. Whereas, in private practice, the practitioner is both clinician and administrator, in a clinic, the functions are split. In a clinic, the clinician sees patients and receives a paycheck that does not depend on the number of patients seen (except in fee-for-service clinics). The administrator worries only about revenue and expenses and, even though often a clinician by training, is somewhat removed from the impact of administrative policies on clinical work. If funding sources, usually a governmental agency, require a new piece of documentation, it is the administrator's job to get that piece of paperwork filled out by clinicians. The clinicians generally already feel overburdened by paperwork, so a conflict is set up between administrators and clinicians. It is the administrator's job to impose governmental regulations and to get clinicians to generate enough revenue to support the expenses of the clinic. It is the clinicians' job to see patients. Clinicians are on the front lines and immersed in the often agonizing experience of trying to connect with, and help, patients with complex, intractable problems. Administrators and clinicians often end up feeling that each does not understand the other. Administrators find clinicians unreasonably resistant to the need to document their work and to work hard. In the extreme they may see clinicians as lazy, as trying to get away with doing as little work as possible. Clinicians see administrators as taskmasters, piling meaningless task after meaningless task on them or being concerned only with quantity of work at the expense of quality.

To illustrate how administrators and clinicians get polarized, consider the situation of a governmental official, not a clinician, whose job is to monitor a public clinic's performance. How does one determine if a clinic staff is doing what it is supposed to do? Cost-effectiveness calculations require some concrete measure of effectiveness, so the first step is to require that clinicians write down (for communication with an auditor) concrete goals for each patient, along with a time frame for achieving these goals. In a comprehensive, multidisciplinary setting, there must be interdisciplinary input on the goals and the progress achieved. The end result, for the clinician, is time spent on meetings in which comprehensive treatment plans must be written for each patient, with input from several staff members; then progress is reviewed every 90 days in an interdisciplinary meeting, with written documentation of treatment progress, complete with signatures of all present.

Another government official may be responsible for ensuring that each clinic lives up to its commitment for "levels of service," that is, numbers of patients seen. If the number of patients seen is low for a period of time, the official requires a written plan for remedial action on the part of clinic administrators. The clinic administrators then require the staff to find ways to schedule more patients.

More meetings, more patients: the staff likely feel beset with demands from all sides, overwhelmed, resentful, misunderstood. Clinicians may point out that the workload makes meaningful psychotherapeutic work impossible. There is simply not enough time to do the work in the quantity required, plus perform all the tasks required for documentation. To further complicate matters, some clinicians, especially psychodynamically oriented ones, may say that concrete behavioral goals cannot capture the essence of what needs to be achieved. Unless such a clinician can come up with some goal that meets the auditor's need for something concrete, the clinician either goes through the motions of writing treatment plans and feels demoralized or is noncompliant. Clinicians spend their time dealing with complex and painful human situations; paperwork seems peripheral, an intrusion, at best faintly reflecting the experience of doing the work. The administrator's priorities often seem to do violence to what makes a clinician's life meaningful.

The low- or middle-level administrator, responding to a multitude of demands from above, does not have the flexibility to respond to the clinicians' concerns with relaxation of a requirement here or there. At best, he may work with the clinicians to find a creative way to get paperwork done quickly or may convey the clinicians' concerns to a government official responsible for the clinic. All too often, such an administrator responds to the multiple pressures of governmental demands and clinician resentment with withdrawal and rigidity. Since his performance is judged by administrators above him, his primary concern is likely to be with quantity and documentation. On a day-to-day basis he has more contact with clinicians and thus is faced continually with their dissatisfaction, anger, and resentment. He may be aware that if he does not respond to their concerns, the clinicians have the power to passively-aggressively undermine him by seeing few patients or failing to do their paperwork. It is a complex organizational and interpersonal situation for which few administrators are adequately trained or prepared. In the absence of outstanding human skills and organizational knowledge and expertise, there is likely to be a spiral of misunderstanding, threats, disciplinary actions, resentment.

In private practice, where clinicians function independently, integration of clinical and administrative functions is inevitable. The private practitioner must be both administrator and clinician. She must balance quality and quantity in terms of the trade-offs in her own life. How much money does she feel she needs? What are the demands of her family, of her own wishes to live in a certain way? What are the consequences of adding another patient at the end of the day or the beginning of the day, of getting out of bed an hour earlier, of being that much more tired at the end of the day? The private practitioner may impose long working hours on herself, in the interest of higher income, and choose to pay the price in terms of her own comfort, time with her family, or the quality of attention she can give her patients. If the same conditions were imposed on her by an administrator in a clinic, it would be cause for protest and resentment. In clinic and governmental bureaucracies, it is not in anybody's job description to perform the kind of integrative function that the private practitioner must exercise within herself in order to make these decisions.

Splits also occur between clinical disciplines and approaches. The biological psychiatrist represents the approach that takes account of the impact of the functional status of the nervous system and chemical means of influencing the nervous system. The psychoanalytically informed therapist (nowadays, often a psychologist or a social worker) represents concern with human experience and feeling, with in-depth contact between patient and analyst as a means of therapy. The family therapist (usually a social worker, sometimes a psychologist) represents an approach that focuses on the impact of context, system, the ways in which human behavior is influenced by the larger systems in which people are embedded. Family therapists, along with biological psychiatrists, can take a quite directive approach to patients, as opposed to the psychoanalyst, who likes to let things unfold. Family therapists, biological psychiatrists, behavior therapists can be symptom-focused, in contrast to the psychoanalyst, who tends to think about that portion of the iceberg that is under water. On treatment-planning teams there is a potential for conflict when the disciplines become polarized, for example, psychologists for therapy versus psychiatrists for medication; psychoanalytically trained clinicians for individual therapy and long-term, in-depth work versus behavior therapists or family therapists for a short-term approach (on which they may ally with administrators interested in short waiting lists); and so on. Treatment-planning meetings can easily become forums for conflict over these issues, in which resolution is achieved through a political process, for example, the assertion of psychiatric authority or the creation of alliances between various staff members with similar points of view about a case. Ideally, an interdisciplinary milieu provides a rich opportunity for integration by bringing together people with diverse perspectives. In many clinic settings, such a cross-fertilization indeed occurs, with productive results. In less fortunate cases, the process of integration is short-circuited by polarization and splitting among staff members.

Private practitioners must integrate the various approaches to treatment for and within themselves. A private clinician, faced with the challenge of working with a very disturbed patient alone, may seek out biological psychiatrists as backup; the same clinician might resist the emphasis on medication in a clinic setting where autonomy becomes more the issue. Many private clinicians working with children, for example, find some way to integrate family work with individual child work, whereas in a clinic setting there can more easily be conflict over treatment modality.

These splits and conflicts reflect, in microcosm, larger social and intellectual currents and crosscurrents deeply embedded in our society. The Western privileging of science is reflected in the dominance of the medical profession and behavioral psychologists in many public clinics. Administrative pressure reflects the capitalist commodification of mental health services. Many therapists feel that this commodification amounts to an alienating dehumanization of psychotherapeutic work. Some object to being termed "providers" (in managed-care lingo) of psychotherapeutic "services," as these terms imply an instrumental, technological, mechanical relationship, rather than an intimate, "I-thou" (Buber, 1948) relationship, between patient and therapist.

Psychoanalysis, among all psychotherapeutic modalities, has the most difficulty with scientism and commodification. Nonetheless, efforts have been made to develop a version of psychoanalysis that would be compatible with the modern medical model. Ego psychology has been particularly successful in this regard, with its diagnostic emphasis on adaptive strengths and weaknesses. Some analytically oriented researchers have recently tried to accommodate to the cost-benefit calculations of insurance companies and managed care providers by demonstrating the cost-effectiveness of psychoanalytic treatment in terms of preventing inpatient psychiatric treatment and unnecessary medical visits. Short-term dynamic therapies have been developed (e.g., Malan, 1963; Mann, 1973) that use psychoanalytic concepts in formulating a method aimed at achieving specific and limited goals. Nonetheless, the fit with modernist science, technology, and technical rationality is not a natural or easy one for psychoanalysis. Psychoanalysis requires the provision of time and space for the emergence of the unconscious on its own terms. Behavioral change is seen as flowing from, and requiring as a precondition, less tangible forms of psychic change. Quick behavior change may even be seen by analysts as defensive, a flight into health. Many psychoanalysts feel that their model gets bent out of shape when adapting their mind-set to come up with a psychiatric diagnosis or a short-term, symptom-focused treatment plan. The basic tension between psychoanalysis and Western science, as manifested by modern medicine, and the bureaucracy of the public clinic make any rapprochement tenuous.

Contradictions abound, however, when one plays out the implications of the view of psychoanalysis I have just presented. For example, does resistance to the commodification of psychoanalysis entail denial of the analyst's entrepreneurial and commercial motives? Can the analyst's objectification of the patient (i.e., seeing the patient as a source of money) be denied only by treating patients so well-to-do that money can be passed without pain? Is the analyst's resistance to public clinic commodification a form of elitism, a refusal to adapt to the conditions required for public funding of psychotherapy and thus for the availability of psychotherapy to the less well-off? Dimen (1993) has written eloquently about some of these contradictions as they arise around money in psychoanalysis. She sees contradictions, such as the ways in which all our relationships simultaneously involve both objectification and intersubjective intimacy, as inherent in human relationships. I return to a consideration of these issues in the final chapter of this book.

Interstaff Relationships and Clinical Interaction:
Return to the Case of José

How do the issues I have discussed in this chapter play themselves out on the microcosmic level of the treatment room? Recall the case of José, whom I could not see when he returned to the clinic at age 18 because my psychiatrist refused to take responsibility for the case. On one level, my team psychiatrist was maintaining one of the clinic's administrative boundaries. José's reapplication to the clinic, from an administrative point of view, was not different from any other application. The patient was too old, so he was to be sent to the adult clinic. From my psychoanalytically informed clinical perspective, what was important to me was that I had an ongoing relationship with José. I saw his earlier termination as an event within this ongoing relationship. The opportunity to process his termination and his decision to return as events between us seemed to me crucial clinically. Dr. B's take on the clinical issue was different from mine, however; he thought that I was infantilizing José by attempting to continue to see him in the child and adolescent clinic. I then had to sort out what was a difference in a clinical point of view and what was an assertion of power of a psychiatrist over a psychologist or an assertion of the primacy of administrative boundaries over "soft-headed" clinical concerns. Was the psychiatrist calling to my attention a countertransferential overprotectiveness of José, my grandiose sense that only I could help him? What if José had terminated with me in private practice, and I did not have time to see him when he came back? Would I not, then, like the psychiatrist, say he had to go elsewhere? Or was it a difference in clinical sensibility that I was confronting with him? Did I give high priority to continuity because I, on theoretical grounds, saw the clinical situation on a parent–child model in which continuity was an essential feature of the holding environment? Perhaps this was incomprehensible to the psychiatrist, with his more symptom-focused model. Then again, perhaps we were each choosing and holding to our models as part of a power game we were playing with each other. If I took this point of view, my consideration of my counter-transference felt like weakness on my part, as if to give credence to what he was saying was part of a surrender to him. To fail to give credence to what he was saying, on the contrary, felt like digging in on my part, with potentially negative consequences. Ultimately, I believe there was a confluence of theoretical, political, and personality factors feeding into this extremely complicated, but not uncommon, situation.

Having determined that I had no recourse, I was now in a difficult clinical situation with José. I expected him to be angry that I could not see him. As I myself was angry that I could not see him, there was danger that the two of us would avoid a disjunctive interaction between us by joining forces against a third party, the clinic bureaucracy and power structure. I felt a temptation to get myself off the hook by explaining to José, resentfully, that I had tried and failed to get him reregistered. Two related considerations gave me pause, however. One was that I did not want to deny José's potential perception of me as part of the clinic system. From my point of view, it was vital for my self-image that I distance myself from what seemed to me an insensitive bureaucratic structure. I did not want to make it more difficult for José, however, who might plausibly and accurately see me as an agent of that very structure. Second, I was concerned not to neglect José's anger at me for abandoning him, for not being powerful enough to be able to arrange to see him there, or, perhaps, for not wanting to see him. I, in turn, was somewhat annoyed with José for having terminated with me when he did and found myself secretly saying, I told you so, when he came back. I could identify with a retaliatory impulse not to see him when he returned to me. I was also concerned not to avoid taking account of José's responsibility for having terminated when he did and thus to take a risk that I would not be able to see him if and when he came back. In terminating, he was making a decision to take a risk. This seemed to me a fact that would be ignored if we both blamed "the clinic" or the psychiatrist for failing to undo the consequences of his decision.

As it happened, José did not express anger at me overtly for not being able or willing to see him. He compliantly took the referral I gave him, seemingly resigned to an impossible situation and denying that he held me responsible in any way. I believe, however, that the subsequent self-destructive behavior with which he returned to me may have unconsciously communicated some of the anger and despair he felt.

What Makes a Clinic Function Well
in an Inner-City Environment?

So far in this chapter I have discussed the ways in which interdisciplinary relationships within a clinic can be considered from an
ecological, systemic point of view. On one hand, interdisciplinary
relationships reflect, in a microcosm, interactions among economic,
social, and intellectual forces in society at large. I now turn to a
consideration of the ways in which the inner-city environment itself
affects the clinic and staff–staff and staff–patient interactions.

Deprivation is an inescapable fact of life in the inner city. A
middle-class clinician coming to work in an inner-city community
often can barely begin to imagine the sense of deprivation that comes
with trying to live and raise children on a poverty-level income.
Nonetheless, the sense of deprivation begins to infiltrate the
clinician's experience in various ways. Bollas (1989) points out how
people create physical and human environments in order to actualize
a preferred sense of self. Attractive, well-cared-for physical environments reflect and create a sense of pride in those who live and work
there. Money and the things it can buy reflect and create a sense of
fullness. People who live and work in the inner city are surrounded
by squalor and neglect a good deal of the time. When the psychology
internship I directed was evaluated by outside consultants, I
remember the shock felt by one of them when he compared the
physical space in which we worked with his own. He worked in a
relatively well funded hospital in a non-inner-city environment. He
said there was plush carpeting on his floor and art on his office walls.
We had worn industrial carpeting on the floors and graffiti on our
outside walls. The view from our windows included abandoned
buildings and stolen and stripped cars. The environment tended to
have a demoralizing effect on those of us who worked there, with
associated feelings of frustration, deprivation, despair, low self-
esteem. Some of our patients neglected themselves physically and in
other ways or were too poor to take care of themselves. Some of
them were sick, had acquired immune deficiency syndrome (AIDS),
smelled of alcohol, wore dirty, old clothes, and so on. Working in
this environment tended to produce staff feelings of demoralization
and devaluation of self and others, including colleagues and patients.
Our administrators were reviled. More subtle was devaluation of
patients through characterization of them as not capable of insight,

as being able to use only concrete services, and so on. In short, staff feelings of demoralization and deprivation were widespread and inevitable as a reflection of the environment in which we worked, with its devalued status in society at large. To work in such an environment with a sense of pride and dignity required extra support from the clinic and from peers. There needed to be special attention paid to in-service training, to sensitive, clinically oriented supervision, to efforts to keep in perspective for the staff the importance of the difficult work they were doing. In short, under deprived conditions, staff need to feel taken care of and appreciated by administration and by each other in order to feel that they have something to give to their patients.

The beleaguered administration tended, instead, to pile further demands and criticisms on the clinicians, who were already feeling drained by their patients. As administrative demands multiplied, clinical supervision was preempted by so-called administrative supervision, which meant having one's paperwork checked. The staff from time to time tried to organize peer supervision groups. The administration, however, would deny clinicians the time to attend such groups unless they were seeing enough patients every week, and their paperwork was already up to date. Those who were allowed to attend peer supervision groups found it hard not to use the time to complain about the administration.

Under these conditions, the needs of patients came to feel ever increasingly like impositions upon staff members. For example, consider the ways in which missed appointments were handled. A missed appointment was often welcomed by a clinician overwhelmed with paperwork, despite anxiety about having reduced levels of service. In addition, it was often the least functional patients who missed appointments. These patients tended to have the most intractable problems and to respond least to the clinician's interventions and thus gave back least to the therapist. When such patients missed appointments, it often stimulated the clinician to hope that the patient would disappear forever, along with his needs and demands. In this context, a decision had to be made about how to follow up. Should one call the patient, write the patient, do nothing and wait for the patient to make the next move? Clinicians often found it tempting to do nothing or to procrastinate and see what would happen. The patient might indeed disappear, perhaps compliantly with the clinician's desire. Often enough, after a delay, the patient would recontact the clinician in crisis. A crisis both accelerated the demands upon the clinician and coerced attention from a clinician who, by now, was quite likely seen as unresponsive. In this way a vicious circle was created of the clinician's feeling overwhelmed and withdrawing from the patient, who would withdraw in turn, only to return with accelerating demands not easily resolved psychotherapeutically.

In the early years of this program, there had been much higher morale and pride among staff. At first, there was a great deal of excitement about community mental health and about the resources that the hospital had committed to this clinic. This child and adolescent program was, in fact, the largest program of its kind in the state in terms of numbers of staff and patients seen. The size reflected the competence of the administration in obtaining government funding. This same responsiveness to the concerns of governmental agencies and bureaucrats led, later, to the unremitting paperwork and levels-of-service pressures on staff. Early on, however, staff felt a strong sense of enthusiasm, derived from a commitment to provide the highest-quality treatment to usually overlooked patients. Clinic-level administrators, at this early time in the history of the program, were seen by staff as quite remote and uninvolved. At this time, this was seen as a kind of benign neglect. Staff really wanted to be left alone to do the work they wanted to do with patients and with each other. For example, at one point some staff came up with an idea to organize the clinic into small, interdisciplinary teams that would do intakes together, then follow the cases in periodic case discussions. The staff met with the clinic administrators from time to time to keep them informed and to forestall their feeling threatened by the staff initiative. The feeling was that the administrators appreciated the staff's taking the initiative as long as their sense of control was not threatened. With tacit administrative blessing, the staff provided for themselves a framework of mutual support. How did this positive situation break down? The turn in a negative direction began when the chief died suddenly. Following this loss, which was not mourned collectively among the staff, there was a power struggle between the chief physician and the social work supervisor. The sense of interdisciplinary collaboration disappeared; The chief physician consolidated his power and banished the social work supervisor from the clinic; he never fully retreated to the position of benign neglect. There was an ongoing effort to assert medical control, in the context of ever-increasing bureaucratic demands, which eventually led to the destruction of morale.

Earlier in my career, I participated in another inner-city clinical setup that worked well, from my point of view. This was a day treatment center for latency-aged children, and was jointly sponsored by a medical school's community mental health center and the city's board of education. There were two classrooms, each with six or eight children, a teacher, and a paraprofessional. A man was hired to sit in the hallway with children who, having been out of control in the classroom, needed "time out." Each child was seen by a therapist twice a week; each child's family was seen once a week. If the child was out of school, and we had not heard from the family, someone from the day treatment center would call or go out to the home to see what was going on, if necessary. There was an in-depth case presentation and discussion once a week. Every child and family would be presented every three months or so. The aim was both to enhance the clinical understanding of each case and to further the ongoing professional development of the staff. In this program the children made remarkable gains; staff morale and sense of pride were high. What made for this success?

One factor here was the director, a young man who was hired directly out of his own internship to run the program. The administration had demonstrated great confidence in him by giving him this position, and he responded by investing himself strongly in his work. He hired people who would create the kind of serious and committed environment he wished to foster. A creative collaboration between the medical school and the board of education demonstrated the commitment of each to this program. The commitment of resources was adequate to provide an intensive level of intervention to each child and family. The case conferences were at a high intellectual level and made staff feel they could not only work productively with their patients but develop professionally at the same time. When children and families responded well to the intensive interventions, staff morale was further reinforced. When the work was more difficult, the discussion in case conferences and in supervision fostered learning from the experience and a sense of accomplishment in the face of formidable difficulties. In short, this program worked because everyone involved felt well cared for, and there was a sense of group support and commitment. Lest I be thought to be painting a Pollyanna-like picture here, I should add that after several years, staff showed up to work one September to find the program abruptly closed down. Someone on the board of education had decided that teachers would no longer be assigned to programs that were not located in school buildings. The day treatment center patients and families became clinic patients overnight, absorbed into the staff's caseload, seen once a week.

In this chapter I have attempted to illustrate an ecological perspective on the public clinic. According to this point of view, there is an interaction between macrocosmic social forces and the dynamics on various microcosmic levels, from the level of therapist–patient interaction, to intraclinic relationships among the various disciplines. The potentially relevant macrocosmic forces include capitalism, in the context of which psychotherapy becomes a commodity, the therapist a provider, the patient a consumer, the outcome of the treatment a product; the dominant philosophy of science and the power structure of science, which determines the relative status of various treatment models; and the hierarchical power structure of society, within which race, class, and gender are constituted. These macrocosmic forces interact with the internal psychic lives of the participants and the interpersonal dynamics between them to produce events such as I have described in this chapter. From the point of view of patient, therapist, or member of an interdisciplinary team, gaining knowledge and awareness of the relevant macrocosmic forces, in their interaction with personal and interpersonal factors, is analogous to making the personal unconscious conscious. For the individual, such knowledge can help to understand and overcome the particular form of psychic splitting fostered according to one's role in a social, economic, or political system.

6 / ON THE FUTURE OF PSYCHOANALYSIS

Psychoanalysis, in many ways, appears to be out of step with the zeitgeist of these closing years of the 20th century. We are witnessing an increasing dehumanization of daily life and a search for simple and inexpensive solutions to complex human problems. The move toward managed health care is a striking example of this trend. Managed care started out as an attempt to eliminate waste in health-related spending by establishing a checkpoint at which a proposed medical intervention, before being carried out, would have to be adjudged necessary. Managed care, however, has evolved into a strategy for cost-cutting and profit maximization on the part of corporations, including the managed care companies themselves. When an insurance company receives a fixed amount of money per covered employee, the company's interest is served in denying authorization for medical procedures whenever possible. State laws that exempt managed care companies from liability for the medical consequences of their denials shield them from negative repercussions of their decisions. There is further inducement for managed care companies to deny authorization as much as possible, in that they can thereby lower the amount per covered employee charged to corporations and thus improve their competitive position vis-á-vis other managed care companies. For the employee, however, the result not infrequently is denial of authorization for medical care. The situation is especially serious in mental health care, where managed care companies routinely authorize as few as four psychotherapy sessions for the treatment of conditions as serious as major depression.[1] A practitioner who is within a managed care network must treat the patient within these parameters even if, in his judgment, more treatment is required. The practitioner, further, takes on all the responsibility, in terms of exposure to liability, for the managed care

---

[1] A relative of mine, depressed after her husband left her, went to her health maintenance organization to see if she would be eligible for psychotherapy. The clerk's first question was, "Are you suicidal?" The answer being no, she was told that psychotherapeutic help was unavailable.

company's decision. For employee/patient and therapist, the system often appears to be driven by the profit motive of the organizations concerned rather than the needs of the individual patient.

In the face of this dehumanization of mental health treatment, psychoanalysis offers a humane and complex-minded response to human suffering. But psychoanalysis is often the villain in the narrative constructed by advocates of managed care to justify the draconian limitations imposed on psychotherapeutic treatment. Psychoanalytic practitioners are portrayed as typically engaged in an endless and futile process of tracking current problems back to their childhood roots for wealthy patients with nothing better to do. The management of mental health care is then justified as saving the corporations and the unwitting public from being exploited by unscrupulous practitioners.

It is of vital importance to put forward the psychoanalytic critique of dehumanized and simple-minded approaches to mental health care. Our effectiveness in putting forward this critique is attenuated, however, by psychoanalytic exclusivity and elitism. To the extent that psychoanalytic treatment is seen as a treatment for a few well-to-do patients, it is not surprising that there is a lack of public support for our field. As medical costs spiral out of control, the politically feasible thing to do is to restrict expensive treatments that benefit only a few. Here, I believe, psychoanalysts have a predicament. Psychoanalysis is so labor-intensive that it can never be available on a large scale. This fact may predispose psychoanalysis to elitism but does not make elitism inevitable. The sources of elitism in psychoanalysis are not inherent in the process; these sources can be changed once we become aware of them. In the rest of this chapter, I outline how I think psychoanalysis has become elitist and how analysts might change the situation to fortify the position of psychoanalysis in society.

Modifiable forms of elitism that I have discussed at length include rigid adherence to a frame for psychoanalytic work that excludes the public clinic as a locus for psychoanalytic work, exclusionary criteria of analyzability, and failure to take account of difference in the realms of race, culture, and social class. This book represents an effort to stimulate thought and action about these aspects of an elitist trend within psychoanalysis.

A second form of elitism is more subtle and relates to our position vis-á-vis other forms of therapy. Ever since Freud (1919, p. 190) described psychoanalysis as "pure gold," in contrast to forms of therapy that utilize "suggestion," the prototypical psychoanalytic

alloy, psychoanalysis has considered itself elite among the psychotherapies. This way of looking at what is pure about psychoanalysis
predisposes analysts to regard as second-class any form of therapy
that aims at change, especially behavioral change. To have a wish or
goal seems too close to trying to influence the patient in particular
ways. The insistence of some analysts on a distinction between
psychoanalysis and psychotherapy seems driven by this desire to
define analysis as concerned solely with understanding, while a
concern with change is the devaluing mark of psychotherapy.
Furthering this impression that psychoanalysts are not interested in
change is the emphasis on process (i.e. transference and countertransference) in the work. The psychoanalytic point of view,
however, ultimately makes questionable any rigid distinction between
process and goal or outcome. Freud's concept of transference
emerged in the context of his realization that one could not attempt
a cure in isolation from the interpersonal process that evolved around
the effort. Not only did Freud find that this process could obstruct
the goal-oriented effort, but it was his genius to conceive that the
process contained within itself the very pathological situation that
needed to be addressed in order for a cure to take place. Goal and
process turned out to reflect each other at a deep level. The process
could not have taken shape except in relation to the cure that was
being attempted. The analytic focus on process is organized by
efforts directed at deep, thoroughgoing outcomes, such as relief of
suffering, enhancement of experience, and behavioral change.
Analysis of process would be meaningless and without moral
significance except in the context of organizing purposes, just as
pursuit of a goal is futile without attention being paid to the process
that frames the effort. If psychoanalysts disown concerns about
effectiveness, they play into the hands of those who would portray
psychoanalysis as the problem. Analysts thus render themselves less
effective in confronting the inherent limitations of a simple-minded,
technical approach to the resolution of human problems.

Psychoanalysts, along with many other therapists, object to
managed care when the patient's interests are placed lower in
priority than the interests of the employer or the managed care
company itself. Such prioritizing can take place either through
unreasonable limitations placed on the treatment or when the goals
of treatment must be formulated primarily in ways that serve the
adaptation of the patient to the work environment. Psychoanalysts
need not object to the emphasis on cost-effectiveness per se. Rather,
the psychoanalytic objection ought to address the mechanistic,

dehumanizing approach to human suffering embodied in managed care. From a psychoanalytic point of view, such an approach is indeed pathogenic. It is more costly in time and money to treat people as human beings, to listen to them, to develop a complex-minded idea of what is wrong and an approach to treatment that is responsive to the patient's reaction to the treatment. Imposing a quick, technical solution is likely to appear cost-effective as long as the patient is sent packing after a few sessions, without follow-up as to long-term effectiveness. From a psychoanalytic perspective, the managed care process constitutes an abandonment of the patient as a person. Such a countertransferential attitude cannot but be reflected in the outcome achieved.

What Is to Be Done?

Countering psychoanalytic elitism means, first and foremost, staying involved in the public sector, even as that sector becomes increasingly dominated by cost-cutters and advocates of technical rationality. Analysts need to expand the niches they can envision themselves usefully filling, for example, as consultants to case managers and to short-term therapists with regard to the inevitable transferential and countertransferential aspects of their work.

Several models have been developed for applying a psychoanalytic perspective to short-term therapy, as previously mentioned. Short-term dynamic therapy uses psychoanalytic understanding and psychoanalytic interpretations in the service of symptom relief (Malan, 1963; Mann, 1973). These therapies are primarily symptom focused, do not encourage open-ended exploration, and do not provide space or time for the emergence of unconscious material in unexpected ways. Nonetheless, they use psychoanalytic understanding of how the mind works to effect symptom relief in an efficient manner. As in more standard psychoanalytic work, the approach to symptoms is not made directly, but rather via underlying conflicts presumably causally related to the symptom. A core issue—a conflict, in most cases—is quickly identified, often in the first session; manifestations of this conflict are interpreted as soon as they appear, and the therapist attempts to do an end run around, or a rush straight through the middle of, resistance. Since separation is inevitably an issue in a brief therapy, Mann (1973), for example, believes that conflicts around separation are the most appropriate focus for a time-limited therapy. Mann also believes that most psychological difficulties are traceable to separation difficulties; thus, for him, the brevity of his treatment is actually a facilitating factor, insofar as it heightens the salience of separation in the clinical situation.

Psychoanalytic consultants can have a crucial role to play in the operation of case management, outreach, and inpatient programs that are not psychoanalytic in goal or method. Psychoanalysts have a great deal more to offer than direct treatment. They have a way of understanding people and their interactions that is an invaluable resource for people using methods of intervention from intensive case management, to behavioral therapies. They have ways of understanding group behavior that can enrich the functioning of clinics and treatment teams. Transference and countertransference are as ubiquitous (and far more difficult to manage) in mental health work in the public sector as they are in private office treatment. From a psychoanalytic perspective, as I have noted, it is difficult to imagine people doing home visits with psychiatric patients without a solid understanding of transference and countertransference. Meek (1994) provides a model for this work. Her "intervention project" provides in-home counseling, case management, and advocacy services to an impoverished clientele considered to be at risk for child abuse or neglect or psychiatric hospitalization. In consulting with the clinical staff of this program, Meek provided a psychoanalytic perspective that helped give meaning to psychiatric symptoms and crises in patients' lives and pointed the way toward interventions. Psychoanalytic consultants can also give crucial support to staff with the formidable countertransferential pressures inherent in in-home work with very troubled people. The consultant role can thus provide a valuable, even essential, place for the psychoanalyst far beyond the consulting room. With so much to offer, psychoanalysts ought not give up the public sector to biological psychiatrists, behavioral psychologists, and community activists. If they join them with their own expertise, psychoanalytically trained clinicians will add a great deal to community mental health and contribute toward establishing a more broad-based and thus a more secure position for psychoanalysis in society.

A second way to respond to the challenge of managed care is to critique the outcome research that might support its assumptions and to do research assessing the effectiveness of psychoanalytic treatment. The approach here is to argue that psychoanalysis is cost-effective in the long term if outcome is measured in complex and sophisticated ways. A typical argument would run as follows. Crisis- or symptom-focused treatment is like a Band-Aid. The underlying source of the crisis or symptom is not addressed; therefore, trouble will reappear in similar or dissimilar guises. Empirical research does not demonstrate such phenomena for a variety of reasons: since researchers are eager to get their work finished and published, they are unlikely to follow up patients long enough to see what are the long-term results of various forms of treatment. Outcome measures are not generally sophisticated or multidimensional enough to pick up on psychological distress expressed in indirect ways, for example, through somatic symptoms.[2] Biological and behavioral treatments aim at specific goals that are easily measured, so that typical outcome research is more likely to demonstrate their efficacy. Psychoanalytic treatment aims at a more comprehensive change in personality that may produce changes in functioning and put symptom relief on a firmer footing. Such an outcome is difficult to demonstrate in standard empirical research, which requires a concrete and quickly and easily measured outcome criterion.

The previous arguments address questions of efficiency in terms of symptom relief. Some patients do come for therapy specifically to remove symptoms and would welcome an approach that addressed only their symptom or dysfunction. Even in medicine, however, most patients want to be addressed as human beings, with symptomatic treatment undertaken in the context of a human relationship. How much more so must this be when the symptoms have to do with psychological distress. In medicine, the questions posed here come under the heading of "compliance." That is, what often happens when physicians address symptoms to the exclusion of the whole human being is that the person fails to comply with the treatment. This type of phenomenon led Freud to focus on interpersonal process in the treatment, what we have come to call transference. The patient frustrates the physician's, and his or her own, goal-oriented effort. In this sense psychoanalysis in its essence, demonstrates the fallacy of any project that presupposes that human problems can be fixed like a mechanical breakdown (any mechanic or owner of a machine that has broken down knows, however, that the fixability of machines is also often mythical). Managed care assumes that symptoms can be isolated from the rest of a human being's functions and relationships, that an outside agent can tinker with one aspect of the person's functioning without getting drawn

---

[2]Cummins (1986) reports that 60% of visits to medical doctors are for complaints for which no organic cause can be found, so that they are presumably based in psychological distress.

into the system with which he is interacting and without influencing, in unanticipated ways, other aspects of that system. The premise of managed care is omnipotent thinking, the modernist delusion of control carried to an extreme. In critiquing this kind of thinking, we are not alone, even in the current climate. There has been a broad increase in ecological awareness throughout our society. People are conscious of how technology, while providing many benefits, has involved costs (e.g., pollution) that cannot be ignored. The associated debates going on in contemporary society provide a context in which the psychoanalytic argument can resonate.

Psychoanalysis, as a theory of mind, has been widely influential in society; it has entered the very fabric of our culture, of our ways of thinking and understanding ourselves. Psychoanalytic theory has profoundly influenced the theory and practice of education, literary criticism, the arts, and social theory. In the current focus on the social relevance of psychoanalysis as therapy, we sometimes take for granted the importance of psychoanalysis as theory and cultural influence. One goal of this book has been to develop the ways in which psychoanalysis can be relevant and useful to our increasingly diverse and multicultural society. Psychoanalysis can offer under-standings of race, culture, and class that can help orient our society in the midst of its current identity crisis. In our current beleaguered position as a clinical practice, we should not overlook the potential for psychoanalysis, as a theory of mind, to take a leadership role in making sense of our world.

REFERENCES

Abel, E. (1990), Race, class, and psychoanalysis? Opening questions. In: *Conflicts in Feminism*, ed. M. Hirsch, & E. F. Keller. New York: Routledge, pp. 184–204.

Abraham, K. (1924), A short study of the development of the libido. *Selected Papers on Psychoanalysis*. London: Hogarth Press, 1948, pp. 418–501.

Alexander, F. (1956), *Psychoanalysis and Psychotherapy*. New York: Norton.

Alford, C. F. (1989), *Melanie Klein and Critical Social Theory*. New Haven, CT: Yale University Press.

Anthony, E. J. & Cohler, B., eds. (1987), *The Invulnerable Child*. New York: Guilford.

Arendt, H. (1958), *The Human Condition*. Chicago: University of Chicago Press.

Aron, L. (1991), The patient's experience of the analyst's subjectivity. *Psychoanalytic Dialogues*, 1:29–51.

Aron, L. (1992), Interpretation as expression of the analyst's subjectivity. *Psychoanalytic Dialogues*. 2:475–508.

Bachofen, J. J. (1968), *Myth, Religion, and Mother Right*. Princeton, NJ: Princeton University Press.

Bakhtin, M. (1981), *The Dialogic Imagination*, ed. M. Holquist. Austin: University of Texas Press.

Barratt, B. (1993), *Psychoanalysis and the Postmodern Impulse*. Baltimore: Johns Hopkins University Press.

Benjamin, J. (1988), *The Bonds of Love*. New York: Pantheon.

Berlin, I. (1969), *Four Essays on Liberty*. Oxford: Oxford University Press.

Betancourt, H. & Lopez, S. R. (1993), The study of culture, ethnicity and race in American psychology. *American Psychologist*, 48:629–637.

Bernstein, R. J. (1993), *The New Constellation*. Cambridge, MA: MIT Press.

Bhabha, H. (1990), *Nation and Narration*. New York: Routledge.

Bion, W. R. (1961), *Experiences in Groups*. New York: Basic Books.

Bion, W. R. (1988a), Attacks on linking. In: E. Bott-Spillius. *Melanie Klein Today,* Vol. 1, ed. E. Bott-Spillius. London: Routledge.

Bion, W. R. (1988b), Notes on memory and desire. In: *Melanie Klein Today*, Vol. 2, ed. E. Bott-Spillius. London: Routledge.

Blechner, M. (1993), Homophobia in psychoanalytic writing and practice. *Psychoanalytic Dialogues*, 3:627–638.

Bollas, C. (1987), *The Shadow of the Object*. New York: Columbia University Press.

Bollas, C. (1989), *Forces of Destiny*. London: Free Association Books.

Brown, G. W. & Harris, T. (1978), *The Social Origins of Depression*. New York: Free Press.

Brown, N. O. (1959), *Life Against Death*. Hanover, NH: Wesleyan University Press.

Buber, M. (1948), *Between Man and Man*. New York: Macmillan.

Burke, W. (1992), Countertransference disclosure and the asymmetry/ mutuality dilemma. *Psychoanalytic Dialogues*, 2:241–270.

Butler, J. (1990), *Gender Trouble*. New York: Routledge.

Caligor, L., Zaphiropoulos, M., Grey, A. & Ortmeyer, D. (1971), The Union project of the William Alanson White Institute of Psychiatry, Psychoanalysis, and Psychology. In: *Psychoanalytic Contributions to Community Psychology*. ed. D. Milman & G. Goldman. Springfield, IL: Thomas.

Chodorow, N. (1992), Heterosexuality as a compromise formation: reflections on the psychoanalytic theory of sexual development. *Psychoanalysis and Contemporary Thought*, 15:267–304.

Chomsky, N. (1968), *Language and Mind*. New York: Harcourt, Brace, World.

Cummins, N. A. (1986), The dismantling of our health system: strategies for the survival of psychological practice. *American Psychologist*, 41:426–431.

Cushman, P. (1994), Confronting Sullivan's spider: Hermeneutics and politics of therapy. *Contemporary Psychoanalysis*, 30:800–844.

Davidson, L. (1987), The cross-cultural therapeutic dyad. *Contemporary Psychoanalysis*. 23:659–675.

Davies, J. M. & Frawley, M. G. (1992), Dissociative processes and transference–countertransference paradigms in the psychoanalytically oriented treatment of adult survivors of childhood sexual abuse. *Psychoanalytic Dialogues*, 2:5–36.

Derrida, J. (1978), *Of Grammatology*, trans. G. C. Spivak. Baltimore, MD: Johns Hopkins University Press.

Derrida, J. (1978), *Writing and Difference*, Chicago: University of Chicago Press.

Dimen, M. (1993), Anxiety and alienation: Class, money, and psychoanalysis. Presented at the spring meeting of the Division of Psychoanalysis, American Psychological Association, New York.

Dimen, M. (1994), Money, love, and hate: Contradiction and paradox in psychoanalysis. *Psychoanalytic Dialogues*, 4:69–100.

Ehrenreich, B. (1989), *Fear of Falling*. New York: Pantheon.

Ehrenreich, B. & Ehrenreich, J. (1979), The professional-managerial class. In: *Between Labor and Capital*, ed. P. Walker. Boston: South End Press, pp. 5–48.

Eissler, K. (1958), Remarks on some variations in psychoanalytic technique. *International Journal of Psycho-Analysis*, 39:222–229.

Fairbairn, W. R. D. (1952), Endopsychic structure considered in terms of object relationships. In: *Psychoanalytic Studies of the Personality*. London: Routledge & Kegan Paul, pp. 82–136.

Fairbairn, W. R. D. (1958), On the nature and aims of psychoanalytic treatment. *International Journal of Psycho-Analysis*, 39:374–385.

Fanon, F. (1963), *The Wretched of the Earth*. New York: Grove Press.

Ferenczi, S. (1932), *The Clinical Diary of Sándor Ferenczi*, ed. J. Dupont (trans, M. Balint & N. Z. Jackson). Cambridge, MA: Harvard University Press, 1988.

Fish, J. M. (1995), Why psychologists should learn some anthropology. *American Psychologist*, 50:44–45.

Fosshage, J. (1992), Self psychology: The self and its vicissitudes within a relational matrix. In: *Relational Perspectives in Psychoanalysis*, ed. N. Skolnick & S. Warshaw. Hillsdale, NJ: The Analytic Press, pp. 21–42.

Foster, R. P. (1994), The social politics of psychoanalysis. Presented at biennial conference, Psychoanalytic Society of the Postdoctoral Program, New York.

Foucault, M. (1980), *The History of Sexuality, Vol. I.* New York: Vintage.

Fraiberg, S. (1987), Ghosts in the nursery: A psychoanalytic approach to the problems of impaired mother–infant relationships. In: *Selected Writings of Selma Fraiberg.* Columbus, OH: Ohio State University Press, pp. 100–136.

Freud, S. (1905), *Three Essays on the Theory of the Sexuality. Standard Edition*, 7:125–245. London: Hogarth Press, 1953.

Freud, S. (1913), *On Beginning Treatment. Standard Edition*, 12:123–144. London: Hogarth Press, 1958.

Freud, S. (1916–17), *Introductory Lectures on Psychoanalysis. Standard Edition*, 15, 16. London: Hogarth Press, 1963.

Freud, S. (1919), Lines of advance in psychoanalytic therapy. *Standard Edition*, 17:157–168. London: Hogarth Press, 1955.

Freud, S. (1920), *Beyond the Pleasure Principle. Standard Edition*, 18:3–64. London: Hogarth Press, 1955.

Freud, S. (1921), *Group Psychology and the Analysis of the Ego. Standard Edition*, 18:65–143. London: Hogarth Press, 1955.

Freud, S. (1922), Encyclopedia article: The libido theory. *Standard Edition*, 18:255–259. London: Hogarth Press, 1955.

Freud, S. (1926), The question of lay analysis: Conversations with an impartial person. *Standard Edition*, 20:177–258. London: Hogarth Press, 1959.

Freud, S. (1930), *Civilization and its Discontents. Standard Edition*, 21:51–145. London, Hogarth Press, 1961.

Friedman, L. (1988), *The Anatomy of Psychotherapy*. Hillsdale, NJ: The Analytic Press.

Fromm, E. (1941), *Escape From Freedom*. New York: Avon.

Fromm, E. (1947), *Man for Himself*. Greenwich, CT: Fawcett.

Fromm, E. (1955), *The Sane Society*. Greenwich, CT: Fawcett.

Fromm, E. (1970), *The Crisis of Psychoanalysis.* New York: Holt.

Frommer, M. (1994), Homosexuality and psychoanalysis: Technical considerations revisited. *Psychoanalytic Dialogues*, 4:215-234.

Gabbard, G. O. (1986), The treatment of the "special" patient in a psychoanalytic hospital. *International Review of Psycho-Analysis*, 13:333-347.

Gabbard, G. O. (1992), Commentary on Davies and Frawley. *Psychoanalytic
Dialogues*, 2:37-47.

Geertz, C. (1973), *The Interpretation of Cultures*. New York: Basic Books.

Gill, M. (1982), *Analysis of Transference*. New York: International Universities Press.

Gilman, S. (1993), *Freud, Race, and Gender*. Princeton, NJ: Princeton
University Press.

Greenberg, J. R. (1986), Theoretical models and the analyst's neutrality.
Contemporary Psychoanalysis, 22:87-106.

Greenberg, J. R. (1991), *Oedipus and Beyond*. Cambridge, MA: Harvard
University Press.

Grey, A. (1966), Social class and the psychiatric patient: A study in compos-
ite character. *Contemporary Psychoanalysis*, 2:87-121.

Grey, A., Ortmeyer, D. & Caligor, L. (1972), Research issues for psychotherapy with blue-collar patients. In: Innovations in Psychotherapy, ed. G. D.
Goldman & D. S. Millman. Springfield, IL: Charles C. Thomas, pp. 134-
145.

Halpern, R. (1993), Poverty and infant development. In: *Handbook of Infant
Mental Health*, New York: Guilford, pp. 73-86.

Harris, A. (1992), Dialogues as transitional space: A rapprochement of
psychoanalysis and developmental psycholinguistics. In: *Relational
Perspectives in Psychoanalysis*, ed. N. Skolnick & S. Warshaw. Hillsdale
NJ: The Analytic Press, pp. 119-145.

Herron, W. G. (1994), The development of ethnic identity. Presented at
spring meeting of the Division of Psychoanalysis, American Psychological
Association, Washington, DC.

Hoffman, I. Z. (1983), The patient as interpreter of the analyst's experience.
Contemporary Psychoanalysis, 19:389-422.

Hoffman, I. Z. (1991), Toward a social constructivist view of the psychoanalytic situation. *Psychoanalytic Dialogues*, 1:74-105

Hoffman, I. Z. (1992), Some practical implications of a social constructivist
view of the psychoanalytic situation. *Psychoanalytic Dialogues*, 2:287-
304.

Hollingshead, A. B. & Redlich, F. C. (1958), *Social Class and Mental Illness*.
New York: Wiley.

Holmes, D. (1992), Race and transference in psychoanalysis and psychotherapy. *International Journal of Psycho-Analysis*, 73:1-11.

Jacoby, R. (1983), *The Repression of Psychoanalysis*. New York: Basic
Books.

Jaques, E. (1955), Social systems as defence against persecutory and
depressive anxiety. In: *New Directions in Psychoanalysis*. ed. M. Klein.
London: Tavistock. pp. 478-498.

Javier, R. (1994), Race does matter: An introduction. Presented at biennial conference, Psychoanalytic Society of the Postdoctoral Program, New York.

Jay, M. (1973), *The Dialectical Imagination*. Boston: Little, Brown.

Joseph, B. (1989), *Psychic Equilibrium and Psychic Change*. New York: Tavistock.

Kernberg, O. (1975), *Borderline Conditions and Pathological Narcissism*. New York: Aronson.

Kernberg, O. (1992), *Aggression in Personality Disorders and Perversions*. New Haven, CT: Yale University Press.

Klein, M. (1975a), Notes on some schizoid mechanisms. In: *Envy and Gratitude and Other Works*. New York: Delacorte, pp. 1–24.

Klein, M. (1975b), The origins of transference. In: *Envy and Gratitude and Other Works*. New York: Delacorte, pp. 48–60.

Klein, M. (1975c), On the theory of anxiety and guilt. In: *Envy and Gratitude and Other Works*. New York: Delacorte, pp. 25–42.

Kovel, J. (1988), *The Radical Spirit*. London: Free Association Press.

Kupers, T. (1981), *Public Therapy*. New York: Free Press.

Lacan, J. (1977), *Ecrits*. trans. Alan Sheridan. New York: Norton.

Langer, M. (1989), *From Vienna to Managua*. London: Free Association Press.

Lesser, R. (1993), A reconsideration of homosexual themes: Commentary on Trop and Stolorow's "Defense Analysis in Self Psychology." *Psychoanalytic Dialogues*, 3:639–641.

Levenson, E. (1972), *The Fallacy of Understanding*. New York: Basic Books.

Levenson, E. (1982), Language and healing. In: *Curative Factors in Dynamic Psychotherapy*, ed. S. Slipp. New York: McGraw-Hill, pp. 91–103.

Levi-Strauss, C. (1963), *Structural Anthropology*. New York: Basic Books.

Lewes, K. (1988), *The Psychoanalytic Theory of Male Homosexuality*. New York: Simon & Schuster.

Lipton, S. D. (1977), The advantages of Freud's technique as shown in his analysis of the Rat Man. *International Journal of Psycho-Analysis*. 58:255–274.

Loewald, H. (1988), *Sublimation*. New Haven, CT: Yale University Press.

Lombardi, K. (1994), Freud, Klein, and the British middle school: Psychoanalytic theories as metaphors for critical social conditions. Presented at spring meeting of the Division of Psychoanalysis, American Psychological Association, Washington, DC.

Lyons-Ruth, K. & Zeanah, C. (1993), The family context of infant mental health I. Affective development in the primary caregiver relationship. In: *Handbook of Infant Mental Health*, ed. C. Zeanah. New York: Guilford Press, pp. 14–37.

Main, T. F. (1957), The ailment. *British Journal of Medical Psychology*, 30:129–145.

Malan, D. (1963), *A Study of Brief Psychotherapy*. New York: Plenum Press.

Mann, J. (1973), *Time-Limited Psychotherapy*. Cambridge: Harvard University Press.

Marcuse, H. (1964), *One-Dimensional Man.* Boston: Beacon Press.
Marcuse, H. (1966), *Eros and Civilization.* Boston: Beacon Press.
Marx, K. (1867), *Capital.* New York: International.
Meek, H. (1994), Ghostbusting: Locating meaning in psychotic symptoms. Presented at the spring meeting of the Division of Psychoanalysis, American Psychological Association, Washington, DC.
Menzies, I. E. P. (1975), A case study in the functioning of social systems as a defense against anxiety. In: *Group Relations Reader I*, ed. A. D. Colman & W. H. Bexton. Jupiter, FL: A. K. Rice Institute, pp. 281–312.
Mitchell, S. A. (1981), The psychoanalytic treatment of homosexuality: Some technical considerations. *International Review of Psycho-Analysis*, 8:63–80.
Mitchell, S. A. (1988), *Relational Concepts in Psychoanalysis.* Cambridge, MA: Harvard University Press.
Mitchell, S. A. (1993), *Hope and Dread in Psychoanalysis.* New York: Basic Books.
Neiman, L. (1987), A critical review of the resiliency literature and its relevance to homeless children. *Childrens' Environments Quarterly*, 5:17–25.
Ogden, T. (1986), *The Matrix of the Mind.* Northvale, NJ: Aronson.
Ogden, T. (1994), *Subjects of Analysis.* Northvale, NJ: Aronson.
Piaget, J. (1954), *The Construction of Reality in the Child.* New York: Basic Books.
Pick, I. B. (1988), Working through in the countertransference. In: *Melanie Klein Today*, ed. E. Bott-Spillius. London: Routledge, pp. 34–47.
Pine, F. (1985), *Developmental Theory and Clinical Process.* New Haven, CT: Yale University Press.
Racker, H. (1968), *Transference and Countertransference.* New York: International Universities Press.
Reich, W. (1945), On character analysis. In: *The Psychoanalytic Reader Vol. 1*, ed. R. Fleiss. New York: International Universities Press, pp. 129–147.
Rendon, M. (1993), The psychoanalysis of ethnicity and the ethnicity of psychoanalysis. *American Journal of Psychoanalysis*, 53:109–122.
Ryle, G. (1949), *The Concept of Mind.* London: Hutchinson.
Samuels, A. (1993), *The Political Psyche.* London: Routledge.
Schachter, J. & Butts, H. (1971), Transference and countertransference in inter-racial analyses. *Journal of the American Psychoanalytic Association*, 16:792–808.
Schafer, R. (1992), *Retelling a Life.* New York: Basic Books.
Schwartz, D. (1993), Heterophilia: The love that dare not speak its aim. *Psychoanalytic Dialogues*, 3:643–652.
Schweder, R. A. (1991), *Thinking through Cultures.* Cambridge, MA: Harvard University Press.
Searles, H. (1979a), The dedicated physician. In: *Countertransference.* New York: International Universities Press, pp. 77–88.
Searles, H. (1979b), The patient as therapist to his analyst. In: *Countertransference.* New York: International Universities Press, pp. 380–459.

Sennett, R. & Cobb, J. (1972), *The Hidden Injuries of Class.* New York: Vintage Books.

Shaw, R. & Eagle, C. J. (1971), Programmed failure: The Lincoln Hospital Story. *Community Mental Health Journal,* Dec.: 5–7.

Smith, A. (1776), *Inquiry into the Nature and Causes of the Wealth of Nations.* London: A. Strahan & T. Cadell.

Speigel, R. (1970), Psychoanalysis—for an elite? *Contemporary Psychoanalysis,* 7:48–63.

Stanton, A. M. & Schwartz, M. (1954), *The Mental Hospital.* New York: Basic Books.

Stone, L. (1961), *The Psychoanalytic Situation.* New York: International Universities Press.

Sullivan, H. S. (1953), *The Interpersonal Theory of Psychiatry.* New York: Norton.

van der Kolk, B. A. (1987), *Psychological Trauma.* Washington, DC: American Psychiatric Press.

Vaughns, K. (1994), Race: Does it matter? Notes from the supervisory underground. Presented at biennial conference, Psychoanalytic Society of the Postdoctoral Program, New York.

Vela, R. & Bluestone, H. (1982), Transcultural aspects of the treatment of the Puerto Rican poor in New York City. *Journal of the American Academy of Psychoanalysis,* 10:269–283.

Vygotsky, L. (1963), *Language and Thought.* Cambridge, MA: MIT Press.

Vygotsky, L. (1975), *Mind in Society.* Cambridge, MA: Harvard University Press.

Wachtel, P. (1989), *The Poverty of Affluence.* Philadelphia: New Society.

Weber, M. (1958), *The Protestant Ethic and the Spirit of Capitalism.* New York: Scribner.

West, C. (1993a), *Prophetic Thought in Postmodern Times.* Monroe, ME: Common Courage Press.

West, C. (1993b), *Prophetic Reflections: Notes on Race and Power in America.* Monroe, ME: Common Courage Press.

Whitson, G. (1990), The effect of the analyst's cultural embeddedness on the treatment of "working-class patients." Presented at a colloquium, Postdoctoral Program in Psychotherapy and Psychoanalysis, New York University.

Winnicott, D. W. (1958a), The depressive position in normal emotional development. In: *Through Pediatrics to Psychoanalysis.* New York: Basic Books, pp. 262–277.

Winnicott, D. W. (1958b), Metapsychological and clinical aspects of regression within the psychoanalytical setup. In: *Through Pediatrics to Psychoanalysis.* New York: Basic Books.

INDEX